AMERICAN
CIVIL
RELIGION

A HARPER FORUM BOOK

AMERICAN CIVIL RELIGION

Edited by RUSSELL E. RICHEY
and DONALD G. JONES

HARPER & ROW, PUBLISHERS
New York, Hagerstown, San Francisco, London

AMERICAN CIVIL RELIGION. Copyright © 1974 by Harper & Row, Publishers, Inc. All rights reserved. Printed in the United States of America. No part of this book may be used or reproduced in any manner whatsoever without written permission except in the case of brief quotations embodied in critical articles and reviews. For information address Harper & Row, Publishers, Inc., 10 East 53rd Street, New York, N.Y. 10022. Published simultaneously in Canada by Fitzhenry & Whiteside Limited, Toronto.

Designed by Gwendolyn O. England

Library of Congress Cataloging in Publication Data

Richey, Russell E
   American civil religion.
   (Harper forum books)
   Bibliography: p.
   1. United States—Religion.   I. Jones, Donald G.,
joint author.   II. Title.
BR515.R5   200′.973   73-18702
ISBN 0-06-066856-3 (pbk)

78 79 80 81 82 10 9 8 7 6 5 4

Contents

III CRITICISM

IV RESPONSE

List of Contributors

ROBERT N. BELLAH is Ford Professor of Sociology and Comparative Studies at the University of California, Berkeley. He is author of *Beyond Belief: Essays on Religion in a Post-Traditional World* (1970), *Tokugawa Religion* (1957), editor of *Religion and Progress in Modern Asia* (1965), and coeditor of *Religion in America* (1968) with William G. McLoughlin.

WILL HERBERG, Andrew V. Stout Professor of Religion and Culture in The Graduate School, Drew University, is author of *Protestant, Catholic, Jew* (1960), *Judaism and Modern Man* (1951), and editor of *Four Existentialist Theologians* (1958).

DAVID LITTLE, Associate Professor of Religion and Sociology, University of Virginia, is author of *American Foreign Policy and Moral Rhetoric: The Example of Vietnam* (1969) and *Religion, Order, and Law: A Study in Pre-Revolutionary England* (1969).

CHARLES H. LONG, Professor of History of Religions, University of Chicago, is editor of *Myth and Symbols* (with Joseph M. Kitagawa) 1969 and author of *Alpha: The Myths of Creation* (1963).

MARTIN E. MARTY is Professor of Modern Church History at the University of Chicago and associate editor of *The Christian Century*. Among his recent books are *Protestantism* (1972), *Righteous Empire: The Protestant Experience in America* (1970), and *The Modern Schism: Three Paths to the Secular* (1969).

LEO MARX, Professor of English and American Studies at Amherst College, is author of *The Machine in the Garden: Technology and the Pastoral Ideal in America* (1964).

SIDNEY E. MEAD is emeritus Professor of Religion in American History, History Department and School of Religion, University of Iowa. He is the author of *Nathaniel William Taylor, 1786-1858: A Connecticut*

Liberal (1942) and *The Lively Experiment: The Shaping of Christianity in America* (1963).

HERBERT RICHARDSON is Associate Professor of Theology at St. Michael's College and the Toronto School of Theology. He is author of *Toward an American Theology* (1967), *Nun, Witch, Playmate* (1971), and editor, with Donald R. Cutler, of *Transcendence* (1969).

W. LLOYD WARNER was University Professor Emeritus, Michigan State University, at his death in 1970. Among his works are The Yankee City Series, *Democracy in Jonesville* (1949), and *Social Class in America* (1949).

JOHN F. WILSON, Professor of Religion at Princeton University, is editor of *Church and State in American History* (1965), editor, with Paul Ramsey, of *The Study of Religion in American Colleges and Universities* (1970), and author of *Pulpit in Parliament: Puritanism during the English Civil Wars, 1640-1648* (1969).

DONALD G. JONES, Associate Professor of Religion, and RUSSELL E. RICHEY, Assistant Professor of Church History, both teach in The Graduate School, Drew University. They planned the Consultation, "Civil Religion in America," at which a number of the papers in this volume were presented.

Introduction

DONALD G. JONES AND RUSSELL E. RICHEY

1 The Civil Religion Debate

General and Particular Religion in America

STUDENTS OF RELIGION in America have discerned two broad types of religion in this country: particular and general. The particular religion has usually been identified with churches, synagogues, missionary movements, denominations, revivals, and the like. General religion has been discussed under such categories as democratic faith, societal religion, the American way, generalized religion, common faith, American Shinto, and now "civil religion."

While the existence of these two broad types of religion in America has been acknowledged by some observers of the American scene from the days of the founding fathers, the close study of religion in America has focused on particular religion, specifically on institutionalized forms of Christianity and Judaism. Secular and theologically oriented historians have studied various visible religious institutions, ideas, and movements or church history. Sociologists of religion have tended to investigate what Thomas Luckmann has called "church religion" with a strong tendency toward "denominational sociologies of religion." This equation between "religion" and "church" in the American mind has tended to obscure the complicated and dynamic history and meaning of religion in America. Specifically, this equation has tended to conceal the presence of particular and general religion and interrelations between the conventional visible faith of churches and the generalized, more invisible civil religion in America.

In the celebrated article by Robert Bellah on "Civil Religion,"

3

which first appeared in 1967 and is the lead article in this volume, the lack of attention to this generalized civil religion was noted. Bellah wondered that "something so obvious should have escaped serious analytical attention." Actually some attention had been given to the various religious phenomena now discussed under the category of civil religion. Historians such as Ralph Gabriel, Yehoshua Arieli, and Daniel Boorstin in different ways assessed the religious dimension of "nationalism," the "American creed," the "democratic faith," and "culture religion." In the mid and late fifties, students of religion J. Paul Williams, Robin Williams, Lloyd Warner, and Will Herberg analyzed the "common faith" of Americans. In the late fifties and early sixties Gibson Winter, Martin Marty, Roy Eckardt, Peter Berger, John Smylie, and Sidney Mead all made a significant advance in the scholarship of general religion, or what has now come to be commonly called civil religion.

In one sense, then, Bellah's claim to discovery and his wonderment at scholarly myopia is unfair. The subject had been given attention. In another sense he is right. The scholarly community had been without a commonly accepted concept in terms of which description, analysis, and interpretation could proceed. Adequate scholarly attention awaited a concept. Bellah's phrase "civil religion" has become that concept. It has renewed the discussion, produced conferences, evoked numerous scholarly papers, and attracted the notice of the press. Some fruits of this discussion are contained in this volume, which itself grew out of a major consultation on Civil Religion at the graduate school of Drew University. The bibliography is a guide to the wider conversations. Also helpful in understanding the older discussion and the more coherent new discussion are the essays by John Wilson and Martin Marty in this volume.

The Current Discussion of Civil Religion

What was it about Bellah's conception that commended attention and renewed the discussion? There were undoubtedly a number of extrinsic factors that would account for its appeal. First, the Kennedy presidency, the apparent source of Bellah's discovery of the phenomenon, lent plausibility to the concept. An activist president, calling the nation to new frontiers, seemed to symbolize the best in the civil religion. At the same time, the first Roman Catholic president, in his invocation of God's guidance of the nation, was clearly appealing to spiritual resources that were common, patently not Roman Catholic, but not Protestant either. Earlier affirmations of a common religion did not dispel from scholarly or popular minds the belief that the nation was still Protestant. Bellah's statement possessed a background of political events sustaining his thesis. In the late 1960s, as activism turned to conflict, civil religion gained further appeal and opprobrium. Both the antiwar movement and the black movement were hostile to the civil religion insofar as it seemed to legitimize the "imperialism" and "racism" of American society. But each in its own way also seemed to draw upon resources that well might be termed civil religious. The appeal of the concept had much to do with the appropriateness of civil religion to both status quo and dissent. It probably also appealed to those searching for some consensus amid the conflict, for some unitive resources to heal the wounds and bridge the divisions in American society.

Scholarly as well as social factors help to explain the popularity of the topic. Two deserve mention. First, there was a change in sociology of religion. In the 1960s the sociology, which had eschewed philosophic and societal concerns to concentrate research on religious institutions, rediscovered Max Weber and Émile Durkheim and thereby interest in the broader societal roles of religion. In the work of Peter Berger, Thomas Luckmann, Clifford Geertz, Andrew Greeley, and others the functions of religion in society came under examination. Bellah's thesis and its reception are very much part of this revolution in sociology. Concurrently a similar revolution was going on in the study of religion generally. The study of religion, once the preserve of denominations and seminaries, had solidified its position in universities and independent colleges. To the academic students of religion, civil religion was an "ideal" topic. Even more than secular cities and godless theology, civil religion made plausible the claim that religion ought to be studied by the nonreligious. Here, God be praised, was a religion that was nonreligious, to which the denominations had no claim and which ought properly to belong to departments of religion. Civil religion sent nonprofessing gurus into spasms of ecstasy (i.e., they began to write papers on the topic).

Such extrinsic factors cannot be gainsaid. But Bellah's essay and his conception of civil religion were appealing for their sheer cogency. Bellah insists that "there actually exists alongside of and rather clearly differentiated from the churches an elaborate and well-institutionalized civil religion in America." Here was a thesis that could be readily understood and which seemed capable of being tested against the fabric and history of American society. Bellah underscores the separateness and integrity of the American civil religion in a variety of ways. He suggests that it is possessed of its own set of sacred persons, events, beliefs, rituals, and symbols quite distinct from those of the denominations. He shows it to be capable of development and enrichment. He argues that it is "a genuine apprehension of universal and transcendent religious reality." It is, in layman's language, a "true" religion with its own access to God. And it contains its own ethic which performs a distinct function in national and individual life.

The essays in Parts II and III, and Bellah's own rethinking in Part IV of this volume, are all in one way or another a response to this essay. The other essays in Part I, by substance or publication, predate Bellah's analysis. If one accepts Bellah's statement as normative, they are then critical stages and important statements preparatory for Bellah's. If one denies to Bellah monopoly in conceptualization, they must be seen as significant alternative conceptions.

One alternative, Sidney Mead's "religion of the Republic" described here in "The 'Nation with the Soul of a Church,'" is on some levels quite close to Bellah's view. Bellah as a sociologist insists on taking American civil religion seriously even though he hypothesizes that civil religion may be common to many societies. Mead, a historian, shares the belief that the civil religion, "religion of the Republic," as he calls it, in its best expressions is worthy of citizens' support and scholarly respect. With Bellah he criticizes detractors' practice of comparing the worst in civil religion with the best in traditional or denominational religion. In his several statements on the religion of the Republic, Mead has seemed very much the advocate of his religion (and not above an occasional comparison of the best in civil religion with the worst in denominational).

As Mead's title indicates, he finds significant analogies between the roles of the nation and those roles exercised by the church in the European past. Mead notes that all nationalisms involve a spirituality, an ideology. His interest is in America's ideology and its development. Among the significant influences on this national religion, in addition to the exigencies of nationalism itself, was the Enlightenment. Mead's phrase "religion of the Republic" suggests the extent of civil religion's indebtedness to the American Enlightenment and the revolutionary period. The nation's synergistic religious cosmopolitanism, the universal religion which provides the nation with its prophetic and transcendent spirituality, is really the Enlightenment faith. The republican beliefs in popular sovereignty and representative government and the deist beliefs in the existence of God, creation, laws of nature, providence, immortality, and judgment are the fundamentals of the religion of the Republic. They unite and transcend the separate sects and ethnic groups. It is the belief system of the religion of the Republic—the "universality inherent in its spiritual core"—that makes it decidedly superior to the divisive creeds of the denominations. Mead, therefore, rejects the charge that civil religion is idolatrous. While conceding that apotheosis of the nation has occurred, Mead argues that ". . . the theology of the synergistic and theonomous religion of the Republic stands against this idolatrous tendency equally with Christianity."

Will Herberg, who represents another alternative, is one for whom the charge of idolatry does indeed hold. Herberg's indictment was most forcefully stated in *Protestant, Catholic, Jew,* where he permits himself theological as well as sociological commentary. In that work American religious history was organized around the reciprocal relations of religion and ethnicity. Herberg discovered that the Protestantism that had once proved unitive and normative for American society had succumbed finally to religious pluralism and that the denominations which had served to sustain ethnic identities had lost that role to the three major religious traditions. Further, undergirding American society and shaping the traditions of Protestantism, Catholicism, and Judaism was a new common religion, the American Way of Life or religion of Americanism. Herberg's judgment on the American Way of Life followed naturally from this discovery of the traditions' betrayals of their central values. It was Neo-Orthodoxy's response to the euphoria and celebrationism of Eisenhower America. In this essay Herberg, as sociologist and citizen, strikes a new note. He concedes to the civil religion a certain noble character as he does also to the similar civil religions of the *polis* and *civitas* in the Greco-Roman world. Herberg's civil religion is "the operative religion of the American people" supplying American society "with its 'overarching sense of unity' amidst conflict." It is this unitive function that differentiates Herberg's civil religion from Bellah's, which like Peter Berger's "sacred canopy" is an overarching structure of values and beliefs. Civil religion is then not a tightly coherent tradition as Bellah would have. Rather, the diffuse American folkways—what Americans are intolerant about—are identified as the common religion. Civil religion is the American Way of Life:

> The American Way is dynamic; optimistic; pragmatic; individualistic . . . and pluralistic. . . . Culturally, the American Way exhibits an intense faith in education, significantly coupled with a disparagement of culture in the aesthetic sense; and, characteristically, an extraordinarily high moral valuation of . . . sanitation . . . !

It is celebrative of democracy, the constitution, and national unity, of free enterprise economics, of social egalitarianism and, most interesting, of religion. Like all civil religions "it is the religionization of the national life and national culture." Having given civil religion a broad definition, Herberg portrays civil religion as possessing also broad foundations. Not the elitist religion of the Enlightenment but Puritanism and Evangelicalism; not the eighteenth century but the seventeenth and nineteenth; not Deism but secularized Protestantism underlies civil religion.

The essays by Bellah, Mead, and Herberg describe the American civil religion. The focus of the essay by W. Lloyd Warner is at once broader and narrower. It is broader in its concern for the entire symbol system of Yankee City, not just those segments which might belong to the civil religion. It is narrower in its focus on Memorial Day and its representation only of the symbol system to the neglect of other dimensions of the national cult. This one sacred ceremony in civil religion, however, and Lincoln as a sacral figure are perceptively analyzed and serve to illustrate further the phenomena associated with civil religion. The character and strengths of Warner's analysis are carefully examined by John Wilson.

The essays by John Wilson and Martin Marty are interpretive of the discussions on civil religion. Wilson's statement demonstrates how a historian assesses interpretive categories. Wilson tests a theological model (Mead's civil religion as an American faith), a ceremonial model (Warner's, "concerned with symbolic behavior in society") and a structural-functional model (Bellah's, "concerned with civil religion as a particular religion within American society") for their usefulness to the historian. The reader should observe how Wilson understands Mead, Warner, and Bellah and upon what bases he is discriminating between these alternatives. Wilson suggests that Bellah's model will best serve the historian. The question naturally arises whether there are other uses or other disciplines for which other models might be preferable. Even as Wilson commends Bellah's conceptualization—civil religion—he raises a serious question about the very existence of civil religion. He asks whether the various elements identified as part of the civil religion do indeed "constitute a differentiated tradition, a particular religion, centered on American polity." His own conclusion seems to be in the negative. He suggests that it is a reality with a more episodic existence.

A different manner of coming to terms with varying types and understandings of civil religion is provided by Martin Marty. Marty begins where Wilson ends by qualifying the existence of civil religion, establishing limits on its unitive functions, noting its episodic character. He calls attention to groups not wholly receptive to the civil religion—ethnics, blacks, women, the sects, and the denominations to some extent. Such hold-outs have been, he insists, common reactions to the civil religion. He raises the interesting possibility that civil religion may be most real to the scholars for whom such a generalization as civil religion is particularly useful. From charging popular ignorance of civil religion Marty moves to the other extreme, hinting that there may be as many civil religions as there are citizens. Having established the

limitations of the concept civil religion, Marty proceeds to identify
four types of civil religion. The typology utilizes the distinction of
priestly and prophetic religious styles. The priestly is celebrative,
affirmative, culture-building; the prophetic is dialectical, judgmental. These styles exist within two kinds of civil religion. The
two kinds differ in the central theological affirmation, that concerning the nation. One kind understands the nation as under God
and therefore responsible to God. In the other, God language is
missing and the nation itself assumes transcendence. With these
two discriminations Marty is able to identify celebrative and self-
critical styles of the civil religion which holds God above the cult
and of the civil religion in which the nation displaces God. The
nation-under-God priests are best represented by Eisenhower, its
prophets by Lincoln. The nation-as-transcendent priests include
Nixon, its prophets Sidney Mead. Marty's typology draws attention, then, to the diversity within civil religion. The typology also
differentiates the interpreters insofar as they identify one of the
types as the civil religion. The reader, in reflecting on the appropriateness of Marty's typology to American civil religion, may want to
explore the possibility that in some of the controversy over civil
religion, disputants were employing quite different definitions
legitimized by different strata or types of civil religion.

The questions raised by the historians and sociologists about
civil religion might be termed epistemological and ontological—
questions about the nature, existence, character, and appearance of
civil religion. In Part III rather serious ethical questions are posed
from the quite separate fields of theology, ethics proper, history of
religions, and literature. Herbert Richardson, David Little, Charles
Long, and Leo Marx are not so much concerned whether civil
religion exists as whether it should. Their essays explore the good
and bad in civil religion.

Richardson's essay is a straightforward theological essay. Richardson does not score the civil religion for its excesses. He questions its right to exist. He begins by suggesting that the linking
of religion with any dimension of human life, in the case of civil
religion with the nation-state, has two results. Ultimacy is conferred
on that human aspect and the ultimate is reconceived to resemble
it. Specifically in civil religion the nation-state is apotheosized and

ultimacy is conceived in political terms and symbols. The former, Richardson denounces in the interests of cultural pluralism. He argues that the pretensions of American nationalism, the national self-idolization, are not civil religion's malfunctioning but are the inevitable expression of civil religion. By historical circumstance, the confusion of state with nation, the destruction of potentially rivaling regional and ethnic loyalties, and the deflation of other religious and cultural values, a national-state civil religion was created which is without religious competition. Idolatry is the natural result. It can be ended only by creating competitive loyalties, allowing self-expression to the various nations, cultures, and regions within the United States. These social groupings in turn will generate ideals countervailing to the civil religion. Richardson, second, attacks the American tendency to conceive ultimacy in political terms, a trait deeply rooted in our Puritan past which invokes one of the ideological strains of the Old Testament. That urban-national political ideology venerates law, national unity, and centralized power. It gives ultimacy to the *civitas*. Opposing that Old Testament model, Richardson suggests, is the New Testament. The New Testament, he argues, compares ultimate reality not to the *civitas* but to the *ecclesia*. It is in the gospel that Richardson locates the values to overcome the idolatry of civil religion and it is in the church where Richardson discovers the viable institutional alternative to civil religion.

David Little examines the moral belief of Thomas Jefferson. The narrow focus is of broad significance. In assessing the viability of Jefferson and the American Enlightenment, Little is testing what according to Bellah and Mead is the central belief structure of civil religion. Little considers the relations between three concerns in Jefferson's thought: religion, morality, and civic responsibility. The three, he argues, need to be related and therefore constitute a triad with three stress points, three tensions which need to be taken seriously. They are the tensions of religious belief and civic responsibility, of moral belief and civic responsibility, and of religion and moral belief. The tensions are vital ones which any civil religion must face, and Little cites Rousseau as an advocate of civil religion who had carefully and successfully addressed all three. Jefferson, so argues Little, failed to deal adequately with any of the tensions. His rhetoric, fundamental to the civil religion, has consequently served to obscure the tensions and render America incapable of dealing with the simplest of moral dilemmas. Religious scruples concerning civil duties, for example, have proved more serious and subtle than the Jeffersonian rhetoric of our civil religion would allow. Pacificism, opposition to education, and resistance to medical treatment deserve to be seen in our national cult as potentially more than national disloyalty.

Charles H. Long brings to the topic of civil religion perspectives derived from the history of religions and the experience of black Americans. He sees in both civil religion and Protestantism traditions and symbolism derived from the experience of the European immigrant. The myths, beliefs, and narratives in terms of which the Protestant religious history is recounted or the civil religion analyzed constitute, Long suggests, a cultural language which gives meaning to the American experience. This language is faulted at the most fundamental levels. It is faulted because it is exclusively European. Indians and blacks, their experience, and the symbols which would place them within America are omitted. Thereby they are denied the status of "American." They are rendered invisible. But the fault runs more deeply. The traditions and symbolism have been preserved, developed, and interpreted in centuries of repression and exploitation of non-Europeans by Europeans. The cultural language has not just omitted this conflict and ignored the presence of the non-Europeans. Borrowing on psychological imagery, Long argues that the language represses these dimensions of the Europeans' own life and history. This language has played (and insofar as it is used by historians in the interpretation of the American past continues to play) an ideological role. It permits European Americans to hide from themselves, to conceal their true experience from themselves, to deny in themselves the inner experience of conquest and suppression. When, thus, the civil religion and Protestantism—Long implicates both in this cultural exploitation—are revealed as the recounting of the mighty works of white conquerors, a double repression is involved. Indians and blacks are repressed symbolically as they were oppressed physically, culturally, spiritually. They are made invisible. The European is at the same time repressing part of himself; he is making invisible part of his own consciousness. From this "hermeneutic" of America there is no easy escape. Simple patching of black and Indian history into American history will not mend the deep fissure. Only a new "hermeneutic," a new civil religion, or perhaps a plurality of "hermeneutics" and civil religions, can overcome the concealment and invisibility. In such a reinterpretation of American religious history, repression in both its meanings will need to be overcome. A transformation of American consciousness and of American society is thus entailed.

Leo Marx discerns two distinct linguistic traditions in American history which, he suggests, constitute two civil religions. One that he associates with the civil religion under discussion is "polite, upper-class, bookish, conventional, churchly," hereditary, and alien. The other is the language of the American vernacular. It is democratic, egalitarian, common, obscene, "cruder, more colloquial, closer to the raw," in short, populist. The latter, he argues, invoking one of the most important folk beliefs (that we have broken with European corruption), is the earthy, native, practical, vernacular response to alien and elitist ideals. As spokesman for this tradition and critics of the official civil religion, Marx heralds Emerson, Whitman, Twain, Hemingway, and Mailer. In their more virulent moments they depict the language of the official civil religion as obscene, offer obscenity as an appropriate response, and so in capturing the people's hopes give a sacred dimension to their obscenity. In some ways like the prophetic strain identified by Marty, these critics and Marx himself uncover the seamier side of the priestly civil religion—its imperialism, nativism, racism—and call for a renewed spirituality and language born of the common American life. Marx's analysis should also be compared with others, for instance with Herberg's. On one level he responds to Herberg's characterization of the civil religion as noble by saying, "Noble, like shit." On another level he affirms, noble, yes, with the alien trappings of nobility in which common Americans have all too frequently found themselves exploited, manipulated, undone.

Bellah's essay "American Civil Religion in the 1970s" is a response to the discussion generated by the first essay. He speaks directly, for instance, to the question of the existence of civil religion and reaffirms the sociological utility of such a construct. To those who would deny reality to civil religion, Bellah responds by appealing to the sociological imagination and a social construction of reality. The question may thereby have been altered. It is not whether civil religion exists; clearly it does for some sociologists. The question is whether and in what ways what is real for the sociologist becomes real to the man in the street and for other disciplines. There may be no more than the conflicting visions of disciplines in the historians' uneasiness about the reality of the tradition of civil religion and the sociologists' insistence on postulating "that all politically organized societies have some sort of civil religion." Less readily resolved are the ethical questions raised in this volume by Richardson, Little, Long, and Marx. Bellah, however, renews his insistence that civil religion be treated as a viable religion, not as a sham. He admits, though, that it has all the ambiguities, generates all the conflicts, and is subject to all the attacks, misunderstandings, and various interpretations of religion generally. Fundamental to this argument for the integrity—religious and ethical—of the civil religion is Bellah's demand that the prophetic dimension of civil religion be acknowledged and cultured. It is this side of the civil religion that makes possible renewal, national self-criticism, the ability and openness to learn from our own and other national traditions and, ultimately, the creation of a new ethic, communal in character and corrective of the abuses criticized. Bellah is not sanguine about this prospect. Critical of the strain of civil religion ascendant in the Nixon administration, Bellah strikes the note of crisis. His essay belongs to what Robert Friedrichs has termed prophetic sociology. Or to put it differently, Robert Bellah is a prophet in his own religion.

Five Meanings of Civil Religion

What precisely is meant by the category "civil religion"? While linguistic precision is not possible in answering that question, it is possible to discern at least five broad and, to some extent, interrelated meanings of civil religion as the concept has been employed by the contributors to this volume and by other scholars in recent years. This fivefold typology may in fact be a useful methodological scheme for analyzing particular expressions of what has been called general religion, but no effort will be made to support such a conclusion; rather, the primary purpose in setting forth these five meanings is to indicate where the discussants of civil religion stand. It should also be noted that in some cases the particular type or particular point of view is more a matter of emphasis; in other cases it is clearly a matter of substance. At times by both emphasis and substance representatives identified with one type can be found in others.

First is the notion of civil religion as *folk religion*. Will Herberg, Robin Williams and, to a degree, Lloyd Warner would fit this category inasmuch as they tend to see the common religion of Americans descriptively as emerging out of the life of the folk. By examining the actual life, ideas, values, ceremonies, and loyalties of the people, conclusions are drawn as to the existence and status of civil religion. The starting point is not a normative view of what civil religion at best is but, rather, what it actually is on the basis of surveys, polls, and empirical studies. Hence, Will Herberg can arrive at the judgment that American civil religion is at bottom "the American Way of Life." Herberg writes:

> It is an organic structure of ideas, values, and beliefs that constitutes a faith common to Americans as Americans, and is genuinely operative in their lives; . . . Sociologically, anthropologically, it is *the* American religion, undergirding American national life and overarching American society. . . . And it is a civil religion in the strictest sense of the term, for in it, national life is apotheosized, national values are religionized, national heroes are divinized, national history is experienced as a *Heilsgeschichte,* as a redemptive history.

Civil religion in this sense emerges out of the ethos and history of the society and inevitably becomes an idolatrous faith competing with particularistic religions rooted in a reality and traditions transcending the common life of a people.

A second meaning of civil religion may be categorized as the *transcendent universal religion of the nation*. Sidney Mead, a major proponent of this view, views the "religion of the Republic" as a "cosmopolitan" faith which is "essentially prophetic." This civil religion stands in judgment over the folkways of the people. Indeed it stands in judgment and as a corrective against the idolatrous tendency of particular forms of Christianity and Judaism. Mead emphatically denies that the "religion of the Republic" means deification of the state or nation and takes vigorous exception to the view that the religion of the nation is "the American Way of Life."

In like fashion, Robert Bellah assumes a normative stance regarding the meaning of civil religion. It is at best a universal and transcendent religion rendering prophetic judgment on the nation. It functions as a source of meaning and social solidarity for the nation. Bellah also rejects the notion of American civil religion as the "American Way of Life" or the worship of the American nation. It is, rather, ". . . an understanding of the *American experience* in the light of ultimate and universal reality." As such he can entertain the possibility that American civil religion could become "simply one part of a new civil religion of the world." This new world civil religion "could be accepted as a fulfillment and not a denial of American civil religion."

While much of the content of civil religion as viewed by Herberg, on the one hand, and Mead and Bellah, on the other, is similar, the starting point, the direction of analysis, and the evaluation are quite antithetical.

A third meaning of the category "civil religion" is indicated by the phrase *religious nationalism*. In this usage the nation is not the church of national religion. It is, rather, the object of adoration and glorification. The nation takes on a sovereign and self-transcendent character. Some have called this kind of civil religion the religion of patriotism. Archbishop John Ireland in the late nineteenth century was articulating a common sentiment for that period when he said: "The religion of patriotism is not sufficiently understood, and yet it is this religion that gives to country its majesty, and to patriotism its sacredness and force."

Martin Marty in his essay notes that this understanding of civil religion functions well in assessing President Nixon's public theology. Citing Charles Henderson's study, Marty says that Nixon "takes the vocabulary of transcendence and applies it chiefly to his personal vision of the nation." Some interpreters and devotees of civil religion would affirm this view as normative and even take

Archbishop Ireland's position that such a patriotic faith is not incompatible with particularistic religion (such as the Roman Catholic Church). Others, from either the standpoint of universalistic concepts of civil religion or classical traditions of Judaism and Christianity, take a pejorative view. For instance, Herbert Richardson represents civil religion as inevitably tending to idolatry, i.e., religious nationalism, through which Americans "express their faith that politics is a matter of ultimate concern." This religionizing of the nation and politics is the heart of what Richardson means when he discusses civil religion.

A fourth meaning of civil religion, which is a slight variation of the above version, may be designated as the *democratic faith*. The implicit normative view of civil religion in Leo Marx's essay is this democratic egalitarian faith. The humane values and ideals of equality, freedom, and justice without necessary dependence on a transcendent deity or a spiritualized nation represent civil religion at its best in the American experience. To some extent the American creed of Gunnar Myrdal, the common faith of John Dewey, the vision of America discerned in progressive-era historiography, and the democracy-as-religion of J. Paul Williams, encompass this concept of civil religion. This meaning of civil religion has its own detractors and devotees, but whatever the evaluation, it represents a distinct usage of the concept of civil religion and requires its own special analysis.

A fifth meaning of civil religion may be called *Protestant civic piety*. Some historians of the nineteenth century have detected the emergence of what Yehoshua Arieli has called "Protestant nationalism." James Smylie, James Maclear, Winthrop Hudson, Robert Michaelsen, among others, have emphasized the fusion of Protestantism and nationalism and the pervading Protestant coloring in the American ethos. Will Herberg employs this meaning in unequivocal terms when he says, ". . . America's civil religion is compounded of the two great religious movements that molded America—the Puritan way, secularized; and the Revivalist way, secularized."

Those scholars who have emphasized Protestant moralism, individualism, activism ("deeds not creeds"), pragmatism, the work ethic, and the grand motif of "missionizing" the world as

American civil religion would be representative of this type. Vincent Harding and Charles Long suggest a kind of Protestant civil religion when they point to deeply and religiously embedded notions of Anglo-American superiority rooted in Protestant theories of race and Protestant versions of national destiny. In some ways the "uncivil civil religion" as discussed by Leo Marx suggests this Protestant meaning of civil religion.

Protestant civic piety is a less comprehensive characterization of civil religion. However, what it loses in general applicability, it may gain in historical and sociological precision. For instance, this categorization has been particularly apt for viewing such phenomena as common religion in frontier America, certain expressions of common religion in the American South, and some cultic aspects of suburban and rural America in the fifties through the seventies.

The five uses of the phrase civil religion, discerned in these essays and in other writings, are all closely connected and in some instances overlapping. The very diversity of conceptualization represented in this fivefold typology illustrates both the complexity of the issue and pioneer character of the study and debate. Our purpose has been to clarify uses and meanings. We think this volume advances and deepens what is yet a nascent stage in the scholarship of American civil religion.

I
Theme

ROBERT N. BELLAH

2 Civil Religion in America

WHILE SOME HAVE ARGUED that Christianity is the national faith, and others that church and synagogue celebrate only the generalized religion of "the American Way of Life," few have realized that there actually exists alongside of and rather clearly differentiated from the churches an elaborate and well-institutionalized civil religion in America. This article argues not only that there is such a thing, but also that this religion—or perhaps better, this religious dimension—has its own seriousness and integrity and requires the same care in understanding that any other religion does.[1]

The Kennedy Inaugural

Kennedy's inaugural address of 20 January 1961 serves as an example and a clue with which to introduce this complex subject. That address began:

> We observe today not a victory of party but a celebration of freedom—symbolizing an end as well as a beginning—signifying renewal as well as change. For I have sworn before you and Almighty God the same solemn oath our forebears prescribed nearly a century and three quarters ago.

Reprinted, with permission, from "Religion in America," the Winter 1967 issue of *Daedalus,* Journal of the American Academy of Arts and Sciences, Boston, Massachusetts.

The world is very different now. For man holds in his mortal hands the power to abolish all forms of human poverty and to abolish all forms of human life. And yet the same revolutionary beliefs for which our forebears fought are still at issue around the globe—the belief that the rights of man come not from the generosity of the state but from the hand of God.

And it concluded:

Finally, whether you are citizens of America or of the world, ask of us the same high standards of strength and sacrifice that we shall ask of you. With a good conscience our only sure reward, with history the final judge of our deeds, let us go forth to lead the land we love, asking His blessing and His help, but knowing that here on earth God's work must truly be our own.

These are the three places in this brief address in which Kennedy mentioned the name of God. If we could understand why he mentioned God, the way in which he did it, and what he meant to say in those three references, we would understand much about American civil religion. But this is not a simple or obvious task, and American students of religion would probably differ widely in their interpretation of these passages.

Let us consider first the placing of the three references. They occur in the two opening paragraphs and in the closing paragraph, thus providing a sort of frame for the more concrete remarks that form the middle part of the speech. Looking beyond this particular speech, we would find that similar references to God are almost invariably to be found in the pronouncements of American presidents on solemn occasions, though usually not in the working messages that the president sends to Congress on various concrete issues. How, then, are we to interpret this placing of references to God?

It might be argued that the passages quoted reveal the essentially irrelevant role of religion in the very secular society that is America. The placing of the references in this speech as well as in public life generally indicates that religion has "only a ceremonial significance"; it gets only a sentimental nod which serves largely to placate the more unenlightened members of the community, before a discussion of the really serious business with which religion has nothing whatever to do. A cynical observer might even say that an American president has to mention God or risk losing votes. A semblance of piety is merely one of the unwritten qualifications for the office, a bit more traditional than, but not essentially different from, the present-day requirement of a pleasing television personality.

But we know enough about the function of ceremonial and ritual in various societies to make us suspicious of dismissing something as unimportant because it is "only a ritual." What people say on solemn occasions need not be taken at face value, but it is often indicative of deep-seated values and commitments that are not made explicit in the course of everyday life. Following this line of argument, it is worth considering whether the very special placing of the references to God in Kennedy's address may not reveal something rather important and serious about religion in American life.

It might be countered that the very way in which Kennedy made his references reveals the essentially vestigial place of religion today. He did not refer to any religion in particular. He did not refer to Jesus Christ, or to Moses, or to the Christian church; certainly he did not refer to the Catholic Church. In fact, his only reference was to the concept of God, a word which almost all Americans can accept but which means so many different things to so many different people that it is almost an empty sign. Is this not just another indication that in America religion is considered vaguely to be a good thing, but that people care so little about it that it has lost any content whatever? Isn't Eisenhower reported to have said, "Our government makes no sense unless it is founded in a deeply felt religious faith—and I don't care what it is,"[2] and isn't that a complete negation of any real religion?

These questions are worth pursuing because they raise the issue of how civil religion relates to the political society, on the one hand, and to private religious organization, on the other. President Kennedy was a Christian, more specifically a Catholic Christian. Thus, his general references to God do not mean that he lacked a specific religious commitment. But why, then, did he not include some remark to the effect that Christ is the Lord of the world or some indication of respect for the Catholic Church? He did not because these are matters of his own private religious belief and of his relation to his own particular church; they are not matters relevant in any direct way to the conduct of his public office. Others with different religious views and commitments to different churches or denominations are equally qualified participants in the political process. The principle of separation of church and state guarantees the freedom of religious belief and association, but at the same time clearly segregates the religious sphere, which is considered to be essentially private, from the political one.

Considering the separation of church and state, how is a president justified in using the word *God* at all? The answer is that the separation of church and state has not denied the political realm a religious dimension. Although matters of personal religious belief, worship, and association are considered to be strictly private affairs, there are, at the same time, certain common elements of religious orientation that the great majority of Americans share. These have played a crucial role in the development of American institutions and still provide a religious dimension for the whole fabric of American life, including the political sphere. This public religious dimension is expressed in a set of beliefs, symbols, and rituals that I am calling the American civil religion. The inauguration of a president is an important ceremonial event in this religion. It reaffirms, among other things, the religious legitimation of the highest political authority.

Let us look more closely at what Kennedy actually said. First he said, ". . . I have sworn before you and Almighty God the same solemn oath our forebears prescribed nearly a century and three quarters ago." The oath is the oath of office, including the acceptance of the obligation to uphold the Constitution. He swears it before the people (you) and God. Beyond the Constitution, then, the president's obligation extends not only to the people but to God. In American political theory, sovereignty rests, of course, with the people, but implicitly, and often explicitly, the ultimate sovereignty has been attributed to God. This is the meaning of the motto, "In God we trust," as well as the inclusion of the phrase "under God" in the pledge to the flag. What difference does it make that sovereignty belongs to God? Though the will of the people as expressed in majority vote is carefully institutionalized as the operative source of political authority, it is deprived of an ultimate significance. The will of the people is not itself the criterion of right and wrong. There is a higher criterion in terms of which this will can be judged; it is possible that the people may be wrong. The president's obligation extends to the higher criterion.

When Kennedy says that "the rights of man come not from the generosity of the state but from the hand of God," he is stressing this point again. It does not matter whether the state is the expression of the will of an autocratic monarch or of the "people"; the rights of man are more basic than any political structure and provide a point of revolutionary leverage from which any state structure may be radically altered. That is the basis for his reassertion of the revolutionary significance of America.

But the religious dimension in political life as recognized by Kennedy not only provides a grounding for the rights of man which makes any form of political absolutism illegitimate, it also provides a transcendent goal for the political process. This is implied in his final words that "here on earth God's work must truly be our own." What he means here is, I think, more clearly spelled out in a previous paragraph, the wording of which, incidentally, has a distinctly Biblical ring.

> Now the trumpet summons us again—not as a call to bear arms, though arms we need—not as a call to battle, though embattled we are—but a call to bear the burden of a long twilight struggle, year in and year out, "rejoicing in hope, patient in tribulation"—a struggle against the common enemies of man: tyranny, poverty, disease and war itself.

The whole address can be understood as only the most recent statement of a theme that lies very deep in the American tradition, namely the obligation, both collective and individual, to carry out God's will on earth. This was the motivating spirit of those who founded America, and it has been present in every generation since. Just below the surface throughout Kennedy's inaugural address, it becomes explicit in the closing statement that God's work must be our own. That this very activist and non-contemplative conception of the fundamental religious obligation, which has been historically associated with the Protestant position, should be enunciated so clearly in the first major statement of the first Catholic president seems to underline how deeply established it is in the American outlook. Let us now consider the form and history of the civil religious tradition in which Kennedy was speaking.

The Idea of a Civil Religion

The phrase "civil religion" is, of course, Rousseau's. In Chapter 8, Book 4, of *The Social Contract*, he outlines the simple dogmas of the civil religion: the existence of God, the life to come, the reward of virtue and the punishment of vice, and the exclusion of religious intolerance. All other religious opinions are outside the cognizance of the state and may be freely held by citizens. While the phrase *civil religion* was not used, to the best of my knowledge, by the founding fathers, and I am certainly not arguing for the particular influence of Rousseau, it is clear that similar ideas, as part of the cultural climate of the late-eighteenth century, were to be found among the Americans. For example, Franklin writes in his autobiography,

> I never was without some religious principles. I never doubted, for instance, the existence of the Deity; that he made the world and govern'd it by his Providence; that the most acceptable service of God was the doing of good to men; that our souls are immortal; and that all crime will be punished, and virtue rewarded either here or hereafter. These I esteemed the essentials of every religion; and, being to be found in all the religions we had in our country, I respected them all, tho' with different degrees of respect, as I found them more or less mix'd with other articles, which, without any tendency to inspire, promote or confirm morality, serv'd principally to divide us, and make us unfriendly to one another.

It is easy to dispose of this sort of position as essentially utilitarian in relation to religion. In Washington's Farewell Address (though the words may be Hamilton's) the utilitarian aspect is quite explicit:

> Of all the dispositions and habits which lead to political prosperity, Religion and Morality are indispensable supports. In vain would that man claim the tribute of Patriotism, who should labour to subvert these great Pillars of human happiness, these firmest props of the

duties of men and citizens. The mere politician, equally with the pious man ought to respect and cherish them. A volume could not trace all their connections with private and public felicity. Let it simply be asked where is the security for property, for reputation, for life, if the sense of religious obligation *desert* the oaths, which are the instruments of investigation in Courts of Justice? And let us with caution indulge the supposition, that morality can be maintained without religion. Whatever may be conceded to the influence of refined education on minds of peculiar structure, reason and experience both forbid us to expect that National morality can prevail in exclusion of religious principle.

But there is every reason to believe that religion, particularly the idea of God, played a constitutive role in the thought of the early American statesmen.

Kennedy's inaugural pointed to the religious aspect of the Declaration of Independence, and it might be well to look at that document a bit more closely. There are four references to God. The first speaks of the "Laws of Nature and of Nature's God" which entitle any people to be independent. The second is the famous statement that all men "are endowed by their Creator with certain inalienable Rights." Here Jefferson is locating the fundamental legitimacy of the new nation in a conception of "higher law" that is itself based on both classical natural law and Biblical religion. The third is an appeal to "the Supreme Judge of the world for the rectitude of our intentions," and the last indicates "a firm reliance on the protection of divine Providence." In these last two references, a Biblical God of history who stands in judgment over the world is indicated.

The intimate relation of these religious notions with the self-conception of the new Republic is indicated by the frequency of their appearance in early official documents. For example, we find in Washington's first inaugural address of 30 April 1789:

It would be peculiarly improper to omit in this first official act my fervent supplications to that Almighty Being who rules over the universe, who presides in the councils of nations, and whose providential aids can supply every defect, that His benediction may consecrate to the liberties and happiness of the people of the United States a Government instituted by themselves for these essential purposes, and may enable every instrument employed in its administration to execute with success the functions allotted to his charge.

No people can be bound to acknowledge and adore the Invisible Hand which conducts the affairs of man more than those of the United States. Every step by which we have advanced to the character of an independent nation seems to have been distinguished by some token of providential agency. . . .

The propitious smiles of Heaven can never be expected on a nation that disregards the eternal rules of order and right which Heaven itself has ordained. . . . The preservation of the sacred fire of liberty and the destiny of the republican model of government are justly considered, perhaps, as *deeply*, as *finally*, staked on the experiment intrusted to the hands of the American people.

Nor did these religious sentiments remain merely the personal expression of the president. At the request of both Houses of Congress, Washington proclaimed on October 3 of that same first year as president that November 26 should be "a day of public thanksgiving and prayer," the first Thanksgiving Day under the Constitution.

The words and acts of the founding fathers, especially the first few presidents, shaped the form and tone of the civil religion as it has been maintained ever since. Though much is selectively derived from Christianity, this religion is clearly not itself Christianity. For one thing, neither Washington nor Adams nor Jefferson mentions Christ in his inaugural address; nor do any of the subsequent presidents, although not one of them fails to mention God.[3] The God of the civil religion is not only rather "unitarian," he is also on the austere side, much more related to order, law, and right than to salvation and love. Even though he is somewhat deist in cast, he is by no means simply a watchmaker God. He is actively interested and involved in history, with a special concern for America. Here the analogy has much less to do with natural law than with ancient Israel; the equation of America with Israel in the idea of the "American Israel" is not infrequent.[4] What was implicit in the words of Washington already quoted becomes explicit in Jefferson's second inaugural when he said: "I shall need, too, the favor of that Being in whose hands we are, who led our fathers, as

Israel of old, from their native land and planted them in a country flowing with all the necessaries and comforts of life." Europe is Egypt; America, the promised land. God has led his people to establish a new sort of social order that shall be a light unto all the nations.[5]

This theme, too, has been a continuous one in the civil religion. We have already alluded to it in the case of the Kennedy inaugural. We find it again in President Johnson's inaugural address:

> They came here—the exile and the stranger, brave but frightened— to find a place where a man could be his own man. They made a covenant with this land. Conceived in justice, written in liberty, bound in union, it was meant one day to inspire the hopes of all mankind; and it binds us still. If we keep its terms, we shall flourish.

What we have, then, from the earliest years of the republic is a collection of beliefs, symbols, and rituals with respect to sacred things and institutionalized in a collectivity. This religion—there seems no other word for it—while not antithetical to, and indeed sharing much in common with, Christianity, was neither sectarian nor in any specific sense Christian. At a time when the society was overwhelmingly Christian, it seems unlikely that this lack of Christian reference was meant to spare the feelings of the tiny non-Christian minority. Rather, the civil religion expressed what those who set the precedents felt was appropriate under the circumstances. It reflected their private as well as public views. Nor was the civil religion simply "religion in general." While generality was undoubtedly seen as a virtue by some, as in the quotation from Franklin above, the civil religion was specific enough when it came to the topic of America. Precisely because of this specificity, the civil religion was saved from empty formalism and served as a genuine vehicle of national religious self-understanding.

But the civil religion was not, in the minds of Franklin, Washington, Jefferson, or other leaders, with the exception of a few radicals like Tom Paine, ever felt to be a substitute for Christianity. There was an implicit but quite clear division of function between the civil religion and Christianity. Under the doctrine of religious liberty, an exceptionally wide sphere of personal piety and voluntary social action was left to the churches. But the churches were neither to control the state nor to be controlled by it. The national magistrate, whatever his private religious views, operates under the rubrics of the civil religion as long as he is in his official capacity, as we have already seen in the case of Kennedy. This accommodation was undoubtedly the product of a particular historical moment and of a cultural background dominated by Protestantism of several varieties and by the Enlightenment, but it has survived despite subsequent changes in the cultural and religious climate.

Civil War and Civil Religion

Until the Civil War, the American civil religion focused above all on the event of the Revolution, which was seen as the final act of the Exodus from the old lands across the waters. The Declaration of Independence and the Constitution were the sacred scriptures and Washington the divinely appointed Moses who led his people out of the hands of tyranny. The Civil War, which Sidney Mead calls "the center of American history,"[6] was the second great event that involved the national self-understanding so deeply as to require expression in the civil religion. In 1835, de Tocqueville wrote that the American Republic had never really been tried, that victory in the Revolutionary War was more the result of British preoccupation elsewhere and the presence of a powerful ally than of any great military success of the Americans. But in 1861 the time of testing had indeed come. Not only did the Civil War have the tragic intensity of fratricidal strife, but it was one of the bloodiest wars of the nineteenth century; the loss of life was far greater than any previously suffered by Americans.

The Civil War raised the deepest questions of national meaning. The man who not only formulated but in his own person embodied its meaning for Americans was Abraham Lincoln. For him the issue was not in the first instance slavery but "whether that nation, or any nation so conceived, and so dedicated, can long endure." He had said in Independence Hall in Philadelphia on 22 February 1861:

All the political sentiments I entertain have been drawn, so far as I have been able to draw them, from the sentiments which originated in and were given to the world from this Hall. I have never had a feeling, politically, that did not spring from the sentiments embodied in the Declaration of Independence.[7]

The phrases of Jefferson constantly echo in Lincoln's speeches. His task was, first of all, to save the Union—not for America alone but for the meaning of America to the whole world so unforgettably etched in the last phrase of the Gettysburg Address.

But inevitably the issue of slavery as the deeper cause of the conflict had to be faced. In the second inaugural, Lincoln related slavery and the war in an ultimate perspective:

> If we shall suppose that American slavery is one of those offenses which, in the providence of God, must needs come, but which, having continued through His appointed time, he now wills to remove, and that He gives to both North and South this terrible war as the woe due to those by whom the offense came, shall we discern therein any departure from those divine attributes which the believers in a living God always ascribe to Him? Fondly do we hope, fervently do we pray, that this mighty scourge of war may speedily pass away. Yet, if God wills that it continue until all wealth piled by the bondsman's two hundred and fifty years of unrequited toil shall be sunk, and until every drop of blood drawn with the lash shall be paid by another drawn with the sword, as was said three thousand years ago, so still it must be said "the judgments of the Lord are true and righteous altogether.

But he closes on a note if not of redemption then of reconciliation: "With malice toward none, with charity for all."

With the Civil War, a new theme of death, sacrifice, and rebirth enters the civil religion. It is symbolized in the life and death of Lincoln. Nowhere is it stated more vividly than in the Gettysburg Address, itself part of the Lincolnian "New Testament" among the civil scriptures. Robert Lowell has recently pointed out the "insistent use of birth images" in this speech explicitly devoted to "these honored dead": "brought forth," "conceived," "created," "a new birth of freedom." He goes on to say:

> The Gettysburg Address is a symbolic and sacramental act. Its verbal quality is resonance combined with a logical, matter of fact, prosaic brevity. . . . In his words, Lincoln symbolically died, just as the Union soldiers really died—and as he himself was soon really to die. By his words, he gave the field of battle a symbolic sig-

nificance that it had lacked. For us and our country, he left
Jefferson's ideals of freedom and equality joined to the Christian
sacrificial act of death and rebirth. I believe this as a meaning that
goes beyond sect or religion and beyond peace and war, and is now
part of our lives as a challenge, obstacle and hope.[8]

Lowell is certainly right in pointing out the Christian quality
of the symbolism here, but he is also right in quickly disavowing
any sectarian implication. The earlier symbolism of the civil religion had been Hebraic without being in any specific sense Jewish.
The Gettysburg symbolism (". . . those who here gave their lives,
that that nation might live") is Christian without having anything
to do with the Christian church.

The symbolic equation of Lincoln with Jesus was made relatively
early. Herndon, who had been Lincoln's law partner, wrote:

> For fifty years God rolled Abraham Lincoln through his fiery
> furnace. He did it to try Abraham and to purify him for his pur-
> poses. This made Mr. Lincoln humble, tender, forbearing, sym-
> pathetic to suffering, kind, sensitive, tolerant; broadening, deepening
> and widening his whole nature; making him the noblest and loveliest
> character since Jesus Christ. . . . I believe that Lincoln was God's
> chosen one.[9]

With the Christian archetype in the background, Lincoln, "our
martyred president," was linked to the war dead, those who "gave
the last full measure of devotion." The theme of sacrifice was in-
delibly written into the civil religion.

The new symbolism soon found both physical and ritualistic
expression. The great number of the war dead required the establishment of a number of national cemeteries. Of these, the Gettysburg National Cemetery, which Lincoln's famous address served
to dedicate, has been overshadowed only by the Arlington National
Cemetery. Begun somewhat vindictively on the Lee estate across
the river from Washington, partly with the end that the Lee
family could never reclaim it,[10] it has subsequently become the
most hallowed monument of the civil religion. Not only was a section set aside for the Confederate dead, but it has received the dead
of each succeeding American war. It is the site of the one important new symbol to come out of World War I, the Tomb of the

Unknown Soldier; more recently it has become the site of the tomb of another martyred president and its symbolic eternal flame.

Memorial Day, which grew out of the Civil War, gave ritual expression to the themes we have been discussing. As Lloyd Warner has so brilliantly analyzed it, the Memorial Day observance, especially in the towns and smaller cities of America, is a major event for the whole community involving a rededication to the martyred dead, to ths spirit of sacrifice, and to the American vision.[11] Just as Thanksgiving Day, which incidentally was securely institutionalized as an annual national holiday only under the presidency of Lincoln, serves to integrate the family into the civil religion, so Memorial Day has acted to integrate the local community into the national cult. Together with the less overtly religious Fourth of July and the more minor celebrations of Veterans Day and the birthdays of Washington and Lincoln, these two holidays provide an annual ritual calendar for the civil religion. The public-school system serves as a particularly important context for the cultic celebration of the civil rituals.

The Civil Religion Today

In reifying and giving a name to something that, though pervasive enough when you look at it, has gone on only semiconsciously, there is risk of severely distorting the data. But the reification and the naming have already begun. The religious critics of "religion in general," or of the "religion of the 'American Way of Life,' " or of "American Shinto" have really been talking about the civil religion. As usual in religious polemic, they take as criteria the best in their own religious tradition and as typical the worst in the tradition of the civil religion. Against these critics, I would argue that the civil religion at its best is a genuine apprehension of universal and transcendent religious reality as seen in or, one could almost say, as revealed through the experience of the American people. Like all religions, it has suffered various deformations and demonic distortions. At its best, it has neither been so general that it has lacked incisive relevance to the American scene nor so particular that it has placed American society above universal human values. I am not at all convinced that the leaders of the churches have consistently represented a higher level of religious insight than the spokesmen of the civil religion. Reinhold Niebuhr has this to say of Lincoln, who never joined a church and who certainly represents civil religion at its best:

> An analysis of the religion of Abraham Lincoln in the context of the traditional religion of his time and place and of its polemical use on the slavery issue, which corrupted religious life in the days before and during the Civil War, must lead to the conclusion that Lincoln's religious convictions were superior in depth and purity to those, not only of the political leaders of his day, but of the religious leaders of the era.[12]

Perhaps the real animus of the religious critics has been not so much against the civil religion in itself but against its pervasive and dominating influence within the sphere of church religion. As S. M. Lipset has recently shown, American religion at least since the early nineteenth century has been predominantly activist, moralistic, and social rather than contemplative, theological, or innerly spiritual.[13] De Tocqueville spoke of American church religion as "a political institution which powerfully contributes to the maintenance of a democratic republic among the Americans"[14] by supplying a strong moral consensus amidst continuous political change. Henry Bargy in 1902 spoke of American church religion as "la poésie du civisme."[15]

It is certainly true that the relation between religion and politics in America has been singularly smooth. This is in large part due to the dominant tradition. As de Tocqueville wrote:

> The greatest part of British America was peopled by men who, after having shaken off the authority of the Pope, acknowledged no other religious supremacy: they brought with them into the New World a form of Christianity which I cannot better describe than by styling it a democratic and republican religion.[16]

The churches opposed neither the Revolution nor the establishment of democratic institutions. Even when some of them opposed the full institutionalization of religious liberty, they accepted the final outcome with good grace and without nostalgia for an *ancien régime*. The American civil religion was never anticlerical or militantly secular. On the contrary, it borrowed selectively from the religious tradition in such a way that the average American saw no conflict between the two. In this way, the civil religion was able to build up without any bitter struggle with the church powerful symbols of national solidarity and to mobilize deep levels of personal motivation for the attainment of national goals.

Such an achievement is by no means to be taken for granted. It would seem that the problem of a civil religion is quite general in modern societies and that the way it is solved or not solved will have repercussions in many spheres. One needs only to think of France to see how differently things can go. The French Revolution was anticlerical to the core and attempted to set up an anti-Christian civil religion. Throughout modern French history, the chasm between traditional Catholic symbols and the symbolism of 1789 has been immense.

American civil religion is still very much alive. Just three years ago we participated in a vivid re-enactment of the sacrifice theme in connection with the funeral of our assassinated president. The American Israel theme is clearly behind both Kennedy's New Frontier and Johnson's Great Society. Let me give just one recent illustration of how the civil religion serves to mobilize support for the attainment of national goals. On 15 March 1965 President Johnson went before Congress to ask for a strong voting-rights bill. Early in the speech he said:

> Rarely are we met with the challenge, not to our growth or abundance, or our welfare or our security—but rather to the values and the purposes and the meaning of our beloved nation.
>
> The issue of equal rights for American Negroes is such an issue. And should we defeat every enemy, and should we double our wealth and conquer the stars and still be unequal to this issue, then we will have failed as a people and as a nation.
>
> For with a country as with a person, "What is a man profited, if he shall gain the whole world, and lose his own soul?"

And in conclusion he said:

> Above the pyramid on the great seal of the United States it says in Latin, "God has favored our undertaking."
>
> God will not favor everything that we do. It is rather our duty to divine his will. I cannot help but believe that He truly understands and that He really favors the undertaking that we begin here tonight.[17]

The civil religion has not always been invoked in favor of worthy causes. On the domestic scene, an American-Legion type of ideology that fuses God, country, and flag has been used to attack non-conformist and liberal ideas and groups of all kinds. Still, it has been difficult to use the words of Jefferson and Lincoln to support special interests and undermine personal freedom. The defenders of slavery before the Civil War came to reject the thinking of the Declaration of Independence. Some of the most consistent of them turned against not only Jeffersonian democracy but Reformation religion; they dreamed of a South dominated by medieval chivalry and divine-right monarchy.[18] For all the overt religiosity of the radical right today, their relation to the civil religious consensus is tenuous, as when the John Birch Society attacks the central American symbol of Democracy itself.

With respect to America's role in the world, the dangers of distortion are greater and the built-in safeguards of the tradition weaker. The theme of the American Israel was used, almost from the beginning, as a justification for the shameful treatment of the Indians so characteristic of our history. It can be overtly or implicitly linked to the idea of manifest destiny which has been used to legitimate several adventures in imperialism since the early-nineteenth century. Never has the danger been greater than today. The issue is not so much one of imperial expansion, of which we are accused, as of the tendency to assimilate all governments or parties in the world which support our immediate policies or call upon our help by invoking the notion of free institutions and democratic values. Those nations that are for the moment "on our side" became "the free world." A repressive and unstable military dictatorship in South Viet-Nam becomes "the free people of South Viet-Nam and their government." It is then part of the role of America as the New Jerusalem and "the last hope of earth" to defend such governments with treasure and eventually with blood. When our soldiers are actually dying, it becomes possible to consecrate the struggle further by invoking the great theme of sacrifice. For the majority of the American people who are unable to judge whether the people in South Viet-Nam (or wherever) are "free like us," such arguments are convincing. Fortunately President Johnson has been less ready to assert that "God has favored our undertaking" in the case of Viet-Nam than with respect to civil rights. But others are not so hesitant. The civil religion has exercised long-term pressure for the humane solution of our greatest domestic problem, the treatment of the Negro American. It remains to be seen how relevant it can become for our role in the world at large, and whether we can effectually stand for "the revolutionary beliefs for which our forebears fought," in John F. Kennedy's words.

The civil religion is obviously involved in the most pressing moral and political issues of the day. But it is also caught in another kind of crisis, theoretical and theological, of which it is at the moment largely unaware. "God" has clearly been a central symbol in the civil religion from the beginning and remains so today. This symbol is just as central to the civil religion as it is to the Judaism or Christianity. In the late-eighteenth century this posed no problem; even Tom Paine, contrary to his detractors, was not an atheist. From left to right and regardless of church or sect, all could accept the idea of God. But today, as even *Time* has recognized, the meaning of the word *God* is by no means so clear or so obvious. There is no formal creed in the civil religion. We have had a Catholic president; it is conceivable that we could have a Jewish one. But could we have an agnostic president? Could a man with conscientious scruples about using the word *God* the way Kennedy and Johnson have used it be elected chief magistrate of our country? If the whole God symbolism requires reformulation, there will be obvious consequences for the civil religion, consequences perhaps of liberal alienation and of fundamentalist ossification that have not so far been prominent in this realm. The civil religion has been a point of articulation between the profoundest commitments of the Western religious and philosophical tradition and the common beliefs of ordinary Americans. It is not too soon to consider how the deepening theological crisis may affect the future of this articulation.

The Third Time of Trial

In conclusion it may be worthwhile to relate the civil religion to the most serious situation that we as Americans now face, what I call the third time of trial. The first time of trial had to do with the question of independence, whether we should or could run our own affairs in our own way. The second time of trial was over the issue of slavery, which in turn was only the most salient aspect of the more general problem of the full institutionalization of democracy within our country. The second problem we are still far from solving though we have some notable successes to our credit. But we have been overtaken by a third great problem which has led to a third great crisis, in the midst of which we stand. This is the problem of responsible action in a revolutionary world, a world seeking to attain many of the things, material and spiritual, that we have already attained. Americans have, from the beginning, been aware of the responsibility and the significance our republican experiment has for the whole world. The first internal political polarization in the new nation had to do with our attitude toward the French Revolution. But we were small and weak then, and "foreign entanglements" seemed to threaten our very survival. During the last century, our relevance for the world was not forgotten, but our role was seen as purely exemplary. Our democratic Republic rebuked tyranny by merely existing. Just after World War I we were on the brink of taking a different role in the world, but once again we turned our back.

Since World War II the old pattern has become impossible. Every president since Roosevelt has been groping toward a new pattern of action in the world, one that would be consonant with our power and our responsibilities. For Truman and for the period dominated by John Foster Dulles that pattern was seen to be the great Manichaean confrontation of East and West, the confrontation of democracy and "the false philosophy of Communism" that provided the structure of Truman's inaugural address. But with the last years of Eisenhower and with the successive two presidents, the pattern began to shift. The great problems came to be seen as caused not solely by the evil intent of any one group of men, but as stemming from much more complex and multiple sources. For Kennedy, it was not so much a struggle against particular men as against "the common enemies of man: tyranny, poverty, disease and war itself."

But in the midst of this trend toward a less primitive conception of ourselves and our world, we have somehow, without anyone really intending it, stumbled into a military confrontation where we have come to feel that our honor is at stake. We have in a moment of uncertainty been tempted to rely on our overwhelming physical power rather than on our intelligence, and we have, in part, succumbed to this temptation. Bewildered and unnerved when our terrible power fails to bring immediate success, we are at the edge of a chasm the depth of which no man knows.

I cannot help but think of Robinson Jeffers, whose poetry seems more apt now than when it was written, when he said:

Unhappy country, what wings you have! . . .
Weep (it is frequent in human affairs), weep for the terrible
        magnificence of the means,
The ridiculous incompetence of the reasons, the bloody and shabby
Pathos of the result.

But as so often before in similar times, we have a man of prophetic stature, without the bitterness or misanthropy of Jeffers, who, as Lincoln before him, calls this nation to its judgment:

When a nation is very powerful but lacking in self-confidence, it is likely to behave in a manner that is dangerous both to itself and to others.

Gradually but unmistakably, America is succumbing to that arrogance of power which has afflicted, weakened and in some cases destroyed great nations in the past.

If the war goes on and expands, if that fatal process continues to accelerate until America becomes what it is not now and never has been, a seeker after unlimited power and empire, then Vietnam will have had a mighty and tragic fallout indeed.

I do not believe that will happen. I am very apprehensive but I still remain hopeful, and even confident, that America, with its humane and democratic traditions, will find the wisdom to match its power.[19]

Without an awareness that our nation stands under higher judgment, the tradition of the civil religion would be dangerous indeed. Fortunately, the prophetic voices have never been lacking. Our present situation brings to mind the Mexican-American war that Lincoln, among so many others, opposed. The spirit of civil disobedience that is alive today in the civil rights movement and the opposition to the Viet-Nam war was already clearly outlined by Henry David Thoreau when he wrote, "If the law is of such a nature that it requires you to be an agent of injustice to another, then I say, break the law." Thoreau's words, "I would remind my countrymen that they are men first, and Americans at a late and convenient hour,"[20] provide an essential standard for any adequate thought and action in our third time of trial. As Americans we have been well favored in the world, but it is as men that we will be judged.

Out of the first and second times of trial have come, as we have seen, the major symbols of the American civil religion. There seems little doubt that a successful negotiation of this third time of trial—the attainment of some kind of viable and coherent world order—would precipitate a major new set of symbolic forms. So far the flickering flame of the United Nations burns too low to be the focus of a cult, but the emergence of a genuine trans-national sovereignty would certainly change this. It would necessitate the incorporation of vital international symbolism into our civil religion, or, perhaps a better way of putting it, it would result in American civil religion becoming simply one part of a new civil religion of the world. It is useless to speculate on the form such a civil religion might take, though it obviously would draw on religious traditions beyond the sphere of Biblical religion alone. Fortunately, since the American civil religion is not the worship of the American nation but an understanding of the American experience in the light of ultimate and universal reality, the reorganization entailed by such a new situation need not disrupt the American civil religion's continuity. A world civil religion could be accepted as a fulfillment and not a denial of American civil religion. Indeed, such an outcome has been the eschatological hope of American civil religion from the beginning. To deny such an outcome would be to deny the meaning of America itself.

Behind the civil religion at every point lie Biblical archetypes: Exodus, Chosen People, Promised Land, New Jerusalem, Sacrificial Death and Rebirth. But it is also genuinely American and genuinely new. It has its own prophets and its own martyrs, its own sacred events and sacred places, its own solemn rituals and symbols. It is concerned that America be a society as perfectly in accord with the will of God as men can make it, and a light to all the nations.

It has often been used and is being used today as a cloak for petty interests and ugly passions. It is in need—as is any living faith—of continual reformation, of being measured by universal standards. But it is not evident that it is incapable of growth and new insight.

It does not make any decision for us. It does not remove us from moral ambiguity, from being, in Lincoln's fine phrase, an "almost chosen people." But it is a heritage of moral and religious experience from which we still have much to learn as we formulate the decisions that lie ahead.

NOTES

1. Why something so obvious should have escaped serious analytical attention is in itself an interesting problem. Part of the reason is probably the controversial nature of the subject. From the earliest years of the nineteenth century, conservative religious and political groups have argued that Christianity is, in fact, the national religion. Some of them have from time to time and as recently as the 1950's proposed constitutional amendments that would explicitly recognize the sovereignty of Christ. In defending the doctrine of separation of church and state, opponents of such groups have denied that the national polity has, intrinsically, anything to do with religion at all. The moderates on this issue have insisted that the American state has taken a permissive and indeed supportive attitude toward religious groups (tax exemption, et cetera), thus favoring religion but still missing the positive institutionalization with which I am concerned. But part of the reason this issue has been left in obscurity is certainly due to the peculiarly Western concept of "religion" as denoting a single type of collectivity of which an individual can be a member of one and only one at a time. The Durkheimian notion that every group has a religious dimension, which would be seen as obvious in southern or eastern Asia, is foreign to us. This obscures the recognition of such dimensions in our society.

2. Quoted in Will Herberg, *Protestant, Catholic, Jew* (New York, 1955), p. 97.

3. God is mentioned or referred to in all inaugural addresses but Washington's second, which is a very brief (two paragraphs) and perfunctory acknowledgement. It is not without interest that the actual word *God* does not appear until Monroe's second inaugural, 5 March 1821. In his first inaugural, Washington refers to God as "that Almighty Being who rules the universe," "Great Author of every public and private good," "Invisible Hand," and "benign Parent of the Human Race." John Adams refers to God as "Providence," "Being who is supreme over all," "Patron of Order," "Fountain of Justice," and "Protector in all ages of the world of virtuous liberty." Jefferson speaks of "that Infinite Power which rules the destinies of the universe," and "that Being in whose hands we are." Madison speaks of "that Almighty Being whose power regulates the destiny of nations," and "Heaven." Monroe uses "Providence" and "the Almighty" in his first inaugural and finally "Almighty God" in his second. See, *Inaugural Addresses of the Presidents of the United States from George Washington 1789 to Harry S. Truman 1949,* 82d Congress, 2d Session, House Document No. 540, 1952.

4. For example, Abiel Abbot, pastor of the First Church in Haverhill, Massachusetts, delivered a Thanksgiving sermon in 1799, *Traits of Resemblance in the People of the United States of America to Ancient Israel*, in which he said, "It has been often remarked that the people of the United States come nearer to parallel with Ancient Israel, than any other nation upon the globe. Hence OUR AMERICAN ISRAEL is a term frequently used; and common consent allows it apt and proper." Cited in Hans Kohn, *The Idea of Nationalism* (New York, 1961), p. 665.

5. That the Mosaic analogy was present in the minds of leaders at the very moment of the birth of the republic is indicated in the designs proposed by Franklin and Jefferson for a seal of the United States of America. Together with Adams, they formed a committee of three delegated by the Continental Congress on July 4, 1776, to draw up the new device. "Franklin proposed as the device Moses lifting up his wand and dividing the Red Sea while Pharaoh was overwhelmed by its waters, with the motto 'Rebellion to tyrants is obedience to God.' Jefferson proposed the children of Israel in the wilderness 'led by a cloud by day and a pillar of fire of night.' " Anson Phelps Stokes, *Church and State in the United States,* Vol. 1 (New York, 1950), pp. 467-68.

6. Sidney Mead, *The Lively Experiment* (New York, 1963), p. 12.

7. Quoted by Arthur Lehman Goodhart in Allan Nevins (ed.), *Lincoln and the Gettysburg Address* (Urbana, Ill., 1964), p. 39.

8. *Ibid.*, "On the Gettysburg Address," pp. 88-89.

9. Quoted in Sherwood Eddy, *The Kingdom of God and the American Dream* (New York, 1941), p. 162.

10. Karl Decker and Angus McSween, *Historic Arlington* (Washington, D. C., 1892), pp. 60-67.

11. How extensive the activity associated with Memorial Day can be is indicated by Warner: "The sacred symbolic behavior of Memorial Day, in which scores of the town's organizations are involved, is ordinarily divided into four periods. During the year separate rituals are held by many of the associations for their dead, and many of these activities are connected with later Memorial Day events. In the second phase, preparations are made during the last three or four weeks for the ceremony itself, and some of the associations perform public rituals. The third phase consists of scores of rituals held in all the cemeteries, churches, and halls of the associations. These rituals consist of speeches and highly ritualized behavior. They last for two days and are climaxed by the fourth and last phase, in which all the separate celebrants gather in the center of the business district on the afternoon of Memorial Day. The separate organizations, with their members in uniform or with fitting insignia, march through the town, visit the shrines and monuments of the hero dead, and, finally, enter the cemetery. Here dozens of ceremonies are held, most of them highly symbolic and formalized." During these various ceremonies Lincoln is continually referred to and the Gettysburg Address recited many times. W. Lloyd Warner, *American Life* (Chicago, 1962), pp. 8-9.

12. Reinhold Niebuhr, "The Religion of Abraham Lincoln," in Nevins (ed.), *op. cit.*, p. 72. William J. Wolf of the Episcopal Theological School in Cambridge, Massachusetts, has written: "Lincoln is one of the greatest theologians of America—not in the technical meaning of producing a system of doctrine, certainly not as the defender of some one denomination, but in the sense of seeing the hand of God intimately in the affairs of nations. Just so the prophets of Israel criticized the events of their day from the perspective of the God who is concerned for history and who reveals His will within it. Lincoln now stands among God's latter-day prophets." *The Religion of Abraham Lincoln* (New York, 1963), p. 24.

13. Seymour Martin Lipset, "Religion and American Values," Chapter 4, *The First New Nation* (New York, 1964).

14. Alexis de Tocqueville, *Democracy in America*, Vol. 1 (New York, 1954), p. 310.

15. Henry Bargy, *La Religion dans la Société aux États-Unis* (Paris, 1902), p. 31.

16. De Tocqueville, *op. cit.*, p. 311. Later he says, "In the United States even the religion of most of the citizens is republican, since it submits the truths of the other world to private judgment, as in politics the care of their temporal interests is abandoned to the good sense of the people. Thus every man is allowed freely to take that road which he thinks will lead him to heaven, just as the law permits every citizen to have the right of choosing his own government" (p. 436).

17. U.S. *Congressional Record,* House, 15 March 1965, pp. 4924, 4926.

18. See Louis Hartz, "The Feudal Dream of the South," Part 4, *The Liberal Tradition in America* (New York, 1955).

19. Speech of Senator J. William Fulbright of 28 April 1966, as reported in *The New York Times*, 29 April 1966.

20. Quoted in Yehoshua Arieli, *Individualism and Nationalism in American Ideology* (Cambridge, Mass., 1964), p. 274.

SIDNEY E. MEAD

3 The "Nation with the Soul of a Church"

THE APT PHRASE, "a nation with the soul of a church," was coined
by G. K. Chesterton in answer to his question, "What is America?"
the title of the autobiographical essay in which he relates how he
came to appreciate what the United States was all about. Being
urged and then amused by the kinds of questions asked him when
he applied for entrance into the United States, he was led to ask
what is it that "makes America peculiar"? He concluded that it
was the fact that

> America is the only nation in the world that is founded on creed.
> That creed is set forth with dogmatic and even theological lucidity
> in The Declaration of Independence. . . . It enunciates that all men
> are equal in their claim to justice, and that governments exist to
> give them that justice, and that their authority is for that reason
> just. It certainly does condemn anarchism, and it does also by
> inference condemn atheism, since it clearly names the Creator as
> the ultimate authority from whom these equal rights are derived.[1]

I think we need to qualify Chesterton's flat statement that the
United States is "the only nation . . . that is founded on a creed."
For there is a sense in which the being of a nation with a distinct
identity implies a tacitly accepted "creed" among its people—what
Ruth Benedict called a constellation of ideas and standards that

Reprinted, with permission, from *Church History*, 36, No. 3 (September
1967).

give a people a sense of belonging together and of being different from those of other nations and cultures.

The idea of the United States, Chesterton decided, was that of an asylum—"a home for the homeless"—of all the world. What made this country different was the "idea of making a new nation literally out of [the people of] any old nation that comes along."[2] Because every nation is a spiritual entity, it was implied that the spiritual entity of this nation must include every religion that these diverse people brought along.

The new nation was "conceived in liberty, and dedicated to the proposition that all men are created equal." It was the idea of actually incarnating this "theory of equality" in the familar practice of a nation that Chesterton found unique about America—the incarnation of "the pure classic conception that no man must aspire to be anything more than a citizen, and that no man shall endure to be anything less."[3]

By the same token, vis-a-vis such a civil commonwealth, no religious sect must aspire to be anything more than equal with all the others, and none should endure to be anything less. The idea of actually incarnating this theory of the equality of all religious sects in relation to the civil authority is what was unique about the American experiment. The persistence of sectarianism indicates how reluctantly the religious groups have been to accept *this* theory of equality in principle. But just as the ideal of America has been that "of moulding many peoples into the visible image of the citizen," so it was implied that the religious ideal was that of melding the many diverse sectarianisms into one cosmopolitan religion. This, I think, is what Philip Schaff meant when he said in 1855 that "America seems destined to be the Phoenix grave not only of all European nationalities, . . . but also of all European churches and sects. . . ." And he predicted that here where all the sects are "fermenting together under new and peculiar conditions" out of their "mutual conflict . . . something wholly new will gradually arise."[4] It is to me as inconceivable as it was to Schaff a century ago "that any one of the present confessions and sects . . . will ever become exclusively dominant" in the United States.

Now, in a series of broad generalizations, we must try to picture the emergence and development of this theory of equality and its implications. We may begin with an examination of the nature of a nation, which suggests that America was less unique in Christendom than Chesterton might lead one to suppose.

In the fullness of time when Christianity was born the Roman Empire was a fact of experience, and subtle philosophers "combining elements of Platonism with the tenets of the Stoics" had suggested the idea of the world as "a single city of God."[5] The experienced and conceptual orders insofar corroborated one another, "unity answered to unity." Then, as Ernest Barker argues:

> When the Emperor was worshipped as a manifest God and saviour by all his subjects, the society of the Empire became a quasi-religious society, cemented by a common allegiance which was also a common cult.[6]

In its conception of the church as a single, organic, society which transcended and included "all earlier distinctions, whether of Jew and Gentile, or of Greek and barbarian, or of bond and free" Christianity represented its own ideal of a universal society permeated by the personal spirit of God. The "political world-society . . . possessed a universality which answered to the aspiring and universal genius of the early Church." In effect, and, to be sure, with much searching, struggle and compromise, Christianity moved into the shell of the Empire. The Church "became a world-society co-extensive with the world-empire" and "Christianity became both a city of God in conception and an organized universal society in action." Thus it was that when "the Roman Empire vanished in the West: the Catholic society remained. . . . It was a fact, and not merely an idea: and yet it was also an idea, and not altogether a fact." For tribal societies with their particularistic tribal cults were being swept into the Catholic society before their people had fully absorbed, and been absorbed into, the true Catholic idea.

The nation as idea and fact sprang from those seeds of tribalism which germinated and were nourished in the soil of the Christian world-society. Nations emerged with the coincidence of a geographical center (e.g., London or Paris) and a strong political authority, usually a monarch or a line of monarchs, powerful and persuasive enough to become symbols of unity, order, and security.

The tie that binds a nation together is "neither a physical fact of common blood [for "all are composite and heterogeneous"], nor a political structure of common law and order" as was, for example, the Roman Empire. National consciousness gradually emerged among the inhabitants of a territory around "a common allegiance, common memories, and a common tradition—a tradition of uniform law and government, uniform speech, a single literature, a common history."

A nation, then, "is what it is in virtue of a common mental substance resident in the minds of all its members—common hopes for the future, and, above all, a common and general will issuing from the common substance of memories, ideas and hopes."[7] John Wise, in his *Vindication of the Government of New England Churches* in 1717, echoes the then current view that with the compact by which government is formed, comes "that submission and union of wills by which a state may be conceived to be but one person." It is "a compound moral person, whose will (united by those compacts . . .) is the will of all . . . as though the whole state was now become but one man. . . ." And in this sense the compacts by which this state is created, "may be supposed, under God's providence, to be the divine fiat pronounced by God, 'Let us make man.' "[8] The similarity to the Christian conception of the church as the body of Christ is obvious. A nation, in brief, is "essentially a spiritual society," its soul created in the compact of the people.

But, and this is most important, unlike the Empire and Catholic society, the nation "in its essence . . . was a negation of universality: it was a particularist society, confined to a given territory and peculiar to a given body of persons."

In this particularist "spiritual society" the Christian church with its concept of "the world-society" met "something new, and something different in kind from the Empire with which it had come to terms a thousand years before." The "struggles between kings and popes had been struggles . . . between rival authorities."[9] The struggles between the universal church and the nations were struggles between rival spiritual societies, and as such, a confrontation of rival theologies.

The emergence of the nations corresponds in time with the

Reformation, so that concurrent with the fragmentation of the Empire into nations came the fragmentation of the universal visible church into many particular churches. And in those areas where reformation churches were established (Scotland, England, Geneva, Holland, the principalities of North Germany, and Scandinavia), the nation assumed its own form of Christianity and established "a national form of religious organization" fusing "the spiritual tradition of the new and secular nation . . . with the spiritual tradition of the old and Christian society. . . ." Thus the essentially spiritual society of the nation was, in effect, Christianized by partially digesting into its spiritual core a particularized version of Christianity. For its people the nation became also their church, and the church became also their nation—church and nation being merely different perspectives on the one society to which they belonged. Such at least, says Ernest Barker, was the vision of Hooker and Laud in England where the identification was most complete, although never absolute.[10] It always stood under the judgment of the ancient and Catholic concept of universalism, and even while Laud and Charles I ruled it was being challenged in England by nonconformists with a different view of the nature of a church and, consequently, of its relation to civil authority. It was the nonconformist view, adapted to the American environment, that was to triumph and be incarnated in the Constitutional and legal structure of the United States.

But by and large, the Reformation churches of the right-wing became the tribal cults of the emerging nations. And because Roman Catholicism vis-a-vis these nation-churches also found its defenders in national societies, it also tended to assume characteristics of a tribal cult in those countries. During the last quarter of the sixteenth century, for example, it was clearly English-Protestantism versus Spanish-Catholicism.[11] And I suppose that Gallicanism means that the Catholic Church in France was speaking to Rome with a decidedly French accent.

The extent to which the Roman Catholic church was "nationalized" in those countries where it remained dominant was revealed when the flood of immigrants poured into the United States from the several nations of Europe. Soon, says Monsignor John Tracy Ellis, they "completely overshadowed the native Catholics

and gave to the Church a foreign coloring that at once baffled
its friends and exasperated its enemies." But the "foreign coloring" was itself a coat of many different colors. In America, Ellis
notes, the Roman Catholic Church was made up of a "congeries
of nationalities" who shared only their foreignness, and their
Catholicism, which (as Will Herberg has argued so persuasively)
was but one element in the definition of their ethnic identity. The
problem for Catholics in America was to mold this heterogeneous
collection of nationals into one church. And it was because of
that necessity, says Monsignor Ellis, that the Roman Catholic
church in the United States "Willy-nilly . . . had [to] become
catholic in the broadest sense. . . ."[12]

Because during the period following the Reformation it seemed
sufficiently demonstrated that religious differences were a chief
cause of internal dissension and international wars, the national
ideal was religious uniformity institutionalized in an Established
church. Thus experience consolidated the nation-church ideal.
In the Protestant England of Elizabeth I to be a Roman Catholic
was presumptive evidence of disloyalty to the nation and its state,
as in Catholic France the reverse was the case.

Both Catholicism and nonconformity refused "to accept the
identification of religious and national society."[13] Perhaps Lord
Baltimore and Roger Williams who founded the first colonies with
religious freedom had at least that much in common! But it would
seem that the writings of those who assumed and accepted such
identification is an unlikely place to go looking for a doctrine of
the church which will enable the American people to understand
their denominations in a land where religious pluralism has been
a fact for three hundred years, where "*the* Church" as such does
not exist in visible institutional form, and where religious freedom
has prevailed for about two centuries. Yet by and large, Americans
of the theological revival evident since around 1930 who went looking for a "doctrine of the church" dug for historical roots primarily
in the writings of representatives of the right-wing national church
tradition. Twenty some years ago I heard a scholar justify this
limitation with the dogmatic declaration that the Baptists, for
example, "never had a doctrine of the church." In one respect at
least, I find myself in agreement with Harvey Cox:

Our doctrines of the church have come to us from the frayed-out period of classical Christendom and are infected with the ideology of preservation and permanence. They are almost entirely past-oriented, deriving their authority from one or another classical period, from an alleged resemblance to some earlier form of church life, or from a theory of historical continuity. But this will no longer do.[14]

In my context, this will not do if we hope ever to understand the institutional forms of Christianity in the United States and/or the relation of the denominations which emerged out of the experience of Christianity in America to the civil authority of the nation. Thomas Jefferson spoke from experience, both when he commended the Baptists for their consistent advocacy of religious freedom, *and* when he said of the right-wing clergy of New England that "the advocate of religious freedom is to expect neither peace nor forgiveness from them."

But meanwhile the Reformers' establishment of the principle that the individual was justified by faith alone, which removed all human mediators between God and man and established a direct and immediate relation between the individual and God in Christ —while it obviously undermined the claim of the clergy of the visible church to be the sole mediators of eternal salvation, tended also though less obviously to undermine the claim of civil rulers to be "*the* powers . . . ordained of God" of Romans 13:1. The result, noted by Philip Schaff, was that historically "with the universal priesthood comes also a corresponding universal kingship."[15] And Kierkegaard exclaimed, "Oh, Luther, Luther; your responsibility is great indeed, for the closer I look the more clearly do I see that you overthrew the Pope—and set the public on the throne."[16]

This development, this inversion in the conceptual order, laid the foundation for modern democracy—the idea that sovereignty, the power of God for the creation of ordered communities, lies in "the people" and is delegated by them to rulers responsible to them.

One sees this development taking place in the vicissitudes of that "due forme of government both civill and ecclesiastical" which those Puritans who established Massachusetts Bay colony envisaged and attempted to bring into familiar and daily practice.

They accepted without question what was then almost universally conceded in their England, that all government must be by the consent of the governed[17]—a concept which they subsumed under the traditional Jewish-Christian image of the covenant of God with his peculiar people. In their transitional conceptual order they merged the idea of the church as the tribal cult with that of the church as a gathered and covenanted people, and attempted to incarnate and preserve the idea in practice by the simple expedient of ruling that only church members could vote in the election of civil magistrates, who in turn, were chosen only from among the Saints. Thus the gathered church was co-extensive with the actual state, the laws of which, it was supposed, coincided with the laws of God. Hence outward obedience to the laws of the commonwealth, whether consciously and willingly as by the Saints, or reluctantly as by the unregenerate, was by definition outward conformity to the laws of God.

They described their church government as "mixt"—in relationship to Christ its head, it was an absolute monarchy; in relationship to its officers who held direct subordinate power under Christ, it was an aristocracy; when viewed from the perspective of the members who also had their direct subordinate power under Christ, it was a democracy.[18] All the parts of their church government, they held, were exactly revealed in the Word of God, and a strong evidence of a true work of grace in an individual's heart was his desire to consent to that church's support and discipline. The government of the church was by the consent of the governed, which consent they were enabled by grace to give.

Whatever one may think of their exegesis of Scripture and the conclusions respecting church government which they deduced therefrom, or of their actual practices, the important thing for the future was that *this church-state was a democracy of the Saints*. Obviously the whole structure rested upon the assumption that, within the judgment of charity, they could distinguish the Saints from the unregenerate with sufficient accuracy to guarantee the perpetuation of the rule of the Saints. And when confidence in that assumption was undermined, as it soon was when morality became indistinguishable from piety, the democracy of the Saints flowed out to embrace the whole community, to include all the people. At the same time, for the biblical orientation of the original covenant was substituted the concept of "the law of nature"—of men in "the state of nature" endowed with natural rights common to all men whether religious or not. John Wise, in his *Vindication of the Government of the New England Churches* in 1717, while he used all the traditional arguments from Scripture and the practice of the primitive church until the apostasy under Constantine, is most remembered for his Demonstration II, "From the Light of Nature." Here he argued that man is "a free-born subject under the crown of heaven, and owing homage to none but God himself." And since God has not ordained any "particular form of civil government" one concludes it "must . . . be the effect of human free-compacts and not of divine institution; it is the produce [sic] of man's reason, of human and rational combinations, and not from any direct orders of infinite wisdom. . . ."[19]

The founders of the United States accepted this view as axiomatic. We should never forget that

> Our foundations were quarried not only from the legal ideas but also from the political, social, philosophical, scientific, and theological learnings of the eighteenth century, "the silver age of the Renaissance." All these were dominated by a belief in "the laws of nature and of nature's God." Faith in a "higher law," which had achieved a venerable place in the history of ideas through the speculations of jurists, monks, and scholars, burst forth toward the end of the eighteenth century into a fanatical creed that took over French and American liberal thinking and led in each case to a violent revolution.[20]

The course of history exhibits the slow, strong power of high generalities to get incarnated in actuality, and our institutions are primarily incarnations of the constellation of myths and ideas that dominated the thinking of the eighteenth century in which the nation was born.

Prominent in that constellation was the view that sovereign power lies in "the people," who by a first compact agree to have a government, and by a second compact agree upon the kind of government they want. In the founders' thinking, the unique opportunity they possessed was to actualize in practice what a long line of thinkers had conceived as proper government for men.

The dissolution of the political bonds that had bound these people to the English state, declared in the Declaration and made good by successful revolution, meant that the sovereign power was returned to the people who, by implication, desired a government more likely to secure their rights. Now the people could choose the kind of government they wanted—a choice that was exemplified in the acceptance of the Constitution.

There were certain "givens" in the situation which had to be recognized and accepted in framing the new government. Prominent among these "givens" was the fact that by the time the Constitutional Convention met religious pluralism had been, willingly or grudgingly, accepted in every colony. Everywhere, religious uniformity had broken down, making the ideal of a national tribal cult institutionalized in one established church impossible. If there was to be a *United* States "there was no choice but to tolerate all Christian denominations, and forbear entering into the particular views of any," Robert Baird noted in 1845.[21] Vis-a-vis each of the many conflicting religious sects, the new nation's central authority had to be neutral, neither favoring nor hindering any sect's beliefs or practices except where the latter might violate socially acceptable conduct.

> The First Amendment was therefore to insure that no one powerful sect or combination of sects could use political or governmental power to punish dissenters whom they could not convert to their faith. Now as then, it is only by wholly isolating the state from their religious sphere and compelling it to be completely neutral, that the freedom of each and every denomination and of all non-believers can be maintained.[22]

It is worth repeating that such neutrality, which is commonly referred to as "secularization," is more accurately described as desectarianization of the civil authority.[23] Pluralism means many different sects, each a religious interest group, and civil neutrality is based on the recognition, as Reinhold Niebuhr put it, that "it is dangerous to give any interest group [in a nation] the monopoly to define the 'truth' " as was the practice in nations with established churches.[24]

Sectarians, and all advocates who cannot disentangle their particular religious forms from the universal essence of religion, are bound to argue that this means that the civil government is unreligious, or irreligious, even anti-religious—which is what they commonly mean by "secular." This is to confuse anti-sectarianism with anti-religious. At the time, and from his point of view Bishop Hughes of New York was right in the early 1840s when he said, "Take away the distinctive dogmas of the Catholics, the Baptists, the Methodists, the Presbyterians, and so on, and you have nothing left but deism," and deism, he thought, was itself sectarian.[25] For, the "deism" exhibited in the Declaration was a positive religious teaching with, as G. K. Chesterton noted, a lucid and even dogmatic theology.

It was a cosmopolitan, inclusive, universal theology. The founders, typical eighteenth century intellectuals oriented to the actualities of the American scene, were cosmopolitans nationally and religiously. They were cosmopolitans nationally in the sense that Franklin meant when he said, ". . . a Philosopher may set his foot anywhere on . . . [the world's] surface, and say, 'This is my country.' "[26] So such a Philosopher might have entered any church, as Franklin symbolically did by contributing his mite to each, and declare, "This is my church."

Because it is so commonly supposed that the theology of these men like Franklin was *syncretistic*—that is, a common-core made up by combining a heterogeneous set of discrete tenets collected from all the sects—it is worth emphasizing that this was not the case. Their view might more precisely be called *synergistic*, which designates the simultaneous action of separate agencies working in combination to effect an end. When Franklin spoke of "the essentials of every religion" he added that these were "to be found in all the religions we had in our country" though in each "mix'd with other articles" peculiar to that sect. This is not to create a syncretistic common-core, but to plumb for the universal which is dressed and insofar disguised in the particularities of doctrine and practice which distinguish one sect from another. This conception enabled them to distinguish between the substance of religion and to forms of the religious sects exemplified in sectarian tenets and observances. They were aware, in Whitehead's words, that "Religious ideas represent highly specialized forms of general notions,"[27] and in their theologizing they plumbed for the "general notions."

When Franklin and those of like mind listened to a sectarian preacher, they might hear through the particular forms of his pronouncements "the essentials of every religion"—the substance of all religion. Although the preacher might preach on the specific plane, Franklin might listen on the general plane; while the preacher preached specific notions, Franklin might be reminded of the high generalities implicit in and behind the speaker's sectarian presentation. This is not *syncretism* but the idea that the universal is encapsulated in the particular and unique.

This conception, as the founders well realized, is eminently compatible with actual religious freedom and consequent pluralism in a *common*-wealth. It provides a basis for a positive explanation and defense of religious pluralism which does not necessarily undermine belief in the efficacy of sectarian forms of expressing the universal. Indeed it encourages the free, open, and uncurbed proclamation of all sectarian specific notions respecting, in Madison's words, "the duty which we owe to our creator, and the manner of discharging it." It encourages even vehement conflict of opinion between them on the premises stated by Jefferson in the Act for Establishing Religious Freedom in Virginia:

> that truth [which is universal] is great and will prevail if left to herself, that she is the proper and sufficient antagonist to error, and has nothing to fear from the conflict, unless . . . disarmed of her natural weapons, free argument and debate, errors ceasing to be dangerous when it is permitted freedly to contradict them.

On this basis religious pluralism and conflict between the sects is promoted under the aegis of a *neutral* civil authority which limits the conflict to "reason and persuasion . . . [as] the only practicable instruments"[28] for mining the universal truth out of the diversity of opinions that prevails. In this situation each sect, whether knowingly or not, is communicating to its members through its particular forms the universal truth in which all religions meet. Believing this, Jefferson could say of Virginia's neighbors, Pennsylvania and New York, that there "Religion is well supported; of various kinds, indeed, but all good enough. . . ."[29]

That somehow they are "all good enough" is ploughed into our tradition.

Of course it is important to distinguish between the universal those eighteenth-century cosmopolitans plumbed for and the specific notions they came up with in defining its content. Those notions, in Franklin's words, were

> the existence of the Deity; that he made the world, and govern'd it by his Providence; that the most acceptable service of God was the doing of good to men; that our souls are immortal; and that all crime will be punished, and virtue rewarded, either here or hereafter.

A century later, in 1885, these notions were so much a part of the American ethos that Josiah Strong, a Congregational pastor and leader, probably thought he was merely repeating a truism when he said that

> The teaching of the three great fundamental doctrines which are common to all monotheistic religions is essential to the perpetuity of free institutions, while the inculcation of sectarian dogmas is not. These three doctrines are that of the *existence of God*, the *immortality of man*, and *man's accountability*.[30]

I repeat, these are specific notions respecting the content of the universal, to which anyone may legitimately oppose and argue for another constellation of specific notions. But if and when he does so he should realize that on the plane of high generality he is in agreement with Franklin and Strong and the sentiment implicit in the whole American experience that the universal, however latent, is encapsulated in the particular forms of the sects.

There is today among Christians a fine flurry of thinking and activity to "tangibilicate"—to borrow that wonderful word from Father Divine—the answer to the prayer of Jesus "that they all may be one . . . that they also may be one in us . . ." (John 17:21). I suppose that this implies the eventual shedding of all belief that any sectarian particularity is in itself of ultimate significance. The goal of Oneness implies a common universal principle inherent in all sects, in which their sectarian identity is seen to be at most penultimate. But I have found few real attempts to define the substance of that universal in the form of specific notions respecting its content. Indeed, most churchmen today, unlike their evangelical grandfathers in the nineteenth century and their Rationalistic great-grandfathers in the 18th, seem commonly to be frightened away from this attempt by fears of a loss of sectarian identity and the bogey of a "common core" of religion. Nevertheless the ideal, the aspiration, persists. In this connection I quote at some length what seems to have been Paul Tillich's final conclusion, stated in his book *Christianity and the Encounter of the World Religions*:

> Does our analysis demand either a mixture of religions or the victory of one religion, or the end of the religious age altogether? We answer: None of these alternatives! A mixture of religions destroys in each of them the concreteness which gives it its dynamic power. The victory of *one* religion would impose a particular religious answer on all other particular answers. The end of the religious age—one has already spoken of the end of the Christian or the Protestant age—is an impossible concept. The religious principle cannot come to an end. For the question of the ultimate meaning of life cannot be silenced as long as men are men. Religion cannot come to an end, and a particular religion will be lasting to the degree in which it negates itself as a religion. Thus Christianity will be a bearer of the religious answer as long as it breaks through its own particularity.
>
> The way to achieve this is not to relinquish one's religious tradition for the sake of a universal concept which would be nothing but a concept. The way is to penetrate into the depth of one's own religion, in devotion, thought and action. In the depth of every living religion there is a point at which the religion itself loses its importance, and that to which it points breaks through its particularity, elevating it to spiritual freedom and with it to a vision of the spiritual presence in other expressions of the ultimate meaning of man's existence.
>
> This is what Christianity must see in the present encounter of the world religions.[31]

Tillich's view seems to me implicit in the whole American experience with religious pluralism.

This sentiment permeates our tradition until, as Chesterton said, America is "a cosmopolitan commonwealth."[32] This means that its synergistic cosmopolitanism lies at the heart of its nationalism

—that a definitive element of the spiritual core which identifies it as a nation is the conception of a universal principle which is thought to transcend and include all the national and religious particularities brought to it by the people who come from all the world to be "Americanized." America, Philip Schaff noted, from Broadway in New York to the markets of San Francisco, presents "an ethnographic panorama," but

> what is most remarkable is, that over this confused diversity there broods after all a higher unity, and that in this chaos of people the traces of a specifically American national character may be discerned.[33]

What is the nature of that brooding "higher unity"? A somewhat plausible answer was suggested by a bright young student from Germany who, to improve his understanding of religion in America, had attended services in many different churches. He reported to me that what struck him most was that the only common symbol he found in all of them was the United States flag. The fact that in so many of our churches the flag of the United Nations is now displayed beside the flag of the United States, suggests the belief that in this nation it is not incongruous or unpatriotic to symbolize the universality inherent in its spiritual core. This stance originated with the Republic. In the First Federalist Paper Alexander Hamilton, arguing for acceptance of the Constitution, described the venture as an experiment to find out if men could have government by reflection and choice. Thus considered, he argued, the inducements of "philanthropy" (love for mankind) are added to those of "patriotism" (love for country) to back the experiment, because the results of the experiment will be of consequence for all humanity.

The United States is a nation. As a nation it has its spiritual core of which the flag is the symbol.[34] To be sure "nations are human societies, created in time, with the imperfections of the temporal." But we must disabuse ourselves of the notion that therefore "nations are also secular—at least in that sense of the word in which it is used as the antithesis and the negation of the religious.[35] No nation can be called "merely secular, or altogether earthly."[36] It is for this reason that nationalism, as the common sense of distinctive identity, is not necessarily absolutistic or idolatrous. It depends upon the spiritual core, the religion of the nation in question.

We may adapt Paul Tillich's view of religion and culture to an understanding of the nation:

> Religion as ultimate concern is the meaning-giving substance of culture, and culture is the totality of forms in which the basic concern of religion expresses itself. In abbreviation: religion is the substance of culture, culture is the form of religion. Such a consideration definitely prevents the establishment of a dualism of religion and culture.[37]

Religion, of course, is expressed in culturally rooted and conditioned language. And "language is the expression of man's freedom from the given situation and its demands. It gives him universals in whose power he can create worlds above the given world. . . ."[38] The "worlds above the given world" are pictured in the great mythologies or dramas of the religions, which hold before the people the ideals and aspirations which define their sense of destiny and purpose. Man, says A. N. Whitehead, is the animal that can cherish aspirations—which is to be religious, to be committed to an ideal world beyond the present world and to the incarnating of that ideal world in actuality. The religion of this, our Republic, is of this nature. Therefore to be committed to that religion is not to be committed to this world as it is, but to a world as yet above and beyond it to which this world ought to be conformed. The "American religion," contrary to Will Herberg's much popularized misunderstanding, is *not* "the American way of life"[39] as we know and experience it, any more than the Christian faith is the way of life that ordinary professing "Christians" commonly exemplify in their everyday activities.

To be sure, all "Great ideas enter into reality with evil associates and with disgusting alliances. But the greatness remains, nerving the race in its slow ascent."[40]

Seen thus the religion of the Republic is essentially prophetic, which is to say that its ideals and aspirations stand in constant judgment over the passing shenanigans of the people, reminding them of the standards by which their current practices and those of their nation are ever being judged and found wanting. One illustration is sufficient—an extract from the *Manila Times* quoted in *The Christian Century* March 2, 1966:

> It is no wonder that America, with every passing year, seems to have fewer and fewer friends in Asia. For, despite the ideals that once made America great and the burning words of quality [equality] and freedom that have made the US declaration of independence a beacon to all the world, these ideals are betrayed and the inspiring testament of the past confounded by the actuations of the higher-pressure business lobbies that now manipulate decisions in Old Foggy Bottom and around Capitol Hill. The American Eagle today brings with it, not a pledge of justice and fair play, but a 20th century version of gunboat diplomacy dedicated to the protection of US big business.[41]

Is not this "prophetic"?

It seems very commonly supposed that this that I call the religion of the Republic means worship of the state or nation. My hunch is that this supposition is rooted in the general fact that the minds of so many American Biblical scholars and theologians have been formed by European Biblical and theological scholarship, which has largely dominated our theological education for a hundred years. At least in my experience most of the seminary graduates who have come to me for graduate work in American church history confess that they know practically nothing about the American experience of Christianity and its consequent modes of thinking and acting.

Professor Joseph Haroutunian in commenting on this in a very perceptive article called "Theology and American Experience" argued that European modes of thought have not "struck a genuinely responsive chord in the mind of the American Christian."

> European philosophies and their logics . . . could not be readily naturalized in America. While professional theologians lived off European theology, the American Christian tried to get along with a minimum of intellectual discipline. When the latter thought, they did so, to a large measure, as Europeans, arguing for natural or revealed theology, or both; and they lived with a minimum of logic, going by some undisciplined if pious pragmatism which made

shambles both of faith and of practice. Thus theology and American experience have been perennially at odds, and the Church in America has had to live to a large extent without the benefit of logic.[42]

What is at issue here is the conception of the intellectual quest itself, and the relation of the theologian to the concrete forms of the visible church of which he is supposedly a responsible member and articulate spokesman. My view is, in Whitehead's words, that "No religion can be considered in abstraction from its followers, or even from its various types of followers."[43] It follows that the task of theology should be to supply a "great intellectual construction explanatory of . . . [the] modes of understanding" which actually characterize a concrete visible church or denomination, and how those modes grew out of the peculiar experience in history of that group.

Is it not the case that many of the great seminal theologians of Christendom have combined in their persons—as did men as far apart and different as Augustine and Jonathan Edwards—the offices of theologian and ecclesiastical administrator? Consequently most of their theological works were, in the grand old phrase, to explain and defend the concrete modes of thinking and practice that actually characterized their group. But in America theology has become a specialized discipline among several others, while the study and explanation of the visible church institutions has largely become the domain of historians, anthropologists and sociologists whose findings are about as distant from the center of the theologian's interest as are the actual faith and practice of church members and parish ministers.

In this context it is not difficult to understand why the contention that the religion of our Republic means worship of the state or nation goes, with a few notable exceptions, unchallenged. I would not be understood to argue that it is the best, or even a viable religious stance for our day. But I would argue that one most constant strand in its theology has been the assertion of the primacy of God over all human institutions.

From John Cotton who argued from this premise that all power that is on earth must be limited, to Mr. Justice Clark's assertion in the Schempp and Murray decision that we "are a religious peo-

ple whose institutions presuppose a Supreme Being"[44] and Dwight
Eisenhower's dictum that our institutions make no sense except
in the context of religious faith, the idea has been ploughed into
our tradition. James Madison in his *Memorial and Remonstrance
on the Religious Rights of Man* (1784) stated the implication
clearly:

> Before any man can be considered a member of civil society, he
> must be considered as a subject of the governor of the universe; and
> if a member of civil society, who enters into any subordinate as-
> sociation must always do it with a reservation of his duty to the
> general authority, much more must every man who becomes a mem-
> ber of any particular civil society do it *with the saving his allegiance
> to the universal sovereign.* We maintain, therefore, that in matters
> of religion no man's right is abridged by the institution of civil
> society. . . .

In 1946 Mr. Justice Douglas, writing the opinion in the Girourd
case,[45] reasserted the same premise:

> The victory for freedom of thought recorded in our Bill of Rights
> recognizes that in the domain of conscience there is a moral power
> higher than the State. Throughout the ages men have suffered death
> rather than subordinate their allegiance to God to the authority of
> the State. Freedom of religion guaranteed by the First Amendment
> is the product of that struggle.

Abraham Lincoln, who has seemed to me the most profound
and representative theologian of the religion of the Republic,
drew upon the universal element brought to him by the Jewish-
Christian tradition for an understanding of the concrete events of
the Civil War. "The war came," he said, and

> Both [sides] read the same Bible and pray to the same God, and
> each invokes His aid against the other. It may seem strange that
> any men should dare to ask a just God's assistance in wringing their
> bread from the sweat of other men's faces, but let us judge not, that
> we be not judged. The prayer of both could not be answered. That
> of neither has been answered fully. The Almighty has His own
> purposes. . . .
> 　　Fondly do we hope, fervently do we pray, that this mighty scourge
> of war may speedily pass away. Yet, if God wills that it continue

until all the wealth piled by the bondsman's two hundred and fifty years of unrequited toil shall be sunk, and until every drop of blood drawn with the lash shall be paid by another drawn with the sword, as was said three thousand years ago, so still it must be said, "The judgments of the Lord are true and righteous altogether."

Can anyone suppose that Madison and Lincoln and Douglas and Eisenhower in these representative pronouncements represented an idolatrous worship of the nation, or the civil state? or of "the American Way of Life"?

Only when we realize the nature of the religion of the Republic can we begin to understand the nature of the struggle between sectarian Christianity and "Americanism" which is commonly confused by calling it a struggle between Church and State, and discussing it under the categories applicable to other nations and a bygone period. "There is no such thing, organizationally, as the American church in the singular"—to quote John E. Smylie's article, "National Ethos and the Church."[46] Traditionally the struggles between church and state were struggles between two institutionalized authorities. But in the United States the contest between what is commonly called "church and state" is actually between the one coherent, institutionalized civil authority, and about three hundred collectively incoherent religious institutions whose claims tend to cancel each other out.[47] And the primary conflicts have not been and are not now between the civil authority and the "churches," but between competing religious groups themselves. Because the civil authority has had to adjudicate these differences when they threatened to disrupt civil order, it was forced to become "neutral"—neither aiding nor hindering any religious group.

I conclude that what is commonly called the relation between church and state in the United States ought to be resolved into the theological issue between the particularistic theological notions of the sects and the cosmopolitan, universal theology of the Republic. In the early days of the Republic during the period of the French Revolution and the rise of the Jeffersonian party, leading defenders of orthodox Christianity so defined the issue.[48] In their terms it was the issue between revealed and natural religion. But in the heat of the controversy they lost sight of the theological issue[49]—

which was never fully discussed on its merits—and defended revealed religion functionally, arguing that it was the only sure ground for morality upon which in turn stable government rested. They lumped all kinds and shades of dissent from their particularistic Christian views under the catchall term "Infidelity." And "infidelity," Timothy Dwight proclaimed, was a plan "for exterminating Christianity" which "presents no efficacious means of restraining Vice, or promoting Virtue, but on the contrary encourages Vice and discourages Virtue." Indeed, he thought, "So evident is the want of morals on the part of Infidels, in this country, generally, that to say—'A man is an Infidel'—is understood, of course, as a declaration that he is a plainly immoral man." Therefore, he continued,

> Infidelity, naturally and necessarily, becomes, when possessed of the control of national interests, a source of evils so numerous, and so intense, as to compel mankind to prefer any state to those evils.[50]

On this basic argument the victory for Christianity over "infidelity" was won during the early days of the Republic. Infidelity, said Roger Sherman of Connecticut, ceased to be respectable. Indeed it did. But this says nothing about the intellectual merits either of Timothy Dwight's representative defense of Christianity, or the intellectual merits of the "infidel" position. It did effectively sidetrack the theological issue for more than a century—indeed, it still does, until as Martin E. Marty argues in his book, *The Infidel*, we are in danger of going through the whole process again substituting for that era's "infidelity" the current catchall term "secularism."[51]

We have noted G. K. Chesterton's suggestion that the United States is a nation with the soul of a church. Now, having placed this suggestion in a broad context, and canvassed some of its implications, we may note how and why in a very real sense the nation for many Americans came to occupy the place in their lives that traditionally had been occupied by the church. Here I find the argument of John E. Smylie in his article "National Ethos and the Church"[52] quite convincing.

Religious freedom means pluralism. Pluralism means denominationalism and sectarianism. And, says Mr. Smylie, "this de-nominational experience has been devastating for attempts in American Protestantism to understand the church theologically." For Americans

> The denominational church, as they saw it, was not for them the New Israel of God's elect. It was a voluntary society, perhaps the most important among others, but hardly the organ through which God made his ultimate historical demands and offered his fullest earthly rewards.

And under religious freedom because no denomination could plausibly claim to be or to function as "the church" in the new nation, *the nation came more and more so to function.*

The easy theological merging of evangelical Protestantism with the religion of the Republic, and the concurrent merging of the traditional conception of the function (or purpose) of the church with that of the nation, is clearly seen in Lyman Beecher's sermon of 1827:

> Indeed, if it had been the design of heaven to establish a powerful nation in the full enjoyment of civil and religious liberty, where all the energies of man might find scope and excitement, on purpose to show the world by experiment, of what man is capable . . . where could such an experiment have been made but in this country, . . . the light of such a hemisphere shall go up to heaven, it will throw its beams beyond the waves—it will shine into the darkness there, and be comprehended; it will awaken desire, and hope, and effort, and produce revolutions and overturnings, until the world is free. . . . Floods have been poured upon the rising flame, but they can no more extinguish it than they can extinguish the flames of Aetna. Still it burns, and still the mountain heaves and murmurs; and soon it will explode with voices, and thunderings, and great earthquakes. Then will the trumpet of jubilee sound, and earth's debased millions will leap from the dust, and shake off their chains, and cry, "Hosanna to the Son of David."[53]

For Beecher, as to many of his contemporaries, the Republic had become for their era the ark of God's redemptive work in the world. Passionately Protestant and Puritan though he was, he apparently saw no incongruity in this position[54]—because, I think,

Protestantism had become for him a principle of high generality which, he thought, permeated and was being incarnated in the democratic institutions of the Republic. To that extent Beecher had in his way and in Tillich's words, penetrated "into the depth of . . . [his] own religion, in devotion, thought and action" to the "point at which the religion . . . [as such, lost] its importance" and that to which it pointed broke through its particularity.

Again, as when reflecting upon the eighteenth-century Rationalists' position, we must be careful to distinguish between the universal that Beecher plumbed for and the specific notions he came up with in defining its content. What those specific notions were need not concern us here. We are concerned to note that for Beecher, and I think he was fairly typical, the nation was assuming the traditional function of the church as he struggled to harmonize his inherited conceptual order with his religious experience as American.

"Thus," says John E. Smylie, "American Protestantism endowed the nation with churchly attributes, with three theological notes in particular."

(1) ". . . the nation emerged as the primary agent of God's meaningful activity in history."[55] For example, when Lyman Beecher wrote *A Plea for the West* in 1835, he was convinced that "the millennium would commence in America" where "by the march of revolution and civil liberty, the way of the Lord is to be prepared," and from this "nation shall the renovating power go forth." Only America can provide the "physical effort and pecuniary and moral power to evangelize the world."[56]

(2) ". . . the nation became the primary society in terms of which individual Americans discovered personal and group identity." This, of course, is what so struck Will Herberg, who popularized in his *Protestant, Catholic, Jew* the mistaken notion that this was something that happened only in the twentieth century.

(3) "As the nation became the primary community for fulfilling historic purposes and realizing personal identity" it also assumed "a churchly function in becoming the community of righteousness" —which Abraham Lincoln clearly compared to the church when he told an audience in Indianapolis on February 11, 1861 that

"when the people rise in masses in behalf of the Union and the liberties of their country, truly may it be said, 'The gates of hell shall not prevail against them.' "[57]

However much one may quarrel with Mr. Smylie's specific notions and the illustrations I have provided for them, I think his high generality must stand in substance.

What outstanding function did the Republic, conceived as "the primary agent of God's meaningful activity in history" perform vis-a-vis the many religious sects? Primarily, I think, the Republic's neutral civil authority set limits on the absolutistic tendencies inherent in every religious sect, preventing any one of them, or any combination of them, from gaining a monopoly of the definition of truth, and imposing its particular forms on all the people. The Bill of Rights and its application has prevented any sect, or combination of sects, from monopolizing the word of God, and insofar kept them from becoming heteronomous in the society. This is the "neutral" civil authority's primary contribution. Sectarianism means that each sect wants its particular forms to be imposed as God's will on all people. Historically the way of the Republic has been the way in which the sects, denied this possibility, were constantly being pushed, in Tillich's words, "to that point at which the religion itself loses its importance, and that to which it points breaks through its particularity, elevating it to spiritual freedom and with it to a vision of the spiritual presence in other expressions of the ultimate meaning of man's existence."[58] The result is that today dogmatic insistence on the ultimate significance of any sect's particular tenets or observances seems to have reached the vanishing point except in citadels of impregnable isolation from the currents moving in the unfolding history of our world. Richard Cardinal Cushing in a statement which exhibits the sincerity and "Christlike charity" for which he pleads, tells how he

> came to recognize that the differences between Catholics and Protestants in America were not so much religious as they were social and cultural. The differences in faith did not divide us so much as the ethnic differences of our parents and grandparents. I discovered that what the ecumenists today call "nontheological factors" were isolating us and setting Catholic against Protestant and Protestant against Catholic more than our doctrines.[59]

It was the civil authority that limited the conflicts between the religious groups in accordance with Jefferson's plea that "reason and persuasion" were "the only practicable instruments." And after more than two hundred years of such limitation, leaders in the churches discovered "dialogue," and in the twentieth century made a shining new virtue out of what civil authority began to force upon them in the seventeenth century. It seems to me that civil authority has been the most consistent and powerful of the "nontheological" factors that have pressed ecclesiastics into what Cardinal Cushing called "this . . . great and wonderful thing" that "we are talking to each other as Christians, as brothers." Theologically I am inclined to agree with him that this

> is a sign that the Holy Ghost is moving in our midst, is jolting us out of our smug and self-made ghettoes and pushing us toward the unity that Our Lord wills, for which He prayed on the night before He died."[60]

But it seems to me that the primary instrument used by the Holy Ghost to administer that "jolting" in the United States has been the "neutral" civil authority.

Of course, when this or any nation assumes the traditional garb of the church it is in danger of becoming heteronomous vis-a-vis other peoples and nations—asserting that they "must be subjected to a law [our law], strange and superior" though it may be to them.[61] One of the clearest exhibitions of a heteronomous attitude in this nation is found in Josiah Strong's book, *Our Country,* first published in 1885 (revised edition in 1891). Strong argued that the Anglo-Saxon, as the representative in history of "civil liberty" and "pure *spiritual* Christianity," was "divinely commissioned to be, in a peculiar sense, his brother's keeper." Therefore "it is chiefly to the English and American peoples that we must look for the evangelization of the world . . . that all men may be lifted up into the light of the highest Christian civilization." Add to these considerations, he continued, the fact of our "rapidly increasing strength in modern times, and we have well-nigh a demonstration" that God is "not only preparing in our Anglo-Saxon civilization the die with which to stamp the people of the earth, but . . . [is] also massing behind that die the mighty power with which to press it." In brief, he concluded that "God with infinite wisdom and skill" is preparing our civilization to "impress its institutions upon mankind. . . ."[62]

The theology of the synergistic and theonomous religion of the Republic stands against this idolatrous tendency equally with Christianity, and Christians—even they cannot Christianize it— might well be advised to recognize a potential ally. Judging from the past experience of the Christian church, one may doubt that any stand will be effective. For, to quote Albert Camus,[63] as in the medieval church the efficacy of the limit in itself, born in the universality of the Christian religion was undermined, and the church "made increasing claims to temporal power and historical dynamism," so the Republic is likely to follow in the church's footsteps. And if sectarians continue to undermine rather than understand the religion of the Republic, it is likely that the nation will become increasingly heteronomous as the church did. But the limit born in the religion of the Republic is not likely to be undermined by increasing "secularism" any more than was the limit born in the religion of the Catholic society. The gates of hell have never prevailed against the church's vision of the universal, but religious particularity possessed of coercive power has. Sectarianism, religious or national, with heteronomous pretensions is a greater threat than secularism or outright atheism, because it often comes disguised in the garb of "the faith once delivered to the Saints."

Our final concern, then, is to assure ourselves that our attitude toward the nation does not become idolatrous; that the state does not become God; that the Republic does not become heteronomous vis-a-vis other nations. In this situation, as Albert Camus argued in *The Rebel*,[64] we shall be saved if at all by men who "refuse . . . to be deified in that they refuse the unlimited power to inflict death"—by men who "learn to live and to die, and, in order to be a man, . . . refuse to be a god." All men, and all sects, must understand "that they correct one another, and that a limit under the sun, shall curb them all. Each tells the other that he is not God."

Is not this what our democratic Republic sought to incarnate in practice in the nation "conceived in liberty and dedicated to the proposition that all men are created equal"—in whose spiritual core was a theonomous cosmopolitanism? As the Christian sects carried the universal vision until it was, largely in spite of them, incarnated in a religiously pluralistic commonwealth, so perhaps that commonwealth is the bearer in history of the cosmopolitanism which, when and if incarnated in world institutions, may compel the nation-churches to live side by side in overt peace under law— as our Republic compelled the heteronomous religious sects to do until they discovered that limitation of their conflicts to reason and persuasion was a viable path to peace and union—that dialogue was a virtue.

And can we not recognize that our individual refusal to be God, and our cherishing and preserving a system that defends the right of each to tell the other "that he is not God" is, perhaps, in Lincoln's words, "the last, best hope of earth" which we may "nobly save or meanly lose"?

NOTES

1. Raymond T. Bond (ed.), *The Man Who Was Chesterton* (Garden City, N. Y.: Doubleday Image Books, 1960), p. 125.

2. *Ibid.*, p. 131.

3. *Ibid.*, p. 132.

4. *America: A sketch of Its Political, Social, and Religious Character*, pp. 80-81. This work was first published in 1855. Reference is to the edition edited by Perry Miller and published by the Belknap Press of the Harvard University Press in 1961.

5. Ernest Barker, "Christianity and Nationalism" [1927], in *Church, State and Education* (Ann Arbor: University of Michigan Press, 1957), p. 131. Hereafter cited as "Barker."

6. Barker, p. 132. The quotations in the following two paragraphs are taken from this book, pp. 133-136.

7. Barker, p. 136.

8. I quote from the edition published by the Congregational Board of Publication, Boston, 1860, pp. 39-40.

9. Barker, p. 138. *William Temple, Citizen and Churchman* (London: Eyre & Spottiswoode, 1941), p. 68.

10. Barker, pp. 138-139.

11. Crane Brinton, *The Shaping of the Modern Mind* (New York: Mentor Books, 1953), pp. 59-61.

12. *American Catholicism* (Chicago: University of Chicago Press, 1955), p. 50.

13. Barker, p. 140.

14. *The Secular City* (New York: The Macmillan Co., 1965), p. 105.

15. *America*, p. 88.

16. Quoted in *New Yorker* magazine, Feb. 26, 1966, p. 112.

17. See Perry Miller and Thomas H. Johnson, *The Puritans* (New York: American Book Co., 1938), p. 187. Perry Miller, *Errand into the Wilderness* (Cambridge: Belknap Press of the Harvard University Press, 1956), pp. 146-147.

18. See the Cambridge Platform of 1648, chap. X., sect. 3, in Williston Walker, *The Creeds and Platforms of Congregationalism* (Boston: The Pilgrim Press, 1960 [first published 1893], p. 217.

19. P. 29.

20. Robert H. Jackson, *The Supreme Court in the American System of Government* (New York: Harper & Row, 1963), pp. 2-3.

21. Quoted in *Religion in America* (New York: Harper & Brothers, 1845), p. 119.

22. Mr. Justice Black's dissenting opinion in *Zorach* v. *Clauson*, in Joseph Tussman (ed.), *The Supreme Court on Church and State* (New York: Oxford University Press, 1962), pp. 270-271. Hereafter this book is cited as "Tussman."

23. Granted that "the fact is that the line which separates the secular from the sectarian in American life is elusive," as Mr. Justice Brennan noted in his concurring opinion in the Schempp and Murray case; in Arthur Frommer (ed.), *The Bible and the Public Schools* (New York: Liberal Press Books, 1963), p. 86. Hereafter this book is cited as "Frommer."

24. "The Commitment of the Self and the Freedom of the Mind," in Perry Miller *et al.*, *Religion and Freedom of Thought* (Garden City, N. Y.: Doubleday and Co., 1954), p. 59.

25. John R. G. Hassard, *Life of the Most Reverend John Hughes D.D., First Archbishop of New York. With Extracts from His Private Correspondence* (New York: D. Appleton and Company, 1866), p. 226.

26. Quoted in H. Shelton Smith, Robert T. Handy, and Lefferts A. Loetscher, *American Christianity* (New York: Charles Scribner's Sons, 1960), Vol. I, p. 394.

27. Alfred North Whitehead, *Adventures of Ideas* (New York: Mentor Books, [first published 1933]), p. 25.

Compare Lancelot Law Whyte, *The Next Development in Man* (New York: Mentor Books, 1949), pp. 220-221; "The universality of the formative process, once recognized and accepted, casts its spell over man. Every element finds its place in the system of nature, and every particular form symbolizes a general form. Man is himself the supreme symbol, the richest of natural systems. Words are symbols spoken by man, but in the unitary world every form is a symbol and speaks to man."

28. Thomas Jefferson, "Notes on Virginia," in Joseph L. Blau (ed.), *Cornerstones of Religious Freedom in America*, Rev. ed. (New York: Harper & Row Torchbooks, 1964), p. 82.

29. *Ibid.*, p. 83.

30. *Our Country: Its Possible Future and Its Present Crisis* (New York: Baker & Taylor Co., 1891), pp. 101-102.

31. New York: Columbia University Press, 1963, pp. 96-97.

32. *The Man Who Was Chesterton*, p. 129.

33. *America*, pp. 45-46.

34. "The ultimate foundation of a free society is the binding tie of cohesive sentiment. Such a sentiment is fostered by all those agencies of the mind and spirit which may serve to gather up the traditions of a people, transmit them from generation to generation, and thereby create that continuity of a treasured common life which constitutes a civilization. 'We live by symbols.' The flag is the symbol of our national unity, transcending all internal differences, however large, within the framework of the Constitution. This Court has had occasion to say that '. . . the flag is the symbol' of the Nation's power, the emblem of freedom in its truest, best sense. . . . it signifies government resting on the consent of the governed; liberty regulated by law; the protection of the weak against the strong; security against the exercise of arbitrary power; and absolute safety for free institutions against foreign aggression.' " Mr. Justice Frankfurter, opinion of the Court in the Gobitis case, 1940. In Tussman, p. 83.

35. Barker, p. 147.

36. Barker, p. 142.

37. *Theology of Culture*, ed. Robert C. Kimball (New York: Oxford University Press Galaxy Books, 1964), p. 42.

38. *Ibid.*, p. 47.

39. *Protestant, Catholic, Jew: An Essay in American Religious Sociology* (New York: Doubleday & Anchor Books, 1960), pp. 74-81.

40. Whitehead, *Adventures of Ideas*, p. 26.

41. P. 85.

42. *Criterion* III (Winter 1964), p. 7.

43. *Adventures of Ideas*, p. 25.

44. In Frommer, p. 65.

45. In Tussman, p. 203.

46. *Theology Today*, XX (October 1963), p. 313.

47. Lucy Mack Smith, mother of the prophet Joseph Smith, stated this effect very clearly. "If," she argued, "I remain a member of no church all religious people will say I am of the world; and, if I join some one of the different denominations, all the rest will say I am in error. No church will admit that I am right, except the one with which I am associated. This makes them witnesses against each other; and how can I decide in such a case as this, seeing they are all unlike the church of Christ, as it existed in former days!" *Biographical Sketches of Joseph Smith the Prophet and His Progenitors for Many Generations* (Lamoni, Iowa: Reorganized Church of Jesus Christ of Latter-Day Saints, 1912), p. 12.

In this context it is not surprising that when the "personages" first appeared to Joseph Smith, he says, "I asked the personages who stood above me in the light which of all the sects was right—and which I should join. I was answered that I must join none of them, for they were all wrong."

48. As did also Thomas Paine, who said in the second paragraph of *The Age of Reason* (1974) that "the circumstance that has now taken place in France, of the total abolition of the whole national order of priesthood and of everything appertaining to compulsive systems of religion, and compulsive articles of faith, has not only precipitated my intention, but rendered a work of this kind exceedingly necessary; lest, in the general wreck of superstition, of false systems of government, and false theology, we lose sight of morality, of humanity, and of the theology that is true."

49. Paine complained in Part 2 of *The Age of Reason* that "all my opponents resort more or less to what they call Scripture evidence and Bible authority to help them out. They are so little masters of the subject as to confound a dispute about authenticity with a dispute about doctrines; . . ."

50. Quoted in Sidney E. Mead, *Nathaniel William Taylor, 1786-1858* (Chicago: University of Chicago Press, 1942), pp. 44, 45-46.

51. *The Infidel: Free Thought and American Religion* (Cleveland: Meridian Books, 1961), pp. 16, 203.

52. *Theology Today*, XX (October 1963), pp. 313-321.

53. "The Memory of Our Fathers," in *Sermons Delivered on Various Occasions* (Boston: T. R. Marvin, 1828), pp. 301-302, 304, 305.

54. Nor did many of his contemporaries. "The American civil religion was never anticlerical or militantly secular. On the contrary, it borrowed selectively from the religious tradition in such a way that the average American saw no conflict between the two." Robert N. Bellah, "Civil Religion in America," *Daedalus*, Winter 1967, p. 13.

55. *Theology Today*, XX (October 1963), p. 314.

56. *A Plea for the West* (Cincinnati: Truman & Smith, 1835), p. 10. Beecher's sentiment was shared by most of the evangelicals. To take one example, his contemporary, S. S. Schmucker, president of the Lutheran seminary at Gettysburg, argued that "this country . . . is the chosen theatre of God for the free, unbiased development of humanity, and the settlement of the highest questions regarding its privileges, capacities and duties, in social, political and religious life." *The American Lutheran Church, Historically, Doctrinally, and Practically Delineated* (Springfield: D. Harbaugh, 1852), p. 235.

57. Roy P. Basler (ed.), *The Collected Works of Abraham Lincoln* (New Brunswick: Rutgers University Press, 1953), Vol. IV, pp. 193-194.

58. *Christianity and the Encounter of the World Religions*, p. 97.

59. "Can Christians Really Unite?" in *Dominion*, January 1966, pp. 21, 19.

60. *Ibid.*, p. 19.

61. Paul Tillich, *The Protestant Era*, trans. James Luther Adams (Chicago: University of Chicago Press, 1948), p. 56.

62. *Our Country*, pp. 208-210, 214, 222.

63. *The Rebel: An Essay on Man in Revolt*, trans. Anthony Bower (New York: Vintage Books, 1958), p. 299.

64. *Ibid.*, pp. 305-306.

WILL HERBERG

4 America's Civil Religion: What It Is and Whence It Comes

WE GET OUR NOTION of civil religion from the world of classical antiquity. In the world of ancient Athens and Rome, "the state and religion were so completely identified that it was impossible even to distinguish the one from the other. . . . Every city had its city religion; a city was a little church, all complete, with its gods, its dogmas, and its worship."[1] In recent years, many observers of American life have come to the conclusion that this country, too, has its civil religion, though not generally recognized as such, but fully operative in the familiar way, with its creed, cult, code, and community, like every other religion. On this there is wide agreement; but there are considerable differences among historians, sociologists, and theologians as to the sources of America's civil religion, its manifestations, and its evaluation in cultural and religious terms. These are precisely the matters I should like to discuss in the following paragraphs, with the hope of reaching some tentative conclusions on the subject.

"Every functioning society," says Robin Williams, in his influential work, *American Society: A Sociological Interpretation* (1951), "has, to an important degree, a common religion. The possession of a common set of ideas, [ideals], rituals, and symbols can supply an overarching sense of unity even in a society otherwise riddled with conflict."[2] This we might call the *operative* religion of a society, the system of norms, values, and allegiances actually functioning as such in the ongoing social life of the community. And, of course, the operative religion of a society emerges out of, and reflects, the history of that society as well as the structural forms that give it its shape and character. If we ask ourselves what is this system of "ideas, [ideals], rituals, and symbols" that serve as the "common religion" of Americans, providing them with an "overarching sense of unity," it is obvious that it cannot be any of the professed faiths of Americans, however sincerely held; I mean Protestantism, Catholicism, or Judaism, or any of the many denominations into which American Protestantism is fragmented. What is it, then, that does serve that all-important function? What is it in and through which Americans recognize their basic unity with other Americans as Americans? What is it that provides that "overarching sense of unity," expressed in the system of allegiances, norms, and values functioning in actual life, without which no society can long endure? It seems to me that a realistic appraisal of the values, ideas, and behavior of the American people leads to the conclusion that Americans, by and large, find this "common religion" in the system familiarly known as the American Way of Life. It is the American Way of Life that supplies American society with its "overarching sense of unity" amid conflict. It is the American Way of Life to which they are devoted. It is the American Way of Life that Americans are admittedly and unashamedly intolerant about. It is the American Way of Life that provides the framework in terms of which the crucial values of American existence are couched. By every realistic criterion, the American Way of Life is the operative religion of the American people.

This is the civil religion of Americans. In it we have—slightly modifying Fustel de Coulanges's classic formulation—religion and national life so completely identified that it is impossible to distinguish the one from the other. I want to make it clear that when I designate the American Way of Life as America's civil religion, I am not thinking of it as a so-called common-denominator religion; it is not a synthetic system composed of beliefs to be found in all or in a group of religions. It is an organic structure of ideas, values, and beliefs that constitutes a faith common to Americans as Americans, and is genuinely operative in their lives; a faith that markedly influences, and is influenced by, the professed religions of Americans. Sociologically, anthropologically, it is *the* American religion, undergirding American national life and overarching American society, despite all indubitable differences of ethnicity, religion, section, culture, and class. And it is a civil religion in the strictest sense of the term, for, in it, national life is apotheosized, national values are religionized, national heroes are divinized, national history is experienced as a *Heilsgeschichte*, as a redemptive history. All these aspects of the American Way as America's civil religion I will illustrate and document. But, first, I want to call attention to the notable difference in structure and content between America's civil religion and the civil religion of classical antiquity, or even the civil religion as conceived of by Jean-Jacques Rousseau. It is a difference that reflects not only the vast difference in historical context, but especially the separation between the culture of pre-Christian antiquity and the culture of Western Christendom, especially America, so thoroughly permeated with Jewish-Christian visions of redemptive history, messianism, and messianic fulfillment.

Let us try to look at the American Way of Life as America's civil religion in the same objective way, in the same detached yet not unfriendly way that an anthropologist looks upon the religion and culture of the primitive society he is studying. I say, let us try; it is a question whether we, as Americans, can really scrutinize ourselves, as Americans, with any very high degree of objectivity. For that, we may need another Tocqueville, though preferably not another Frenchman.

America's civil religion has its spiritual side, of course. I should include under this head, first, belief in a Supreme Being, in which Americans are virtually unanimous, proportionately far ahead of any other nation in the Western world. Then I should mention idealism and moralism: for Americans, every serious national effort is a "crusade" and every serious national position a high moral issue. Among Americans, the supreme value of the individual takes its place high in the spiritual vision of America's civil religion: and, with it, in principle, if not in practice—and, of course, principle and practice frequently come into conflict in every religion—the "brotherhood" of Americans: "After all, we're all Americans!" is the familiar invocation. Above all, there is the extraordinarily high valuation Americans place on religion. The basic ethos of America's civil religion is quite familiar: the American Way is dynamic; optimistic; pragmatic; individualistic; egalitarian, in the sense of feeling uneasy at any overtly manifested mark of the inequalities endemic in our society as in every other society; and pluralistic, in the sense of being impatient with the attempt of any movement, cause, or institution to take in "too much ground," as the familiar phrase has it. Culturally, the American Way exhibits an intense faith in education, significantly coupled with a disparagement of culture in the aesthetic sense; and, characteristically, an extraordinarily high moral valuation of—sanitation! This is a good example of how what would appear to be rather ordinary matter-of-fact values become thoroughly religionized in the American Way as civil religion. A printed placard displayed in hundreds, perhaps thousands, of restaurants all over the country reads: "Sanitation is a way of life. As a way of life, it must be nourished from within and grow as a spiritual ideal in human relations." Here cleanliness is not merely next to godliness; it is virtually on the same level, as a kind of equivalent.

But, of course, it is the politico-economic aspect of the American Way as America's civil religion that is most familiar to us, as, indeed, in its own way, it was in the civil religions of the ancient world. If America's civil religion had to be defined in one phrase, the "religion of democracy" would undoubtedly be the phrase, but democracy in a peculiarly American sense. It exalts national unity, as, indeed, every civil religion does. On its political side, it means the Constitution. I am reminded of Socrates' deification of the Laws of Athens in the Platonic dialogue, the *Crito*. On its economic side, it means "free enterprise." On its social side, an egalitarianism which, as I have indicated, is not only compatible with, but indeed actually implies, vigorous economic competition and high social mobility. Spiritually, it is best expressed in the very high valuation of religion, and in that special kind of idealism which has come to be recognized as characteristically American. But it is in its vision of America, in its symbols and rituals, in its holidays and its liturgy, in its Saints and its sancta, that it shows itself to be so truly and thoroughly a religion, the common religion of Americans, America's civil religion.

But a word of caution. I have listed a number of aspects of the
American Way that do not seem, at first sight, to be religious in a
certain narrow sense of the word. But that is exactly the character
of a civil religion; it is the religionization of the national life and
national culture. You may be sure that the great annual Panathenaic Procession from the lower agora to the Acropolis, in which the
youths of seventeen or eighteen received their arms and became
adult citizens, entering the Athenian armed forces, would have
seemed to us, accustomed as we are to the idea, though not to the
reality, of the separation of national life and religion, to be really
a political ceremony. But it was the archaic image of Athena that
was carried at the head of the procession, and the procession
moved on to the Parthenon, the temple of Athena. Do you want
the contemporary equivalent of this symbolization? Then think
back to the presidential inauguration ceremony of 1973. Who
came forward as the intensely prestigious figures symbolizing this
great civil ceremony of ours? The Warrior and the Priest, the
soldier and the clergyman. Here is the perfect synthetic symbol of
our civil religion, thoroughly traditional and immensely potent—
and, if I may say so, not altogether unlike the Panathenaic Procession of ancient Athens.

But let us get back to what I would take to be the culminating
aspects of this account of America's civil religion—its view of
America, its Saints and sancta, its redemptive history. What is
America in the vision of America's civil religion? Look at the
reverse of the Great Seal of the United States, which is on the
dollar bill. You see an unfinished pyramid, representing the Ameri-
can national enterprise, and over it the all-seeing eye of God.
Most impressive are the mottoes, in Latin naturally: "Annuit
Coeptis," "He (God) has smiled upon our beginnings"; and
"Novus Ordo Seclorum," "A New Order of the Ages." That is
America in America's civil religion: a new order, initiated under
God, and flourishing under his benevolent providence. Could the
national and the religious be more combined; is it at all possible
to separate the religious and the national in this civil religion, any
more than it was in ancient Greece or Rome?

It is this vision that gives substance to American history as
redemptive history in America's civil religion. For this we can
borrow the felicitous phrase of Oscar Handlin, "Adventure in

Freedom." That is how Americans see the ultimate meaning of American history.

A redemptive history has, of course, its messianism. And so does America's civil religion. Over a century ago, in 1850, in an impassioned outburst in *White Jacket*, Herman Melville formulated this messianic vision in these tremendous words:

> God has predestined, mankind expects, great things from our race; and great things we feel in our souls. The rest of the nations must soon be in our rear. We are the pioneers of the world, the advance guard, sent on through the wilderness of untried things to break a new path in the New World that is ours. . . . Long enough have we debated whether, indeed, the political Messiah has come. But he has come in us. . . . And, let us remember that, with ourselves, almost for the first time in history, national selfishness is unbounded philanthropy.

One recalls Pericles' celebrated funeral oration, givin by Thucydides.

Similarly Charles Fleischer, at the turn of the twentieth century, observed: "We of America are the 'peculiar people,' consecrated to the mission of realizing Democracy, [which] is potentially a universal spiritual principle, aye, a religion."[3] Or Hugh Miller, in 1948: "America was not created to be supreme among the 'great powers.' It was created to inaugurate the transition of human society to just society. It is a missionary enterprise, propagating a gospel for all men."[4]

With its redemptive history and its messianism, America's civil religion has its liturgy and its liturgical year. The traditional Christian year and the Jewish religious year have been virtually eroded in American popular religion, reduced to Christmas and Easter on the Christian side, and to Passover and the High Holy Days on the Jewish side. But, as W. Lloyd Warner tells us, "all societies, simple or complex, possess some form of ceremonial calendar. . . ."[5] In America it is the ceremonial calendar of America's civil religion, our yearly round of national holidays. Lloyd Warner explains:

> The ceremonial calendar of American society, this yearly round of holidays and holy days, . . . is a symbol system used by all Ameri-

cans. Christmas, [New Year,] Thanksgiving, Memorial Day, [Wash-
ington's and Lincoln's birthdays,] and the Fourth of July are days
in our ceremonial calendar which allow Americans to express common sentiments . . . and share their feelings with others on set days
preestablished by the society for that very purpose. This [ceremonial]
calendar functions to draw all people together, to emphasize their
similarities and common heritage, to minimize their differences,
and to contribute to their thinking, feeling, and acting alike.[6]

Recall Robin Williams's characterization of civil religion as the
common religion of a people that is quoted at the outset of this
essay.

America's civil religion, too, has its Saints—preeminently Washington and Lincoln—and its sancta and its shrines—think of
Washington, D.C. and Hyde Park. Some examination of the
Saints of our civil religion is, I think, in place here. I turn to
Lloyd Warner again. He is describing, as an anthropologist would,
a Memorial Day service in Yankee City. First, as to the religio-
national function of Memorial Day: "The Memorial Day ceremonies and subsidiary rites . . . are rituals which are a sacred
symbol system, which functions periodically to integrate the whole
community, with its conflicting symbols and its opposing autonomous churches and associations. . . . Memorial Day is a cult of
the dead which organizes and integrates the various faiths, ethnic
and class groups into a sacred unity."[7] That is what a civil religion
is about. And then he continues, quoting the chief Memorial Day
orator at the ceremony he is reporting: " 'No character except the
Carpenter of Nazareth,' this orator proclaimed, 'has ever been
honored the way Washington and Lincoln have been in New
England. Virtue, freedom from sin, and righteousness were qualities possessed by Washington and Lincoln and, in possessing these
qualities, both were true Americans. . . .' "[8] It will not escape
notice, I hope, that Washington and Lincoln are here raised to
superhuman level, as true Saints of America's civil religion. They
are equipped with the qualities and virtues that, in traditional
Christianity, are attributed to Jesus alone—freedom from sin, for
example. And they are endowed with these exalted qualities
simply by virtue of the fact that they were—true Americans! I
don't know any more impressive illustration of the deeply religious nature of America's civil religion.

What are the sources of America's civil religion? Only in the most general way need we refer to civil religion in the ancient world, or even to the clearly articulated notion of civil religion projected by Jean-Jacques Rousseau as the civil religion of his ideal society so carefully described in his *Social Contract*. First, we must recognize, and I want to repeat, that, in Robin Williams's words, "Every functioning society has, to an important degree, a common religion, . . . a common set of ideas, [ideals,] rituals, and symbols. . . ."[9] And then we have to look to American history and American experience for the sources of the particular form and features of America's civil religion as the American Way of Life. After careful study and scrutiny I have come to the conclusion that the American Way of Life, and therefore America's civil religion, is compounded of the two great religious movements that molded America—the Puritan way, secularized; and the Revivalist way, secularized. The legacy of Puritanism has endowed us with its strenuous, idealistic, moralistic character; but deprived, through pervasive secularization, of the Puritan sense of sin and judgment. The Revivalist legacy has given us its active, pragmatic, what I might term its promotional, character; the slogan "Deeds not creeds!" comes not from John Dewey, but from mid-nineteenth-century revivalism; but again, through drastic secularization it is a pragmatism, a promotionalism, an expansivism no longer "in the cause of Christ."

We do not know how against what earlier background, if any, the civil religion of Athens or Rome emerged into historical times; but we can see the emergence of America's civil religion out of the earlier Protestant Christianity some time toward the middle of the nineteenth century. Here we may be guided by Sidney Mead. "What was not so obvious at the time," Professor Mead writes, referring to the second half of the nineteenth century,

> was that the United States, in effect, had two religions, or at least two different forms of the same religion, and the prevailing Protestant ideology represented a syncretistic mingling of the two. The first was the religion of the [Protestant] denominations. . . . The second was the religion of the American society and nation. This . . . was articulated in terms of the destiny of America, under God, to be fulfilled by perfecting the democratic way of life for the example and betterment of mankind.[10]

In these percipient words, we can recognize the outlines and substance of America's civil religion.

These words suggest that there have been various stages in the emergence of civil religion in America and in the varying relations of this religion to the more conventional religions of Christianity and Judaism. Unfortunately, this aspect of the problem of the development of America's civil religion has not yet received adequate study. Yet we are in a position to distinguish very generally certain phases. There is, first of all, the emerging syncretism to which Mead refers in the passage I have just read. After that, apparently, comes a very explicit and unembarrassed religionization of the American Way. And finally, some time in this century, the explicit exaltation of the American Way, or democracy, as the super-religion, over and above all other religions. Consider these two statements. The first is from J. Paul Williams, a distinguished scholar and professor of religion: "Americans must come to look upon the democratic ideal (not necessarily the practice of it) as the Will of God, or, if they please, of Nature. . . . Americans must be brought to the conviction that democracy is the very Law of Life. . . . The state must be brought into the picture; governmental agencies must teach the democratic idea *as religion*. . . . Primary responsibility for teaching democracy as religion must be given to the public schools."[11] The civil religion as established religion with the public schools as its seminaries. But it is Horace M. Kallen, the well-known philosopher, who has put the matter most clearly and most strikingly. "For the communicants of the democratic faith," Kallen proclaims, "it [democracy] is the religion *of* and *for* religions. . . . [It is] the religion of religions; all may freely come together in it."[12] America's civil religion, democracy, is the overarching faith, in which the particular religions may find their particular place, provided they don't claim any more. Think of the Roman overarching civil religion with its Pantheon, and with the niches in the Pantheon so generously awarded by Rome to the particular ethnic religions, so long as they did not come into collision with the overarching faith of Rome.

How shall we envisage the relation of America's civil religion to the various versions of Christianity and Judaism professed by Americans? This was a problem for the world of classical antiquity as well. Romans and Greeks of those days had at least four different kinds of religion in coexistence: (1) the very ancient Indo-European religion of the high gods, the Olympian deities for the Greeks—the religion of Zeus-Jupiter; (2) the domestic religion, compounded of the cult of ancestors and the household gods, the *lares* and *penates* of Rome; (3) the so-called mystery religions, the personal salvationary cults, largely though not entirely of foreign, oriental origin; and, finally, (4) the great civil religion of the *polis* and the *civitas*, expanded into empire. We know, from unfortunately too fragmentary data, that the relations among these coexisting religions were always uneasy, sometimes hostile. In the Rome of the late republic and early empire, repeated attempts were made to outlaw the oriental salvation cults as incompatible with "true Roman piety," but to no effect. Even when the various bans were lifted or fell into disuse, however, the relations remained far from cordial.

In this country today, there seems to be, for the great mass of Americans, no sense of conflict, or even of tension, between America's civil religion and the traditional religions of Christianity and Judaism professed by almost all Americans. The civil religion is, of course, affirmed as the American Way, but is neither seen nor denominated as a religion by the great mass of Americans; and that makes coexistence all the easier. Yet there are some points of tension, perhaps even of conflict, at the periphery, what I have elsewhere called the "hold-out groups." There are, first, here and there, groups of incompletely enculturated—that is, incompletely Americanized—immigrants; quite naturally they stand on the margins of the American Way, and therefore have not yet come under the coverage of America's civil religion. It would not be difficult to specify names and places, but that is hardly necessary. These groups are very small, and are rapidly diminishing.

Second, there are what are sometimes called the "old-fashioned" churches, churches with a strong creedal or confessional tradition, which tend to look askance at some of the manifestations and expressions of America's civil religion. But this attitude, too, is rapidly eroding, and will not, I think, last very long. Finally, among the "hold-out" groups are the theologians and theologically inclined laymen, a rather small group in this country, but the group from which the various attemps to identify, examine, and criticize America's civil religion have mostly come. All in all, however, these "hold-out groups" comprise a very small proportion of the American people. By and large, the great mass of Americans are not aware of any tension, or friction, or conflict between America's civil religion and their professed faiths, whatever they may be.

I come now to the last, and perhaps most difficult, question that I have set myself in examining this problem of civil religion. And that question is double: how are we to evaluate America's civil religion culturally, on the one hand, and theologically, on the other? Some of my friendly critics, such as Sidney Mead and Andrew Greeley, gently upbraid me for treating America's civil religion too harshly. I plead Not guilty, and I will try to make my case. First, I, of course, regard America's civil religion as a genuine religion; and so was the Athenian civil religion and the Roman— in fact, all the various civil religions of the ancient world. The fact that they were, and America's civil religion is, congruent with the culture is no argument against it; all religions, even the most sectarian, are embedded in, and display some congruence with, some concretion of culture, simply because all religions, in their human dimension (and they all possess a human dimension) must necessarily reflect some aspects of human society and social life. Furthermore, America's civil religion, as it has emerged during the past two centuries, strikes me as a noble religion, celebrating some very noble civic virtues. But so was the Roman civil religion in its best period, and so was Confucianism turned into religion in classical China. On its cultural side, I would regard the American Way of Life, which is the social face of America's civil religion, as probably the best way of life yet devised for a mass society—with the proviso that even the best way of life, if it is the way of life of a mass society, will have its grave defects. And, if Abraham Lincoln, for instance, is to be taken as an exemplar of our civil religion, then we can see what a powerful strain of genuine Christian spirituality, in this case Calvinist, has entered into it. So I certainly would not want to disparage America's civil religion in its character as religion.

But, if it is an authentic religion as civil religion, America's civil religion is not, and cannot be seen as, authentic Christianity or Judaism, or even as a special cultural version of either or both. Because they serve a jealous God, these biblical faiths cannot allow any claim to ultimacy and absoluteness on the part of any thing or any idea or any system short of God, even when what claims to be the ultimate locus of ideas, ideals, values, and allegiance is the very finest of human institutions; it is still human, man's own construction, and not God himself. To see America's civil religion as somehow standing above or beyond the biblical religions of Judaism and Christianity, and Islam too, as somehow including them and finding a place for them in its overarching unity, is idolatry, however innocently held and whatever may be the subjective intentions of the believers. But this is theology, which I have discussed elsewhere, and which I have tried to avoid here. In this essay it has been my intention to set down my thinking, and some of the conclusions I have reached, on the nature, sources, purposes, structure, and functioning of America's civil religion, and to call attention to some of the questions that need urgent attention for a clarification of the overall problem. To some degree, I hope, I have contributed to this end, so important for a real understanding of our culture, society, and religion.

NOTES

1. Numa Denis Fustel de Coulanges, *La Cité antique* (1864), chap. VII, *ad finem*; chap. VI, *ad finem*.
2. Robin Williams, *American Society: A Sociological Interpretation* (New York: Alfred A. Knopf, 1952), p. 312.
3. Quoted in Arthur Mann, "Charles Fleischer's Religion of Democracy," *Commentary*, June 1954.
4. Hugh Miller, *An Historical Introduction to Modern Philosophy* (New York, 1948), p. 570.
5. W. Lloyd Warner, *Structure of American Life* (Edinburgh, 1952), p. 2.
6. *Ibid.*
7. *Ibid.*, p. 214.
8. *Ibid.*, p. 220 .

9. Williams, *op. cit.*, p. 312.

10. Sidney E. Mead, "American Protestantism since the Civil War: From Denominationalism to Americanism," *The Lively Experiment* (New York, 1963), p. 135.

11. J. Paul Williams, *What Americans Believe and How They Worship* (New York: Harper & Row, 1951), pp. 71, 78, 368, 374.

12. H. M. Kallen, "Democracy's True Religion," *Saturday Review of Literature*, July 28, 1951.

W. LLOYD WARNER

5   An American Sacred Ceremony

Memorial Day and Symbolic Behavior

Every year in the springtime when the flowers are in bloom and the trees and shrubs are most beautiful, citizens of the Union celebrate Memorial Day. Over most of the United States it is a legal holiday. Being both sacred and secular, it is a holy day as well as a holiday and is accordingly celebrated.

For some it is part of a long holiday of pleasure, extended outings, and great athletic events; for others it is a sacred day when the dead are mourned and sacred ceremonies are held to express their sorrow; but for most Americans, especially in the smaller cities, it is both sacred and secular. They feel the sacred importance of the day when they, or members of their family, participate in the ceremonies; but they also enjoy going for an automobile trip or seeing or reading about some important athletic event staged on Memorial Day. This chapter will be devoted to the analysis and interpretation of Memorial Day to learn its meanings as an American sacred ceremony, a rite that evolved in this country and is native to it.

Memorial Day originated in the North shortly after the end of the Civil War as a sacred day to show respect for the Union soldiers who were killed in the War between the States. Only since the last two wars has it become a day for all who died for their country. In the South only now are they beginning to use it to

Reprinted, with permission, from *American Life: Dream and Reality* (Chicago: University of Chicago Press, 1953). © 1953 and 1962 by The University of Chicago.

express southern respect and obligation to the nation's soldier dead.

Memorial Day is an important occasion in the American ceremonial calendar and as such is a unit of this larger ceremonial system of symbols. Close examination discloses that it, too, is a symbol system in its own right, existing within the complexities of the larger one.

Symbols include such familiar things as written and spoken words, religious beliefs and practices, including creeds and ceremonies, the several arts, such familiar signs as the cross and the flag, and countless other objects and acts which stand for something more than that which they are. The red, white, and blue cloth and the crossed sticks in themselves and as objects mean very little, but the sacred meanings which they evoke are of such deep significance to some that millions of men have sacrificed their lives for the first as the Stars and Stripes and for the second as the Christian Cross.

Symbols are substitutes for all known real and imaginary actions, things, and the relations among them. They stand for and express feelings and beliefs about men and what they do, about the world and what happens in it. What they stand for may or may not exist. What they stand for may or may not be true, for what they express may be no more than a feeling, an illusion, a myth, or a vague sensation falsely interpreted. On the other hand, that for which they stand may be as real and objectively verifiable as the Rock of Gibraltar.

The ceremonial calendar of American society, this yearly round of holidays and holy days, partly sacred and partly secular, but more sacred than secular, is a symbol system used by all Americans. Christmas and Thanksgiving, Memorial Day and the Fourth of July, are days in our ceremonial calendar which allow Americans to express common sentiments about themselves and share their feelings with others on set days pre-established by the society for this very purpose. This calendar functions to draw all people together to emphasize their similarities and common heritage; to minimize their differences; and to contribute to their thinking, feeling, and acting alike. All societies, simple or complex, possess some form of ceremonial calendar, if it be no more than the seasonal alternation of secular and ceremonial periods, such as that used by the Australian aborigines in their yearly cycle.

The integration and smooth functioning of the social life of a modern community are very difficult because of its complexity. American communities are filled with churches, each claiming great authority and each with its separate sacred symbol system. Many of them are in conflict, and all of them in opposition to one another. Many associations, such as the Masons, the Odd Fellows, and the like, have sacred symbol systems which partly separate them from the whole community. The traditions of foreign-born groups contribute to the diversity of symbolic life. The evidence is clear for the conflict among these systems.

It is the thesis of this chapter that the Memorial Day ceremonies and subsidiary rites (such as those of Armistice or Veterans' Day) of today, yesterday, and tomorrow are rituals of a sacred symbol system which functions periodically to unify the whole community, with its conflicting symbols and its opposing, autonomous churches and associations. It is contended here that in the Memorial Day ceremonies the anxieties which man has about death are confronted with a system of sacred beliefs about death which gives the individuals involved and the collectivity of individuals a feeling of well-being. Further, the feeling of triumph over death by collective action in the Memorial Day parade is made possible by re-creating the feeling of well-being and the sense of group strength and individual strength in the group power, which is felt so intensely during the wars, when the veterans' associations are created and when the feeling so necessary for the Memorial Day's symbol system is originally experienced.

Memorial Day is a cult of the dead which organizes and integrates the various faiths and national and class groups into a sacred unity. It is a cult of the dead organized around the community cemeteries. The principal themes are those of the sacrifice of the soldier dead for the living and the obligation of the living to sacrifice their individual purposes for the good of the group, so that they, too, can perform their spiritual obligations.

Memorial Day Ceremonies

We shall first examine the Memorial Day ceremony of an American town for evidence. The sacred symbolic behavior of Memorial Day, in which scores of the town's organizations are involved, is ordinarily divided into four periods. During the year separate rituals are held by many of the associations for their dead, and many of these activities are connected with later Memorial Day events. In the second phase, preparations are made during the last three or four weeks for the ceremony itself, and some of the associations perform public rituals. The third phase consists of the scores of rituals held in all the cemeteries, churches, and halls of the associations. These rituals consist of speeches and highly ceremonialized behavior. They last for two days and are climaxed by the fourth and last phase, in which all the separate celebrants gather in the center of the business district on the afternoon of Memorial Day. The separate organizations, with their members in uniform or with fitting insignia, march through the town, visit the shrines and monuments of the hero dead, and, finally, enter the cemetery. Here dozens of ceremonies are held, most of them highly symbolic and formalized. Let us examine the actual ritual behavior in these several phases of the ceremony.

The two or three weeks before the Memorial Day ceremonies are usually filled with elaborate preparations by each participating group. Meetings are held, and patriotic pronouncements are sent to the local paper by the various organizations which announce what part each organization is to play in the ceremony. Some of the associations have Memorial Day processions, memorial services are conducted, the schools have patriotic programs, and the cemeteries are cleaned and repaired. Graves are decorated by families and associations and new gravestones purchased and erected. The merchants put up flags before their establishments, and residents place flags above their houses.

All these events are recorded in the local paper, and most of them are discussed by the town. The preparation of public opinion for an awareness of the importance of Memorial Day and the rehearsal of what is expected from each section of the community are done fully and in great detail. The latent sentiments of each individual, each family, each church, school, and association for its own dead are thereby stimulated and related to the sentiments for the dead of the nation.

One of the most important events observed in the preparatory phase in the community studied occurred several days before

Memorial Day, when the man who had been the war mayor wrote an open letter to the commander of the American Legion. It was published in the local paper. He had a city-wide reputation for patriotism. He was an honorary member of the American Legion. The letter read: "Dear Commander: The approaching Poppy Day [when Legion supporters sold poppies in the town] brings to my mind a visit to the war zone in France on Memorial Day, 1925, reaching Belleau Wood at about 11 o'clock. On this sacred spot we left floral tributes in the memory of our town's boys—Jonathan Dexter and John Smith, who here had made the supreme sacrifice, that the principle that 'might makes right' should not prevail."

Three days later the paper in a front-page editorial told its readers: "Next Saturday is the annual Poppy Day of the American Legion. Exerybody should wear a poppy on Poppy Day. Think back to those terrible days when the red poppy on Flanders Field symbolized the blood of our boys slaughtered for democracy." The editor here explicitly states the symbolism involved.

Through the early preparatory period of the ceremony, through all its phases and in every rite, the emphasis in all communities is always on sacrifice—the sacrifice of the lives of the soldiers of the city, willingly given for democracy and for their country. The theme is always that the gift of their lives was voluntary; that it was freely given and therefore above selfishness or thoughts of self-preservation; and, finally, that the "sacrifice on the altars of their country" was done for everyone. The red poppy became a separate symbol from McCrae's poem "Flanders Felds." The poem expressed and symbolized the sentiments experienced by the soldiers and people of the country who went through the first war. The editor makes the poppy refer directly to the "blood of the boys slaughtered." In ritual language he then recites the names of some of the city's "sacrificed dead," and "the altars" (battles) where they were killed. "Remember Dexter and Smith killed at Belleau Wood," he says. "Remember O'Flaherty killed near Château-Thierry, Stulavitz killed in the Bois d'Ormont, Kelley killed at Côte de Châtillion, Jones near the Bois de Montrebeaux, Kilnikap in the Saint Mihiel offensive, and the other brave boys who died in camp or on stricken fields. Remember the living boys of the Legion on Saturday."

The names selected by the editor covered most of the ethnic and religious groups of the community. They included Polish, Russian, Irish, French-Canadian, and Yankee names. The use of such names in this context emphasized the fact that the voluntary sacrifice of a citizen's life was equalitarian. They covered the top, middle, and bottom of the several classes. The newspapers throughout the country each year print similar lists, and their editorials stress the equality of sacrifice by all classes and creeds.

The topic for the morning services of the churches on the Sunday before Memorial Day ordinarily is the meaning of Memorial Day to the town and to the people as Christians. All the churches participate. Because of space limitations, we shall quote from only a few sermons from one Memorial Day to show the main themes; but observations of Memorial Day behavior since the second World War show no difference in the principal themes expressed before and after the war started. Indeed, some of the words are almost interchangeable. The Rev. Hugh McKellar chose as his text, "Be thou faithful until death." He said:

> Memorial Day is a day of sentiment and when it loses that, it loses all its value. We are all conscious of the danger of losing that sentiment. What we need today is more sacrifice, for there can be no achievement without sacrifice. There are too many out today preaching selfishness. Sacrifice is necessary to a noble living. In the words of our Lord, "Whosoever shall save his life shall lose it and whosoever shall lose his life in My name shall save it." It is only those who sacrifice personal gain and will to power and personal ambition who ever accomplish anything for their nation. Those who expect to save the nation will not get wealth and power for themselves.
>
> Memorial Day is a religious day. It is a day when we get a vision of the unbreakable brotherhood and unity of spirit which exists and still exists, no matter what race or creed or color, in the country where all men have equal rights.

The minister of the Congregational Church spoke with the voice of the Unknown Soldier to emphasize his message of sacrifice:

> If the spirit of that Unknown Soldier should speak, what would be his message? What would be the message of a youth I knew

myself who might be one of the unknown dead? I believe he would speak as follows: "It is well to remember us today, who gave our lives that democracy might live, we know something of sacrifice."

The two ministers in different language expressed the same theme of the sacrifice of the individual for national and democratic principles. One introduces divine sanction for this sacrificial belief and thereby succeeds in emphasizing the theme that the loss of an individual's life rewards him with life eternal. The other uses one of our greatest and most sacred symbols of democracy and the only powerful one that came out of the first World War—the Unknown Soldier. The American Unknown Soldier is Everyman; he is the perfect symbol of equalitarianism.

There were many more Memorial Day sermons, most of which had this same theme. Many of them added the point that the Christian God had given his life for all. That afternoon during the same ceremony the cemeteries, memorial squares named for the town's dead, the lodge halls, and the churches had a large number of rituals. Among them was the "vacant chair." A row of chairs decorated with flags and wreaths, each with the name of a veteran who had died in the last year, was the center of this ceremony held in a church. Most of the institutions were represented in the ritual. We shall give only a small selection from the principal speech:

Now we come to pay tribute to these men whose chairs are vacant, not because they were eminent men, as many soldiers were not, but the tribute we pay is to their attachment to the great cause. We are living in the most magnificent country on the face of the globe, a country planted and fertilized by a Great Power, a power not political or economic but religious and educational, especially in the North. In the South they had settlers who were there in pursuit of gold, in search of El Dorado, but the North was settled by people seeking religious principles and education.

In a large city park, before a tablet filled with the names of war dead, one of our field workers shortly after the vacant-chair rite heard a speaker in the memorial ritual eulogize the two great symbols of American unity—Washington and Lincoln. The orator said:

No character except the Carpenter of Nazareth has ever been honored the way Washington and Lincoln have been in New England. Virtue, freedom from sin, and righteousness were qualities possessed by Washington and Lincoln, and in possessing these characteristics both were true Americans, and we would do well to emulate them. Let us first be true Americans. From these our friends beneath the sod we receive their message, "Carry on." Though your speaker will die, the fire and spark will carry on. Thou are not conqueror, death, and thy pale flag is not advancing.

In all the other services the same themes were used in the speeches, most of which were in ritualized, oratorical language, or were expressed in the ceremonials themselves. Washington, the father of his country, first in war and peace, had devoted his life not to himself but to his country. Lincoln had given his own life, sacrificed on the altar of his country. Most of the speeches implied or explicitly stated that divine guidance was involved and that these mundane affairs had supernatural implications. They stated that the revered dead had given the last ounce of devotion in following the ideals of Washington and Lincoln and the Unknown Soldier and declared that these same principles must guide us, the living. The beliefs and values of which they spoke referred to a world beyond the natural. Their references were to the supernatural.

On Memorial Day morning the separate rituals, publicly performed, continued. The parade formed in the early afternoon in the business district. Hundreds of people, dressed in their best, gathered to watch the various uniformed groups march in the parade. Crowds collected along the entire route. The cemeteries, carefully prepared for the event, and the graves of kindred, covered with flowers and flags and wreaths, looked almost gay.

The parade marched through the town to the cemeteries. The various organizations spread throughout the several parts of the graveyards, and rites were performed. In the Greek quarter ceremonies were held; others were performed in the Polish and Russian sections; the Boy Scouts held a memorial rite for their departed; the Sons and Daughters of Union Veterans went through a ritual, as did the other men's and women's organizations. All this was part of the parade in which everyone from all parts of the community could and did participate.

Near the end of the day all the men's and women's organizations assembled about the roped-off grave of General Fredericks. The Legion band played. A minister uttered a prayer. The ceremonial speaker said:

> We meet to honor those who fought, but in so doing we honor ourselves. From them we learn a lesson of sacrifice and devotion and of accountability to God and honor. We have an inspiration for the future today—our character is strengthened—this day speaks of a better and greater devotion to our country and to all that our flag represents.

After the several ceremonies in the Elm Hill Cemetery, the parade re-formed and started the march back to town, where it broke up. The firing squad of the American Legion fired three salutes, and a bugler sounded the "Last Post" at the cemetery entrance as they departed. This, they said, was a "general salute for all the dead in the cemetery."

Here we see people who are Protestant, Catholic, Jewish, and Greek Orthodox involved in a common ritual in a graveyard with their common dead. Their sense of separateness was present and expressed in the different ceremonies. but the parade and the unity gained by doing everything at one time emphasized the oneness of the total group. Each ritual also stressed the fact that the war was an experience where everyone sacrificed and some died, not as members of a separate group, but as citizens of a whole community.

The full significance of the unifying and integrative character of the Memorial Day ceremony—the increasing convergence of the multiple and diverse events through the several stages into a single unit in which the many become the one and all the living participants unite in the one community of the dead—is best seen in Figure 1. It will be noticed that the horizontal extension at the top of the figure represents space; and the vertical dimension, time. The four stages of the ceremony are listed on the left-hand side, the arrows at the bottom converging and ending in the cemetery. The longer and wider area at the top with the several well-spread rectangles represents the time and space diversities

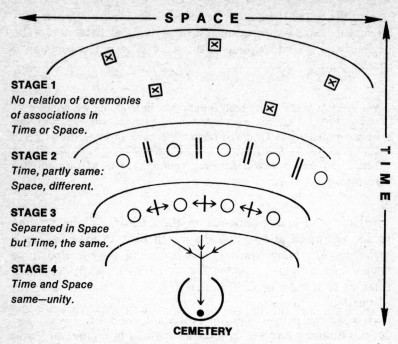

Fig. 1. Progress of the Memorial Day ceremony

of stage 1; the interconnected circles in stage 3 show the closer integration that has been achieved by this time.

During stage 1 it will be recalled that there is no synchronization of rituals. They occur in each association without any reference to one another. All are separate and diverse in time and space. The symbolic references of the ceremonies emphasize their separateness. In general, this stage is characterized by high diversity, and there is little unity in purpose, time, or space.

Although the ceremonies of the organizations in stage 2 are still separate, they are felt to be within the bounds of the general community organization. There is still the symbolic expression of diversity, but now diversity in a larger unity (see Fig. 1). In stage 3 there are still separate ceremonies but the time during which they are held is the same. Inspection of the chart will show that time and space have been greatly limited since the period of stage 1.

The ceremonies in stage 4 become one in time and one in space. The representatives of all groups are unified into one procession. Thereby, organizational diversity is symbolically integrated into a unified whole. This is not necessarily known to those who participate, but certainly it is felt by them. The chart is designed to symbolize the progressive integration and symbolic unification of the group.

Moreover, at the conclusion of the ceremony, when the entire collectivity moves physically from diversity and extension, spread thinly throughout the city, into the enclosed, confined, consecrated unity of the receptacle (the cemetery as depicted in the chart), the celebrants themselves and their great ceremony symbolically incorporate the full spiritual power of the cemetery as a sacred symbol system.

Yankee City cemeteries are themselves collective representations which reflect and express many of the community's basic beliefs and values about what kind of society it is, what the persons of men are, and where each fits into the secular world of the living and the spiritual society of the dead. Whenever the living think about the deaths of others, they necessarily express some of their own concern about their own extinction. The cemetery provides them with enduring visible symbols which help them to contemplate man's fate and their own separate destinies. The cemetery and its gravestones are the hard, enduring signs which anchor each man's projections of his inner-most fantasies and private fears about the certainty of his own death—and the uncertainty of his ultimate future—on an external symbolic object made safe by tradition and the sanctions of religion.

Although the cemetery is a place of the dead, it is also dependent on the living for its own existence. Yankee City, being a very old city, has many graveyards, some of which are ancient and no longer used. These were not part of the Memorial Day celebrations. As long as the cemetery is being filled with a fresh stream of the recently dead, it stays symbolically alive and a vital emblem, telling the living the meaning of life and death. But when the family, the kindred, and other members of the community gradually discontinue burying their loved ones there, the cemetery, in a manner of speaking, dies its own death as a meaningful symbol of life and death, for it ceases to exist as a living sacred emblem and, through time, becomes a historical monument. As a symbolic object it, too, is subject to the meaning of time. Its spirituality then resides in a different context, for it becomes an object of historical value in stable communities rather than a sacred collective representation effectively relating the dead to the living.

When cemeteries no longer receive fresh burials which continue to tie the emotions of the living to the recently dead and thereby connect the living in a chain of generations to early ancestry, the graveyards must lose their sacred quality and become objects of historical ritual. The lifetime of individuals and the living meanings of cemeteries are curiously independent, for both are dependent on an ascription of sacred meaning bestowed upon them by those who live. The symbols of death say what life is and those of life define what death must be. The meanings of man's fate are forever what he makes them.

Lincoln—An American Collective Representation Made by and for the People

Throughout the Memorial Day ceremony there were continual references to Lincoln and his Gettysburg Address. The symbol of Lincoln obviously was of deep significance in the various rituals and to the participants. He loomed over the memorial rituals like some great demigod over the rites of classical antiquity. What is the meaning of the myth of Lincoln to Americans? Why does his life and death as conceived in the myth of Lincoln play such a prominent part in Memorial Day?

Some of the answers are obvious. He was a great war president. He was the President of the United States and was assassinated during the Civil War. Memorial Day grew out of this war. A number of other facts about his life might be added; but for our present purposes the meaning of Lincoln the myth is more important to understand than the objective facts of his life-career.

Lincoln, product of the American prairies, sacred symbol of idealism in the United States, myth more real than the man himself, symbol and fact, was formed in the flow of events which composed the changing cultures of the Middle West. He is the symbolic culmination of America. To understand him is to know much of what America means.

In 1858, when Lincoln ran against Stephen Douglas for the United States Senate, he was Abraham Lincoln, the successful lawyer, the railroad attorney, who was noted throughout the state of Illinois as a man above common ability and of more than common importance. He was a former congressman. He was earning a substantial income. He had married a daughter of the superior classes from Kentucky. His friends were W. D. Green, the president of a railway, a man of wealth; David Davis, a representative of wealthy eastern investors in western property, who was on his way to becoming a millionaire; Jesse Fell, railway promoter; and other men of prominence and prestige in the state. Lincoln dressed like them; he had unlearned many of the habits acquired in childhood from his lowly placed parents and had learned most of the ways of those highly placed men who were now his friends. After the Lincoln-Douglas debates his place as a man of prestige and power was as high as anyone's in the whole state.

Yet in 1860, when he was nominated on the Republican ticket for the presidency of the United States, he suddenly became "Abe Lincoln, the rail-splitter," "the rude man from the prairie and the river-bottoms." To this was soon added "Honest Abe," and finally, in death, "the martyred leader" who gave his life that "a nation dedicated to the proposition that all men are created equal" might long endure.

What can be the meaning of this strange transformation?

When Richard Oglesby arrived in the Republican convention in 1860, he cast about for a slogan that would bring his friend, Lincoln, favorable recognition from the shrewd politicians of New York, Pennsylvania, and Ohio. He heard from Jim Hanks, who had known Lincoln as a boy, that Lincoln had once split fence rails. Dick Oglesby, knowing what appeals are most potent in getting the support of the politicians and in bringing out a favorable vote, dubbed Lincoln "the rail-splitter." Fence rails were prominently displayed at the convention, to symbolize Lincoln's lowly beginnings. Politicians, remembering the great popular appeal of "Old Hickory," "Tippecanoe and Tyler too," and "The Log Cabin and Cider Jug" of former elections, realized that this slogan would be enormously effective in a national election. Lincoln, the rail-splitter, was reborn in Chicago in 1860; and the Lincoln who had become the successful lawyer, intimate of wealthy men, husband of a wellborn wife, and man of status was conveniently forgotten.

Three dominant symbolic themes compose the Lincoln image. The first—the theme of the common man—was fashioned in a form pre-established by the equalitarian ideals of a new democracy; to common men there could be no argument about what kind of a man a rail-splitter is.

"From log cabin to the White House" succinctly symbolizes the second theme of the trilogy which composes Lincoln, the most powerful of American collective representations. This phrase epitomizes the American success story, the rags-to-riches *motif*, and the ideals of the ambitious. As the equal of all men, Lincoln was the representative of the Common Man, as both their spokesman and their kind; and, as the man who had gone "from the log cabin to the White House," he became the superior man, the one who had not inherited but had earned that superior status and thereby proved to everyone that all men could do as he had. Lincoln thereby symbolized the two great collective but opposed ideals of American democracy.

When Lincoln was assassinated, a third powerful theme of our Christian society was added to the symbol being created by Americans to strengthen and adorn the keystone of their national symbol structure. Lincoln's life lay sacrificed on the altar of unity, climaxing a deadly war which proved by its successful termination that the country was one and that all men are created equal. From the day of his death, thousands of sermons and speeches have demonstrated that Lincoln, like Christ, died that all men might live and be as one in the sight of God and man. Christ died that this might be true forever beyond the earth; Lincoln sacrificed his life that this might be true forever on this earth.

When Lincoln died, the imaginations of the people of the eastern seaboard cherished him as the man of the new West and translated him into their hopes for tomorrow, for to them the West was tomorrow. The defeated people of the South, during and after the Reconstruction period, fitted him into the dark reveries of what might have been, had this man lived who loved all men. In their bright fantasies, the people of the West, young and believing only in the tomorrow they meant to create, knew Lincoln for what they wanted themselves to be. Lincoln, symbol of equalitarianism, of the social striving of men who live in a social hierarchy, the human leader sacrificed for all men, expresses all the basic values and beliefs of the Middle West and of the United States of America.

Lincoln, the superior man, above all men, yet equal to each, is a mystery beyond the logic of individual calculators. He belongs to the culture and to the social logics of the people for whom contradiction is unimportant and for whom the ultimate tests of truth are in the social structure in which, and for which, they live. Through the passing generations of our Christian culture the Man of the Prairies, formed in the mold of the God-man of Galilee and apotheosized into the man-god of the American people, each year less profane and more sacred, moves securely toward identification with deity and ultimate godhead. In him Americans realize themselves.

The Effect of War on the Community

A problem of even greater difficulty confronts us on why war provides such an effective context for the creation of powerful national symbols, such as Lincoln, Washington, or Memorial Day. Durkheim gives us an important theoretical lead. He believed that the members of the group felt and became aware of their own group identity when they gathered periodically during times of plenty. For his test case, the Australian aborigines, a hunting and gathering tribe, this was the season when food was plentiful. It was then when social interaction was most intense and the feelings most stimulated.

In modern society interaction, social solidarity, and intensity of feelings ordinarily are greatest in times of war. It would seem likely that such periods might well produce new sacred forms, built, of course, on the foundations of old beliefs. Let us examine the life of American communities in wartime as a possible matrix for such developments.

The most casual survey supplies ample evidence that the effects of war are most varied and diverse as they are reflected in the life of American towns. The immediate effect of war is very great on some towns and very minor on others. During its existence it strengthens the social structure of some and greatly weakens the social systems of others. In some communities it appears to introduce very little that is new, while in others the citizens are compelled by force of circumstances to incorporate whole new experiences into their lives and into the social systems which control them.

In some communities during the second World War there was no decided increase or decrease in the population, and war did not change the ordinary occupations of their people. Their citizens made but minor adjustments in their daily lives; no basic changes occurred in their institutions. For example, there were many small market towns servicing rural areas about them when the round of events substantially repeated what had occurred in all previous years from the time the towns grew to early maturity. A few of their boys were drafted, possibly the market crops were more remunerative, and it may be that the weekly paper had a few more war stories. Changes there were, but they were few and minor in their effect on the basic social system.

At the other extreme, most drastic and spectacular changes occurred in the second World War. Small towns that had formerly existed disappeared entirely, and their former localities were occupied by industrial cities born during the war and fathered by it. Sleepy rural villages were supplanted by huge industrial populations recruited from every corner of America. Towns of a few hundred people, traditionally quiet and well composed, suddenly expanded into brawling young cities with no past and no future. Market towns became industrial areas. The wives and mothers in these towns left their homes and joined the newcomers on the assembly line. The old people went into industry to take jobs they had to learn like the youngest boy working beside them. This and that boy and some of their friends left high school because they received tacit encouragement from their elders and the school authorities to go to work to help in the war effort. In some communities the whole system of control that had formerly prevailed ceased to function or was superseded by outside authority. The influx of population was so great that the schools could teach but a small portion of the children. The police force was inadequate. The usual recreational life disappeared, to be supplanted by the "taxi dance hall," "juke joint," "beer hall," and "gambling dive." Institutions such as the church and the lodge almost ceased to function. In some towns one could drive through miles of trailer camps and small houses pressed against one another, all recently assembled, where the inhabitants lived in squalid anonymity with, but not of, the thousands around them. They were an aggregate of individuals concentrated in one area, but they were not a community.

We have described only the two extremes of the immediate influence of war on the community. Soon, however, those communities which had been little affected by the war felt some of its effects, and those which had been disorganized developed habits of life which conformed to the ordinary pattern of American town life. The two extremes soon approached the average.

But wars influence the average town quite differently. Changes take place, the institutional life is modified, new experiences are felt by the people, and the townsmen repeatedly modify their behavior to adapt to new circumstances brought them by new events. These modifications do not cause social breakdown. The contrary is true. The war activities strengthen the integration of many small communities. The people are more systematically organized into groups where everyone is involved and in which there is an intense awareness of oneness. The town's unity and feeling of autonomy are strengthened by competition in war activities with neighboring communities.

It is in time of war that the average American living in small cities and towns gets his deepest satisfactions as a member of his society. Despite the pessimistic events of 1917, the year when the United States entered the first World War, the people derived deep satisfaction from it, just as they did from the last war. It is a mistake to believe that the American people, particularly the small-towners, hate war to the extent that they derive no satisfaction from it. Verbally and superficially they disapprove of war, but at best this is only partly revealed in their deeper feelings. In simpler terms, their observed behavior reveals that most of them had more real satisfaction out of the second World War, just as they did in the previous one, than they had had in any other period of their lives. The various men's and women's organizations, instead of inventing things to do to keep busy, could choose among activities which they knew were vital and significant to them and to others.

The small-towner then had a sense of significance about himself, about those around him, and about the events which occurred, in a way that he had never felt before. The young man who quit high school during the depression to lounge on the street corner and who was known to be of no consequence to himself or to anyone else in the community became a seasoned veteran, fighting somewhere in the South Pacific—a man obviously with the qualities of a hero (it was believed), willing to give up his life for his country, since he was in its military forces. He and everyone else were playing, and they knew they were playing, a vital and significant role in the present crisis. Everyone was in it. There was a feeling of unconscious well-being, because everyone was doing something to help in the common desperate enterprise in a co-operative rather than in a private spirit. This feeling is often the unconscious equivalent of what people mean when they gather to celebrate and sing "Hail, hail, the gang's all here." It also has something of the deep significance that enters into people's lives only in moments of tragedy.

The strong belief that everyone must sacrifice to win a war greatly strengthens people's sense of their importance. Everyone gives up something for the common good—money, food, tires, scrap, automobiles, or blood for blood banks. All of it is contributed under the basic ideology of common sacrifice for the good of the country. These simple acts of giving by all individuals in the town, by all families, associations, schools, churches, and factories, are given strong additional emotional support by the common knowledge that some of the local young men are representing the town in the military forces of the country. It is known that some of them may be killed while serving their country. They are sacrificing their lives, it is believed, that their country may live. Therefore, all acts of individual giving to help win the war, no matter how small, are made socially significant and add to the strength of all the social structure by being treated as sacrifices. The collective effect of these small renunciations, it is believed, is to lessen the number of those who must die on the altars of their country.

Another very strong integrative factor contributed by a war that strengthens the social structure of the small town and city is that petty internal antagonisms are drained out of the group onto the common enemy. The local antagonisms which customarily divide and separate people are largely suppressed. The feelings and psychic energies involved, normally expended in local feuds, are vented on the hated symbols of the enemy. Local groups which may have been excluded from participation in community affairs are given an honored place in the war effort, and the symbols of unity are stressed rather than the separating differences. The religious groups and the churches tend to emphasize the oneness of the common war effort rather than allow their differing theologies and competitive financing to keep them in opposing groups. The strongest pressure to compose their differences is placed against management and labor. (The small number of strikes is eloquent proof of the effectiveness of such pressure.) A common hate of a common enemy, when organized in community activities to express this basic emotion, provides the most powerful mechanism to energize the lives of the towns and to strengthen their feelings of unity. Those who believe that a war's hatreds can bring only evil to psychic life might well ponder the therapeutic and satisfying effects on the minds of people who turn their once private hatreds into social ones and join their townsmen and countrymen in the feeling of sharing this basic emotion in common symbols. Enemies as well as friends should be well chosen, for they must serve as objects for the expression of two emotions basic to man and his social system—hatred and love.

The American Legion and other patriotic organizations give form to the effort to capture the feelings of well-being when the society was most integrated and feelings of unity were most intense. The membership comes from every class, creed, and nationality, for the soldiers came from all of them.

Only a very few associations are sufficiently large and democratic in action to include in their membership men or women from all class levels, all religious faiths, and most, if not all, ethnic groups. Their number could be easily counted on the fingers of one hand. Most prominent among them are the patriotic associations, all of them structural developments from wars which involved the United States. The American Legion is a typical example of the patriotic type. Less than 6 per cent of several hundred associations which have been studied include members from all social classes. Of the remaining 94 per cent, approximately half have representatives from only three classes, or less than three, out of the six discussed in Chapter 3 [of *American Life: Dream and Reality*. The classes described are upper-upper, lower-upper, upper-middle, lower-middle, upper-lower, and lower-lower.] Although the associations which include members from all levels of the community are surprisingly few, those which stress in action as well as in words such other principles of democracy as the equality of races, nationalities, and religions are even fewer. Only 5 per cent of the associations are composed of members from the four principal religious faiths in America—Protestant, Catholic, Jewish, and Greek Orthodox—and most of their members come from the lower ranks of the society.

Lincoln and Washington and lesser ritual figures (and ceremonies such as Memorial Day) are the symbolic equivalent of such social institutions as the patriotic societies. They express the same values, satisfy the same social needs, and perform similar functions. All increase the social solidarity of a complex and heterogeneous society.

How Such Ceremonies Function in the Community

Memorial Day and similar ceremonies are one of the several forms of collective representations which Durkheim so brilliantly defined and interpreted in *The Elementary Forms of the Religious Life*. He said: "Religious representations are collective representations which express collective realities." Religious collective representations are symbol systems which are composed of beliefs and rites which relate men to sacred beings. Beliefs are "states of opinion and consist in representations"; rites are "determined modes of action" which are expressions of, and refer to, religious belief. They are *visible* signs (symbols) of the invisible belief. The visible rite of baptism, for example, may express invisible beliefs about cleansing the newborn infant of sin and relating him to the Christian community.

Ceremonies, periodically held, serve to impress on men their social nature and make them aware of something beyond themselves which they feel and believe to be sacred. This intense feeling of belonging to something larger and more powerful than themselves and of having part of this within them as part of them is symbolized by the belief in sacred beings, which is given a visual symbol by use of designs which are the emblems of the sacred entities, e.g., the Cross of the Christian churches.

That which is beyond, yet part of, a person is no more than the awareness on the part of individuals and the collectivity of individuals of their participation in a social group. *The religious symbols, as well as the secular ones, must express the nature of the social structure of the group of which they are a part and which they represent.* The beliefs in the gods and the symbolic rites which celebrate their divinity are no more than men collectively worshiping their own images—their own, since they were made by themselves and fashioned from their experiences among themselves.

We said earlier that the Memorial Day rites of American towns are sacred collective representations and a modern cult of the dead. They are a cult because they consist of a system of sacred beliefs and dramatic rituals held by a group of people who, when they congregate, represent the whole community. They are sacred because they ritually relate the living to sacred things. They are a cult because the members have not been formally organized into an institutionalized church with a defined theology but depend on informal organization to bring into order their sacred activities. They are called a "cult" here, because this term most accurately places them in a class of social phenomena which can be clearly identified in the sacred behavior of non-European societies.

The cult system of sacred belief puts into the organized form of concepts those sentiments about death which are common to everyone in the community. These sentiments are composed of fears of death, which conflict with the social reassurances that our culture provides us to combat such anxieties. These assurances, usually acquired in childhood and thereby carrying some of the authority of the adults who provided them, are a composite of theology and folk belief. The deep anxieties to which we refer include anticipation of our deaths, of the deaths or possible deaths of loved ones, and, less powerfully, of the deaths or possible deaths of those we know and of men in general.

Each man's church provides him and those of his faith with a set of beliefs and a way of acting to face these problems; but his church and those of other men do not equip him with a common set of social beliefs and rituals which permit him to unite with all his fellows to confront this common and most feared of all his enemies. The Memorial Day rite and other subsidiary rituals connected with it form a cult which partially satisfies this need for common action on a common problem. It dramatically expresses the sentiments of unity of all the living among themselves, of all the living to all the dead, and of all the living and dead as a group to the gods. The gods—Catholic, Protestant, and Jewish—lose their sectarian definitions, limitations, and foreignness among themselves and become objects of worship for the whole group and the protectors of everyone.

The unifying and integrating symbols of this cult are the dead. The graves of the dead are the most powerful of the visible emblems which unify all the activities of the separate groups of the community. The cemetery and its graves become the objects of sacred rituals which permit opposing organizations, often in conflict, to subordinate their ordinary opposition and to co-operate in expressing jointly the larger unity of the total community through the use of common rites for their collective dead. The rites show extraordinary respect for all the dead, but they pay particular honor to those who were killed in battle "fighting for their country." The death of a soldier in battle is believed to be a "voluntary sacrifice" by him on the altar of his country. To be understood, this belief in the sacrifice of a man's life for his country must be judged first with our general scientific knowledge of the nature of all forms of sacrifice. It must then be subjected to the principles which explain human sacrifice whenever and wherever found. More particularly, this belief must be examined with the realization that these sacrifices occur in a society whose deity was a man who sacrificed his life for all men.

The principle of the gift is involved. In simple terms, when something valuable is given, an equally valuable thing must be returned. The speaker who quoted Scripture in his Memorial Day speech, "Whosoever shall save his life shall lose it and whosoever shall lose his life in My name shall save it," almost explicitly stated the feelings and principles involved. Finally, as we interpret it, the belief in "the sacrifice of American citizens killed in battle" is a social logic which states in ultimate terms the subordinate relation of the citizen to his country and its collective moral principles.

This discussion has shown that the Memorial Day ceremony consists of a series of separate rituals performed by autonomous groups which culminate in a procession *of all of them as one group* to the consecrated area set aside by the living for their dead. In such a place the dead are classed as individuals, for their graves are separate; as members of separate social situations, for they are found in family plots and formal ritual respect is paid them by church and association; and as a collectivity, since they are thought of as "our dead" in most of the ceremonies. The fences surrounding the cemetery place all the dead together and separate all the living from them.

The Memorial Day rite is a cult of the dead, but not just of the dead as such, since by symbolically elaborating sacrifice of human life for the country through, or identifying it with, the Christian church's sacred sacrifice of their god, the deaths of such men also become powerful sacred symbols which organize, direct, and constantly revive the collective ideals of the community and the nation.

II
Method

JOHN F. WILSON

6 A Historian's Approach to Civil Religion

IN THIS ESSAY I shall try to display how a historian thinks about a topic like "civil religion," and to suggest what kinds of usefulness it has in his broader concern with the study of American religious history. This, then, is a methodological approach in which I try to be self-consciously the historian. Let me begin with some reflections about the historical task.

One misconception about historical studies, less widespread now than formerly (thanks to the waves of revisionism which have eroded much of the false confidence in the certainty of historical knowledge), is that historians are primarily if not exclusively concerned with "facts"—what happened on July 4, 1776, or on November 18, 1963. One pole of the historian's work always is data, hard, concrete, stubborn. Who gave this address? Is the version we have accurate? Who was in the audience? The historian has a repertoire of questions, probing, seeking, flinty, skeptical. This is, necessarily, one side of him and his work. But there is another pole in the work of a historian also, a side which recognizes that without interpretation, without a framework, without a context known or presumed, the most irreducible "fact" is insignificant. In this sense data taken alone are mute. Interpretation is required, and at a variety of levels, to make data "speak"—that is to say, for them to have historical significance. Indeed in the most basic sense, data are made real—because intelligible—*only* through an interpretive framework. Let us take a hypothetical address. What was the cultural role of formal speech? Do we fully understand the language

115

and its nuances? What meaning was carried by the words, especially in the context of the event? Without conceptions about the context of the address, it does not enter usefully into historical interpretation as a "fact." Of course a hypothetical speech is a very simple and low-level example. Ordinarily the historian takes for granted the cultural context and does not go through asking the sets of questions suggested above. But this kind of self-consciousness about data is required for interpretation of events, however small-scale and mundane or large-scale and consequential; the interpretation of social movements is no less a matter requiring the kind of heightened self-consciousness suggested.

This line of reflection about historical studies has been amply explored in recent years. My point is not to do it again, for I think that the general level of knowledgeability about historical studies, recognizing all of the fluctuation from one academic generation to the next, is at an all-time high. Rather, my point is to make it clear that even the mundane historian, like the theologian, the sociologist, the ethicist, and others, is, willy-nilly, always in the business of establishing and using concepts—although that may not always be clear to outsiders who depend upon the historian's work; it may be done not even entirely self-consciously by practitioners. What does distinguish the historian's approach, then, is not the necessity of using concepts—that he shares with many others. Nor is it the commitment to test and refine—and finally to be ready to reject—particular concepts, for that too is a burden others share as well. It is the criteria of judgment which set him apart, for he does not primarily rely on the canons of logic, or the coherence of doctrinal formulations, or accepted sociological theories, or data available with respect to contemporary societies. The historian is distinguished by his insistence that the concepts he utilizes be proved against data made available out of the social past, tested and tried against those data, so to speak. Thus, in the perspective of the historian no less than in those of the philosopher, student of literature, or anthropologist, there is a reflexive movement, a self-searching review, a refinement of the particular perspective. Logically the initial step taken by a historian is to inventory the models or concepts available to him. As his work proceeds, it involves their continuous assessment and reworking, and finally a perfection—or rejection—of them. These moves are performed effortlessly "behind" classical historical writing so that they are unobtrusive and frequently unobserved. In more pedantic work these steps are either not present at all (that is to say, the concepts or models are taken for granted) or they lie closer to the surface. In this is the art, as opposed to the science, of historiography.

In the perspective of a historian concerned with civil religion in America, an initial and necessary step is to ask for clarification of what we might mean by that concept. Perhaps it is not accidental that "civil religion" seems to have become a generic category, an umbrella term which includes or covers several rather different concepts or models of the subject. (Of course the fruitfulness of concepts sometimes does lie in their ambiguity.) For the major part of this essay I think it is important to explore three chief "models" of civil religion so as to be clear about some of the different meanings of the term as it has been rendered into concepts useful for historical work. According to their different meanings, the models operate in rather different ways at the point of interpreting historical data. There may very well be additional models beyond the three I wish to consider, or it may be that some consolidation of these models would be desirable. An initial and necessary step, however, is the clarification of the models available. Without such an inventory the working historian who turns to study the phenomena alleged to represent civil religion is at the mercy of competing claims and counterclaims, all made on the basis of alleged data. Adjudication between them can come only in terms of adequacy. The three models I propose for consideration may be designated in shorthand form as a theological model concerned with an "American faith," a ceremonial model concerned with symbolic behavior in society, and a structural-functional model concerned with civil religion as a particular religion within American society. Rather than proceed through direct comparison, I will comment on each in turn in order to emphasize the discreteness of each, that is, the very real differences between these separate models for the historical exploration of civil religious phenomena in American history.

The theological model might better be referred to as civil religion conceived as an American faith. The classic delineation of this conception came at the hands of Professor Sidney Mead in an article he published with the title, "The 'Nation with the Soul of a Church.' "[1] He made it clear that the title was derived from G. K. Chesterton, and that fact decisively indicates how Professor Mead understood himself to be building upon and giving articulation in the contemporary world to an interpretation of the American nation which had a distinguished history in 1967. He was recalling America to her true past. Fundamental to this interpretation was a long-range view of the development of Western society. In classical antiquity and the early Middle Ages there took place a substitution of the idea of universal Christian society for that of an empire ruled by Rome. Against this conception, nations emerged in the modern West as particularistic societies identified with territories and based upon compacts wrought by citizen-peoples. The nations of early modern Europe adapted the universalistic Christian social ideals to their own particularistic ends. Thus the tradition of one Christendom was transmuted into varieties of modern European Christian nations.

However secure this pattern proved to be in early modern Europe, it could not serve as the basis for the collective self-understanding required by the new United States of America. Our separation of particular churches and federal governmental institutions in the post-revolutionary era was a negative departure from prevailing European conceptions. What Professor Mead stressed was a particular aspect of this development. The refusal to establish any of the sects had also an important implication in the American context—namely, the affirmation of an essential and universal religious faith expressed in and through the differentiated manifestations of it. He gave this an impressive designation—"synergistic cosmopolitanism"—and identified it as the heart of American nationalism, that which served to set it apart from all others:

> a definitive element of the spiritual core which identifies it [America] as a nation is the conception of a universal principle which is thought to transcend and include all the national and religious particularities brought to it by the people who come from all over the world to be "Americanized."[2]

This he proceeded to identify as "the religion of the Republic." Emphatically it is not essentially this-worldly, it is not normatively expressed through worship of the state, it is not to be equated with crass American nationalism. Rather, it stands for the highest aspiration of the Christian West, the realization of which is—in the present time at least—possibly to be achieved through American history. This is the true faith of the Republic, and America is the only nation embracing as its own *telos* Christian universalism. Accordingly, the faith stands as a prophetic challenge to both particularistic sectarian versions of Christianity on the one hand, and self-serving and ultimately self-defeating versions of American nationalism on the other. For Professor Mead it is virtually axiomatic that the "theologians" of this faith—those who will explore its inner logic and give it articulation—will not be identified with any of the separate religious (sectarian) traditions but, rather, they will be laymen, and especially those elevated to leadership of this new Israel which strains toward the fulfillment of human history, e.g., a Madison, a Lincoln, an Eisenhower. From its early years the new nation "was assuming the traditional function of the church."[3] This function is identified as the providing of meaning for the national life, and that in at least three settings: (1) the nation as God's agent in history; (2) the nation as locus of personal and group identity; (3) the nation as community of righteousness (which in light of the history of American theological reflection must be taken to mean both justification and sanctification).[4] Professor Mead does little with this hint, but moves his essay into an extended peroration or ode to civil authority in the Republic which, in the neutral stance it has taken between warring sects and in fostering reconciliation between them, has rendered a transcendent judgment upon sectarian perversions of essential and universal Christian truth. The article concludes with a kind of prayer (deity not altogether clear) that the "religion of the Republic" not fall into idolatry.

This summary of a rather elegant essay, which became a classic at publication, cannot do it full justice in such short compass. It may enable us to ask, however, whether an essentially theological delineation of the "synergistic and theonomous religion of the Republic"[5] might be translated into a theoretical model to facilitate historical inquiry. The author himself provided us with a lead in suggesting *specific kinds of contexts* in which he believed that the meaning derived from the religion of the Republic has played decisive roles in the national life. One context has been that of international relationships wherein the religious mission of this nation has colored or informed, if not given structure to, interaction with other states, Christian and non-Christian, developed and modernizing. A second context has been that of community-building within the Republic, in the sense of providing a necessary if not sufficient condition for there to be one nation in light of its radical expansion of territory, the ingestion (if not digestion) of various ethnic groups, the staggering mobility which has been so much a characteristic of our society from colonial beginnings. A third context would be that of American social morality construed in the broadest terms—our common ideals and their institutional expression.

In these few sentences I have meant to suggest how the theological meaning concept of civil religion might begin to translate into a variegated model for the purposes of historical research, that is, the analysis and interpretation of relevant phenomena within appropriate time and space matrices. What fascinates me is the degree to which the *kinds* of topics toward which this model directs our attention, the *kinds* of subject matter it brings into focus, while important and fundamental, are nonetheless surprisingly well explored, even old-hat. American self-conceptions vis-a-vis the other nations of the world, the melting-pot once more set to boil as a historical problematic, the broadly Christian values suffusing our officially neutral social life. These are not trivial historical topics. They do represent, however, very well-explored territories, figuratively speaking; and numerous articles, monographs, and studies illuminate even the darker reaches of them. I conclude reluctantly that this kind of a model of civil religion as a particular religious faith undergirding the Republic seems not to have much utility in the doing of history except for possibly providing some marginal enrichment of perspectives on topics much studied in more restricted compass, e.g., under ethnic church life, or revivalism, or movements for the reform of the national life in different periods, and other similar topics.

This essentially negative result makes me think that we were led astray in presuming to discover here the germ for a conception through which to isolate, identify, and study a tradition of civil religion in American history. Perhaps this was not the real point of that essay by Professor Mead, however much, in the ways suggested above, it connects with fundamental work of several generations of American religious historians. It is more nearly exact to say that Professor Mead insisted upon the possibility of transcendent criticism of society in the American context, a criticism not based on any of the positive creeds or sectarian traditions but rooted in universalistic political affirmations perhaps classically summarized in the Declaration of Independence. In an aside let me offer the opinion, and it is simply a personal judgment, that on the basis of the last years of national life it can only be through the eyes of faith that one may affirm this possibility for the national community as opposed to individual prophets or faithful remnants. For the purpose at hand, however, another observation is more appropriate, namely, that essentially theological conceptions or models of civil religion do not hold much promise for working historians save in the application of insights derived from them to such specific projects as exploration of Abraham Lincoln's profound religious reflections.[6] Charles Henderson's book *The Nixon Theology* makes that point very well, although perhaps inadvertently. There simply isn't much theological reflection undergirding the ready and relatively numerous presidential references to morality and the deity.[7] *Ad hoc* God allusions simply do not constitute a theology; there must be some consistent exploration of relevant issues in such a way that a frame of reference oriented to the deity or to the fundamental premises of a culture—whatever the particular coloration—has a logical status or plays an effective and shaping role.

Thus I conclude that a model of civil religion based on the hypothesis of theological meaning for the national life may enable us to learn to love our country, so to speak, but it will probably shed very little light on the issue of whether there are in our national past and present phenomena to be interpreted as constituting a civil religion. Surely it is significant that Lincoln is invariably cited as the *prima facie* evidence when the case is being made that in a "religion of the Republic" there is articulated a transcendent meaning for the American nation which constitutes a positive religious tradition apart from and independent of the sectarian Christian traditions. In many ways Lincoln's case argues just the other side of this issue—here is the exception, the religiously literate, marvelously sympathetic, critical and self-critical soul who expresses in matchless prose the agony he experiences so acutely in presiding over the Union cause during the fierce war between the states which are contending over divergent interpretations of the American destiny. If the theological-meaning model did help us to bring to focus a "religion of the Republic," then we might presume to find other presidents or lay leaders in other periods of national turmoil returning to and even deepening the Lincolnian legacy. It seems to me, however, that the legacy stands alone as a remarkable monument to a tortured soul. I do not intend disrespect to his successors in the White House when I say that such transcendent reflection upon the meaning of this national experiment is absent from their formal and informal declarations. The present incumbent is far more typical than Lincoln in the quality and depth of religious reflection he exhibits.

In sum, one model of civil religion construes it as an American faith. While in a Lincoln there is articulated a profound and transcendent perspective upon the American nation, his insight is virtually in a class by itself and without parallel. The implication of such a faith in terms of the kind of a role it would play in social history as a positive tradition or a religion is another matter. Specifically the concept adds little if anything to long-established interests in American ideas of mission and destiny, the development of a national life as opposed to sectional or class-based social life, and the reality of a common value system. A model of civil religion based upon the idea of an American faith seems to me, at least, to be redundant, promising little more in "pay-off" than the more established and empirically based concepts indicated above.

A second model might be termed "ceremonial-ritual" or even "cultic." W. Lloyd Warner and associates developed this approach to American society most fully. They demonstrated its considerable utility especially in their work on "Yankee City" but also in more generic ways in terms of interest in the role of media in modern society. Warner was especially concerned with the social role of symbolism, and his conceptions were self-consciously derived from and to some degree dependent upon Durkheim's theoretical perspectives. In brief, he attempted to identify and analyze fundamental aspects of collective life in American society in terms of certain representations and symbols which embody it.

In the setting of the present discussion Warner is probably best known for his analysis of the Memorial Day ceremonies in "Yankee City" at the end of the 1930s.[8] These essayistic materials have had a life independent of the more extensive background studies in the symbolic life of Newburyport—or American society. In certain ways this has been unfortunate. The Memorial Day ceremonies of Yankee City were so rich and they dramatized so fully a complex civic ritual that, where such highly developed and explicit ceremonial seemed not to exist, the conclusion has been too readily drawn that the conception was not more generally applicable or fruitful. In this sense it is unfortunate that the analysis of Memorial Day rites has been taken out of context. Even the large paperback, *The Family of God*, which presents the bulk of the content of Volume 5 of the Yankee City Series, passes over rather lightly the theoretical perspectives which underlie the specific interpretation of the content of American symbol life. These perspectives, of course, provide the materials for a model of civil religion based upon Warner's work. At root he is concerned with the collective, symbolic, social-psychologically defined content of American common life as over against the segmentary outcome of associational life in this society. This is to say that he is concerned to identify and analyze the deeper structures of symbolic meaning which provide a cultural unity as against the more superficial differentiation of our society along religious-sectarian, ethnic, class, and perhaps status lines.

Warner posits three adaptive subsystems—technological, moral, and one constituting a "sacred order."[9] He emphasizes that the third subsystem, consisting of rites and beliefs, is a necessary and direct response to the uncontrollable environment which finally subsumes both natural life and species life which underlie the first two adaptive subsystems. The power of the third subsystem is not only that it directly confronts the irrational fears and hostilities of collective life, but that through it the technological and moral levels of experience are coordinated. Thus for Warner it is necessary to interpret the collective symbol life of a community as more than reified concepts of the social life. However we might finally assess Warner's theoretical position, it is clear that his rich conceptions amount to a powerful case for the reality of symbol life in all human collectivities and they force direct attention to the ceremonies and rites which on his terms quite literally make social life possible. If Mead wrestled, so to speak, with the question of what faith about his nation is possible for the American with a sensitive soul, Warner asks another question: given the heterogeneity and vast scale of our society how can there be an American nation?

Within this theoretical perspective the ceremony surrounding Memorial Day, especially as displayed in Yankee City some three decades ago, clearly exemplifies religious rites which are instrumental in the continuance of civil society:

> . . . in the Memorial Day ceremonies the anxieties man has about death are confronted with a system of sacred beliefs about death which give the individuals involved and the collectivity of individuals a feeling of well-being. Further, the feeling of triumph over death by collective action is made possible in the Memorial Day parade by re-creating the feeling of euphoria and the sense of group strength in the group power which is felt so intensely in time of war. . . .
>
> Memorial Day is a cult of the dead which organizes and integrates the various faiths and ethnic and class groups into a sacred unity. It is a cult of the dead organized around the community cemeteries. Its principal themes are those of the sacrifice of the soldier dead for the living and the obligation of the living to sacrifice their individual purposes for the good of the group so that they, too, can perform their spiritual obligations.[10]

Conrad Cherry sympathetically extended or applied Warner's analysis of the Day to Boalsburg, Pennsylvania, which modestly claims to be the birthplace of the celebration.[11] Far more important, he proposed the essential similarity between the underlying themes of Memorial Day and the ceremonies and rituals at the death of Senator Robert F. Kennedy in June 1968. Clearly the national observances at the deaths of the Reverend Martin Luther King and President John F. Kennedy lend themselves to the same interpretation.[12] The clarity and brilliance of Warner's analysis of

Yankee City's Memorial Day has tended to obscure the more generic insights which he surely intended to be derived from his work, namely, that at least the following problematic experiences of collective life call forth symbolic responses entailing patterns of both belief and behavior: finitude, powerlessness, guilt, social uncertainty. In this perspective American society is shot through with institutionalized patterns of behavior which are fundamentally symbolic.

Analysis of social ceremonial or ritual developed by Warner is certainly applicable to both contemporary and historical materials. As an example of the former, interest in professional sports, perhaps especially football, is trivial if read on a literal level only. Viewed in symbolic terms, the regular and dramatic conflicts in large stadiums, before enormous throngs, which stand for countless witnesses by virtue of radio and the video tube, are cultural rites of enormous significance. What clearer celebration of our national commitment to technical expertise melded with the adversary mentality so that as excellence produces victory, error and ineptitude are linked to defeat. It was not accidental that Warner's analysis turned to the content of the media—at the time radio. The possibilities afforded by television programming for the analysis of cultural symbolism stagger the mind.[13] These theoretical insights no less directly illumine many historical aspects of our cultural life as well. For example, the pathetic struggle between generations of nativists and immigrants was carried on, finally, in terms of deep levels of hostility toward and fear for the unknown on the part of both sides. This was coupled with perceived threats to the familiar and secure established values and ways of doing things and defensiveness about foreign ways. Warner's analytic perspective, it seems to me, provides an important approach to extensive ranges of phenomena usually not associated with either civic order or religious concerns. On the basis of his work it is possible to develop a model for the study of religion in American society which may center on obvious rituals like Memorial Day and other explicit ceremonies within the life of the Republic but which also construes much if not all of the collective symbol life of the community as integral to it.

There is fine irony here, if one wishes to see it. The first model of civil religion we reviewed was so highly theological that it proved to have little if any usefulness for the historian intent on working with the very mixed materials presented to him in American history. As a filter, one might say, its mesh was too large, it proved inadequate to capture and retain much evidence for civil religion. This second model proves to be strong at precisely the point the other was flawed, namely, in capturing and retaining—and thus making accessible—an extensive range of phenomena. Its flaw is the converse: it proves to be too fine a filter or mesh for our purposes. Not only does it identify symbolic behavior and belief which is directly concerned with civil society, it captures virtually all kinds of symbolic behavior and belief. This is part of its definition; Warner's third subsystem embraces all cultural rites and beliefs. If civil religion is viewed as coterminus with all rites and beliefs it truly is generic religion and is not specifically useful in differentiating the set of rites and beliefs primarily concerned with civic polity. His work does enable the historian, particularly the one interested in religion and culture, to recognize symbolic aspects or dimensions in events which are usually viewed literalistically. Therefore a historian finds this approach provocative and important but not necessarily productive in refining study of the civil religion in our society. Differentiating criteria for civil religious symbolism are absent from the model implicit in the analysis of Memorial Day ceremonies, however much that consideration has been overlooked in the widespread dependence on Warner's work. This comment is not to find fault with Warner on this point but to indicate that his work cannot be taken over as providing an already developed model of what we might view as civil religion in America. It requires extensive specification to be useful for analyzing that phenomenon. On his own terms Warner has identified "cultic" aspects of American society for study. He has not, however, dealt with "churchly aspects" in the sense that Durkheim insisted every religion would produce a church.

To this point our discussion is at least superficially reminiscent of the story of "Goldilocks and the Three Bears." Taking the role of the heroine, so to speak, we have wandered into the forest of symbol life in American society. We have found a dwelling with a legend over the door to the effect that here those who enter will find a religious means of understanding the symbols concerned with the civil polity, and after a wholesome meal we have lain in two different beds to try them out. Predictably one was hard, much too hard, perhaps useful only for a tough frontiersman like Abraham Lincoln—and then perhaps only after his death and the transfiguration which accompanied it. The other was comfortable and thus inviting—but finally too soft, our heads were filled with fantasies and daydreams and sleep was impossible. Take heart, friends, for there is a third bed which will prove to be "just right" —at least as a conceptualization of what civil religion must be if we are to locate it in our society. This is, of course, Robert Bellah's analysis.

The original essay by Professor Bellah was a skillful presentation of a sophisticated view of civil religion. It was cast in terms of an argument that there is such an "elaborate and well-institutionalized" phenomenon in American social history.[14] Let me indicate the kind of model or conception of civil religion which appeared to underlie his development of the argument. He specifically referred to certain distinct elements or aspects of the phenomenon and implicitly suggested another one.

The first element or aspect is the one most fully developed in the essay, and it invariably receives most attention in general discussions of civil religion. We may term it the "ideological" aspect or the element of "symbolic content." The deep theme or grand motif is that of the American nation carrying out God's will on earth. According to the essay, the idea was generated in the Revolutionary era with the birth of the nation, and imagery taken over from the biblical history of Israel was fused with essentially unitarian conceptions of the deity. This theme was decisively enriched and augmented in the crisis of the War between the States. The experience of civil conflict brought in the whole symbolism relating to death, sacrifice, and rebirth. At once Abraham Lincoln articulated these new insights and became, in a martyr's death, embodiment of them. Finally, in the contemporary context, which is a decisively international epoch, this ideology is under trial as to whether or not it can sublimate what has been an essentially Manichaean view of the world to the necessary building of a viable world order.

Ranged around and expressive of this central ideology or symbolic content of civil religion are other characteristic features of religion. A second element is a series of "religious figures" identified with or instrumental in the development of this religious tradition. Washington and Lincoln are obviously important to the cult. So too are both more recent leaders—Roosevelt, Eisenhower, Kennedy—and ones whose roles in the national life may have been less political, e.g., poets who have celebrated American destiny, a Whitman, a Sandburg perhaps. Major and minor saints abound as exempla of the faith, e.g., in an earlier era the anonymous four chaplains of World War II or the heroic MacArthur, an ambiguous figure as a result of the Korean affair and the reprimand he received at the hands of Truman. Conversions have been celebrated and converts embraced, a Lafayette for instance, while those whose faith has wavered have been rendered as displays of deviate behavior—witness current passions with respect to the question of amnesty arising out of our military entanglement in Vietnam.

A third element is that of a series of specific events which serve to give symbolic definition to the American faith. Typically the events celebrate the times of trial in which the ideological component of the religion was created: the revolutionary struggle, and subevents within it, the conquest of a continent, the hegemony over adjacent seas, in this century alone a twice instrumental role in the triumph of liberal Anglo-American democracy over the forces of degenerate European civilizations, decisive confrontation with the Eastern forces of darkness, forces which have directly threatened European civilization for a millennium. Sacred events are remembered by the faithful through observance of a calendar which sets a frame around profane time. So our temporal seasons are punctuated by commemoration of the formative events in the national life.

Places associated with religious events are also set apart. So it is with countless locations sacred to the American polity. Hallowed ground at Gettysburg; Washington a sacred mecca; New Orleans; the Alamo; the list is endless. If the sacred territory of a misnamed Bunker Hill is vandalized, perhaps by residents of the immediate neighborhood for whom the traditions relating to the birthpangs of the nation are less real than their present frustrations in the national society, the faithful *will* to preserve the place as a means of displaying national unity and resolve in spite of the objections of minorities. So real are the religious feelings associated with a Gettysburg that a commercially inspired observation tower overlooking the battlefield is felt to be a sacrilege.

A final specific element in this complex model of American civil religion is its ritual expression. Ceremonies attendant upon the inauguration of a president, deferential behavior toward the flag and civic officials, solemn proceedings on Memorial Day or the Fourth of July, days of mourning or prayer at the conclusion of divisive wars, months of sorrow upon the deaths of former presidents—these and other similar events represent the kinds of patterned behavior which constitute yet another related aspect of this civil religion.

From the foregoing rehearsal of the case it is clear that this third model of civil religion is far more internally complex than the other two outlined above. This kind of model incorporates much of the range of phenomena identified in the Warner model, but it succeeds in factoring out of it, so to speak, or successfully differentiating the *particular kinds* of symbolic behavior and belief centered on the national polity. In the same way this third model takes account of the role of theology as ideology but does not either insist upon normative judgments about its specific content or conceive of the theology as transcendent over the rather mixed field of religious observance which is also part of its true content. Considered strictly in theoretical terms as a model, this third option represents a clear advance over both of those previously outlined. Like Goldilocks we seem to have found a bed, or at least the model of a bed, which is "just right," neither too hard nor too soft. At this theoretical level the most serious challenge to the conception has concerned its social-structural aspect. Before asking about its practical "fit," brief attention to this matter is warranted.

Professor Philip Hammond, commenting on the original essay when it was reprinted in *The Religious Situation 1968*, praised Bellah's work as a cultural analysis.[15] He suggested, however, that "the parallel structural analysis" received "considerably less attention."[16] Some of the elements or aspects factored out in the preceding paragraphs suggest that Professor Bellah was very much aware of this matter, but Hammond's friendly critique urged the importance of giving more attention to the specific social structures which support civil religion. This was to push Durkheim's insistence that a "church" is associated with a "religion." Hammond in particular proposed that serious attention should be given to the public schools as the primary institution in and through which civil religion has continuous cultural presence in American life. In his view it was less through the curriculum of the schools than through the kind of patterning or structuring of life in competitive sports, student elections, inculcation of fair play, etc., that "civil religious" training was offered.[17] In sum he viewed the school as a socializing institution. Incidentally, this line of thought was pursued much earlier by Professor J. Paul Williams in a somewhat different context.[18]

The preceding attempt at extensive sympathetic exposition will make it evident that I hold this third model or conception of civil religion in high regard. Analytically it is clearly superior to that of civil religion as a virtually disembodied faith option, and it manages to incorporate and build upon the real strengths of the ceremonial-symbolic model while restricting it at the critical point of differentiating the symbolic support for civic order and meaning from the more extensive fabric of symbols and meaning which Warner posited. Here is a model of civil religion which, it seems to me, is eminently serviceable for the historian. The important question thus shifts somewhat to become one of its actual utility as opposed to its theoretical promise: to what degree does the model succeed in bringing into focus appropriate phenomena of American history so as to demonstrate its relevance to this particular context of American historical data? Does it work?

In brief compass let me report a judgment worked out over time which does not lend itself to easy demonstration at any one point. The judgment takes the following form: the concept in question does indeed call attention to, in this sense make visible and even intelligible, ranges of phenomena in American history, some previously overlooked, some viewed in other ways. In this manner the concept or model is productive. It is not as evident, however, that these phenomena necessarily constitute a differenti-ated tradition, a particular religion, centered on the American polity. At the most the phenomena so identified would seem to cohere, according to the model, in a kind of generic civil religion which might be analogous, for instance, to what we mean when reference is made to generic Christianity or generic Judaism in the American context. In an abstract way we acknowledge the reality of Christianity within our culture. As a historian goes to work upon, shall we say, Christianity in America, or even American Christianity, he necessarily proceeds to specification of the generic in terms of ideologies, traditions, figures, events, places, rituals, and structures. American Christianity empirically exists only in par-ticular "sets," and while we may generalize, and do it freely, about Christianity, no historical work succeeds in isolating the subject. Perhaps the closest we come is in the empirically based discussions of social movements—like revivalistic-evangelical Protestantism or nineteenth-century liberal Roman Catholic Christianity. Any his-torical analysis of American Judaism requires the same kind of specification. This same point may be made by contrasting two general formulations which might be offered by a historian: The first: "American culture embodies religious elements derived from Christianity (or Judaism—or civic faith) . . . ." The second: "Christianity (or Judaism—or civic faith) is a specific religion in American society."

I suggest that the historian finds the first statement intelligible and useful, the second he finds impossible to test empirically and thus it is meaningless for his purposes. Why should this be? It is evident that the term "Christianity" (read Judaism, civic faith, etc.,) has undergone a decisive shift of meaning. It has become so highly specified in the second sentence as to mean something rather different. Implicit in the first statement is the view that sym-bolic and behavioral elements get detached from specific traditions and continue to be a part of the culture with identities no longer dependent upon their genesis. Under the second kind of state-ment lies an assumption that the genetic derivation of an element or aspect of a culture continues to determine its cultural identity. This is to take at face value, from the point of view of the his-torian, the fantasies of hierocrats throughout the ages who in saner moments have recognized the independence of culture from even its most determined managers.

I have offered a general judgment as a historian and owe you, at the very least, illustrations of some of the reasons I reach it. If we take at face value the assertion that there is "an elaborate and well-institutionalized" civil religion in America of the kind set out in the model,[19] then the model ought to direct our attention to phenomena which become empirical evidence for such a religion. In addition these same and related phenomena, when reviewed in detail, ought not to seem to require alternative hypotheses to explain them. As an example, the original article placed great, perhaps disproportionate, reliance upon several inaugural addresses of American presidents as providing hard evidence for the ideological aspect of civil religion. It will not be enough, in my view, for the historian to discover in some addresses references which confirm this part of the model. Rather, the model has implicit within it an explanation for *why* it is that the inaugural address is important in the context of the civil religion, namely, that in assuming this particular office an individual is placed under constraints which in some sense require him to act and speak symbolically—i.e., from the viewpoint of the cult. In the case of the American presidency the inaugural addresses and the State of the Union message would seem to be especially central. In sum the genre of address, derived from the role taken by the individual in assuming office, becomes the controlling explanation for why we should find in a particular inaugural statement—John F. Kennedy's for instance—articulation of the faith central to civil religion. Unless the appropriate *class* of official pronouncements in some sense becomes the evidence which must plausibly bear this weight of interpretation, the citation of certain texts from specific speeches is very questionable evidence for an elaborate and well-institutionalized American civil religion.

From this point of view, for the fun of it, I searched rather thoroughly through the public presidential documents, asking whether the weight of evidence seemed to support the judgment that at least in one of his official roles the incumbent becomes a central cult figure constrained to speak for the national faith as part of a civil religion. The most promising evidence is indeed in the inaugural addresses and in the State of the Union messages, although there are other kinds of occasion on which the holders of the office have made interesting declarations of public faith. Heeding Professor Bellah's cautionary word that the ideological element might appear only as a horizon within which to perceive American society, or as the articulation of frame around it, in my opinion the evidence is inadequate to sustain the hypothesis. I do not include tabulation and analysis of the references at this point, but report that, taken as a whole, they seem to me to reflect prevailing cultural epochs and immediate social circumstances far more than they sustain the position that they are evidence for a tradition of civil religion. Indeed, the relative infrequency of the references, their variety and conventional content, and the apparent absence of a framework or set of conventions constraining each incumbent not only comprises inadequate evidence for a differentiated civil religion but serves to disconfirm the hypothesis. It is evidence for a negative judgment.

As a second example of the basis for my general judgment, the model invites attention to the characteristic rituals (or sacred events, or holy places) which seem to be identified and interpreted as significant in light of the conception of civil religion. It is less easy to assemble hard evidence for these genre—cultural observances are evanescent at least until the historian in some future age can depend on reliable samples of video-recordings of such events. It is possible to review more carefully, however, the assumption unreflectively made that phenomena like that of Memorial Day rites, so lucidly analyzed by Warner, should be readily interpreted as *prima-facie* evidence for a civil religious tradition. In the Warner analysis the primary references of the rituals were at once more universal and more particular, in both aspects not focused primarily on the nation and the continuance of civil polity. The references were more universal in dealing explicitly with the fact of human death (the death of all humans)—and more particular in serving to dramatize the tensions arising out of the ethnic, class, and associational differentiation of Yankee City and to resolve them so that the common life of the city might continue. The universality of death in human experience and the social differentiation of American communities—at whatever level—are not unrelated to the possibility of a civil religion, but neither is the meaning for them, from the point of view of culture, necessarily centered there. The great variation of Memorial Day celebrations across time and in different social contexts argues, I think, that if these rites are generically central rituals in a national civil religion, they also function at least as fundamentally in other ways too.

The same kind of observation might be made about other ritual occasions as well, for example, the deaths of either incumbent or retired national leaders, and also the calendar of our national life. Those austere holidays which we associate with our ancestors, to wit, the birthdays of Washington and Lincoln, the Fourth of July as well as Memorial Day, Armistice Day, Thanksgiving, have fared very differently indeed. Those in which there is any potential for commercial exploitation—Washington's Birthday is a minor instance—are chiefly marked by great merchandising promotions rather than community observance. If there is in our social life an elaborate and well-institutionalized civil religion to an appreciable degree fulfilling the specifications of our elegant model, would such indifference and crass exploitation be permitted? We have the examples of Christmas and Easter festivals, the manifest symbolism of which is Christian, in which commercial development is marked. But note how strong and deep are the inhibitions derived from the tradition so that the days themselves are marked by the cessation of worldly activity. Thanksgiving is an interesting case in point, since it can be argued that at least in origins a strand contributing to definition of the day celebrated national destiny under God, a conception finally derived from covenant theology. But surely the modern version of the day celebrates, not national dependence upon a divinely ordained destiny, but family fellowship and enjoyment of the bounties of the land and society. Inhibitions in our culture about that ritual occasion derive more from the sacredness of family than from that of nation. In my judgment there has been a decisive diminution in the civil religious ideology with respect to that particular "day."[20]

The preceding paragraphs indicate how it is that a historian may go about utilizing a promising conception, how he tries it out, so to speak, on kinds of data in our common past. When assessing the utility of models, however, a historian also tries "thought experiments" with respect to the plausibility of the conceptions in the present and the future—whenever possible seeking out the advice and counsel of sociologists and other kindred souls. It seems to me that if there is validity, or analytic utility, in the conception of a differentiated civil religion in our society, then we have the good fortune to be located in a remarkably appropriate temporal laboratory. During the 1972 presidential campaign the nation was treated with rather different interpretations of the essence and destiny of America. One interpretation won a decisive victory, and the president so reelected was installed in office. This coincided with extrication of the nation from the most disastrous and prolonged foreign entanglement in its history. The effective reestablishment of national unity would seem to be the first order of business. In the same period two surviving former presidents died—and were buried with state funerals. At the 1976 presidential election the nation will take note of the bicentennial year of its independence, and planning for appropriate celebration of the event has been underway for some time. It is difficult to imagine, I suggest, a set of circumstances which would render a period more likely to manifest civil religion within this nation—if such a differentiated and well-institutionalized tradition may be said to exist parallel to and alongside more conventionally designated traditions. Perhaps I am "tone deaf" with respect to the relevant evidence for civil religion in our present time. Or perhaps I fail to see deep-going currents of civil religion present in, through, and under the attempts to plan for celebration of the two hundredth anniversary of this nation as a new order of society in the world. Alternatively the conception of a differentiated and developed tradition of civil religion may be intellectually exciting and productive of partial insights—but prove not to be a model which is flight-worthy. With respect to the bicentennial celebrations in particular, Warner's analysis of Yankee City's celebrations of its three hundredth year probably provides us with a more useful instrument than the conception of a developed civil religion. His model, of course, in the modern jargon emphasizes social control functions of collective rituals in a highly differentiated society.

Rather than belabor the point that the historian finally assesses a model on the basis of its productivity and not by virtue of its aesthetic qualities, I should emphasize that models which fail to live up to their potential may in fact have great utility. There are numerous ways in which this can be the case. First, in the kaleidoscope which is history a particular model may prove to "fit" one era but not others. In certain respects the elements posited as constitutive of civil religion in America were probably more a reality in certain periods than others. In the very early years of the new Republic, for example, or more so perhaps in the last decades of the nineteenth and the first two of the twentieth centuries. It is possible to imagine conditions developing in the next decades which might lead to a resurgence of elements we have noted, perhaps even a differentiated civil religion. Should this be the case Robert Bellah would appear to have been a John the Baptist, perhaps, or at least a prophet crying in the wilderness. Parenthetically, should this scenario become reality, I fear that the ideological content of the civil religion is more likely to be highly nationalistic as opposed to the internationalism which he so eloquently advocates. In the first place, then, a model may be partially or even episodically useful.

Second, a compelling model may lead to the reformulation of older problems. More precisely, conceptions which may have seemed adequate may appear less so, and older problems may be more fruitfully studied in new sets, and some worthless discussions may be ended. In the present case, the civil religion proposal has suggested more useful perspectives on the relationships between religious traditions and public political issues, and it has lead to deemphasis of the rather sterile categories of church and state which for so long dominated discussion of the nexus between religious symbols, traditions, and authority on the one hand, and political power and institutions on the other. Let me mention a third constructive outcome, namely, the new or different lines of research implicit in a conception. In the present case there was already beginning in the field of American religious history a movement toward the perspectives developed out of history of religions. Discussion of civil religion in the United States necessarily drives to more comparative work, both in the sense of comparison with other specific societies in which there might be such traditions and in terms of a more adequate theoretical basis for the study of religions in different cultures.

In a historical perspective I think it is difficult to arrive at the judgment that there is in American society an institutionalized, well-developed, and differentiated civil religion, a tradition parallel to and interrelated with other religious traditions in our culture. The proposal that there is such, however, has proved to be enormously stimulating and provocative in the best sense. No doubt discussion engendered by it will be carried on for some time.

NOTES

1. *Church History,* 36 (September 1967), pp. 262-283.
2. *Ibid.,* p. 273.
3. *Ibid.,* p. 280.
4. In this section of his essay Professor Mead indicates indebtedness to writings of John E. Smylie, *ibid.,* pp. 277ff. The parenthetical expression is a reminder that insofar as reflection about the American nation as a religious community has been informed by the traditions of Christian (especially Protestant) thought about both justification and sanctification, conditions have existed under which religious authority might be marshaled for an extraordinary range and variety of American nationalisms.
5. *Ibid.,* p. 282.
6. The literature on Lincoln's religion is extensive; it varies greatly in quality, purpose, and reliability, and it is not too helpful. Two very different, interesting discussions are, Edmund Wilson, "Abraham Lincoln: The Union as Religious Mysticism," *Eight Essays* (Garden City, 1954), pp. 181-202, and William J. Wolf, *The Almost Chosen People* (Garden City, 1959), republished as *The Religion of Abraham Lincoln* (New York, 1963).
7. New York, Harper & Row, 1972.
8. W. Lloyd Warner and various associates published the separate volumes of the Yankee City Series beginning in 1941 (New Haven, Yale University Press). Volume 5 concerns "American Symbol Systems" and was published with the title *The Living and the Dead; A Study of the Symbolic Life of Americans* (New Haven, 1959). Large sections of volume 5 were issued in a paperback shortly thereafter: *The Family of God: A Symbolic Study of Christian Life in America* (New Haven, 1961).
9. See *The Living and the Dead,* pp. 481ff.

10. *Ibid.*, pp. 248-249.

11. See *God's New Israel* (Englewood Cliffs, N. J., 1971), Introduction, pp. 1-4.

12. *Ibid.*, pp. 4-6.

13. See "Mass Media: A Social and Psychological Analysis," *American Life: Dream and Reality*, rev. ed. (Chicago, 1962), pp. 247-273.

14. I have used the version published in *Daedalus,* Vol. 96, No. 1 (Winter 1967), pp. 1-21. The essay is also the first in this volume.

15. Ed. Donald R. Cutler (Boston 1968); Hammond's "Commentary" is found on pp. 381-388; Bellah's brief appreciative response is on pp. 388-389.

16. *Ibid.,* p. 384.

17. *Ibid.*

18. See J. Paul Williams, *What Americans Believe and How They Worship* (New York, 1952), pp. 355ff., following *The New Education and Religion* (New York, 1945), pp. 134ff.

19. Bellah, *Daedalus,* p. 1.

20. Frederic Fox has published an article on "The National Day of Prayer," *Theology Today,* Vol. XXIX, No. 3 (October 1972), which indicates very effectively how dubious it is to cite this occasion as an ingredient in a developed and well-institutionalized civil religion. The exercise is more plausibly interpreted without hypostatizing a tradition of civil religion.

MARTIN E. MARTY

7 Two Kinds of Two Kinds of Civil Religion

CIVIL RELIGION does not exist in the same sense as, say, the Roman Catholic Church exists. It was possible for the late comic Lenny Bruce to say that the Catholic Church "is the only *the* Church." Its dogma, liturgy, authority, and tradition were specific and represented a kind of "given." Civil religion is not the only "*the* religion." It represents no defined or agreed-upon faith at all, nor does it suggest the only way of being "civil." No doubt it is a species of a genus which might be called "Way-of-Life Religion." Somewhere between the attention given the specific religion of the sects and the general religious apprehension of reality is a zone where symbols are bartered, in Thomas Luckmann's picture of a "sacred cosmos."[1] Somewhere in that zone civil religion purportedly lies.

I should like to stress that not everything having to do with how one puts a life together—even in the patriotic or nationalistic realm of life—must be viewed religiously. Some anthropologists and sociologists define religion so broadly that nothing can escape it.[2] If everything is religious nothing is religious. In this sphere as in others it is important to allow for a cool, agnostic, disinterested approach.

Having noticed the nonreligious possibility, it is also important to suggest that the civic realm makes room for what Albert Cleage calls "religiocification" more readily than do most other modes or locales of human activity. In historical definitions, the religious would include man's preoccupation with ultimacy, especially when this is accompanied by the language of myth and symbol, is ceremonially and ritually reinforced, appealed to with metaphysical or quasi-metaphysical sanctions, compelling some sort of socialization, and exacting some sort of behavioral consequences. It is sometimes suggested that such a definition of religion lacks the universal ingredient, deity. Such a definition, however, is Western, influenced by biblical religion; numerous world religions including many schools of Buddhism and—unless one wishes to call it only a philosophy—Confucianism, lack reference to a deity.

The nation, state, or society is one of the most potent repositories of symbols in the modern world, and can often replace religious institutions in the minds of people. The nation has its shrines and ceremonies, demands ultimate sacrifice, and specifies behavioral patterns (e.g., the care and handling of the flag, saying the pledge of allegiance),[3] and in other ways takes the place which formal religions once did. Thus when in 1964 Ernest Gellner restored the concept of civil religion he saw it as a rival to and replacement of the specific traditional faiths. He relates this to a kind of ideology with which a society comes to its new approved social contract, with which it moves "over the hump of transition" to that new status. Ordinarily the civil religion will have admixtures of old faiths; in Russia, Marxism served, and in the West Jewish-Christian resources were fused. The result is a division of labor between, on the one hand, symbolic, unifying ideas, communal banners, which once were fullbloodedly cognitive but whose "cognitive import is now shrouded in semi-deliberate ambiguity; and on the other hand, the cognitively effective but normatively not very pregnant or insistent beliefs about the world." Thus it is contemporary Christianity and Judaism itself that

> have now become *civic* religions, inculcating primarily devotion to the values of the community in which they exist (rather than a selfish and anti-social concern with personal and extramundane salvation); and they are held in a manner which allows complete toleration of rival objects of worship.[4]

Needless to say, not all civil religion has that much Judaic or Christian reminiscence.

Civil religion as a species has been referred to with sufficient frequency that it somehow now "exists"; it has subspecies, much as the Christian faith has its denominations. The presence of internal varieties is not a special problem for such a religion. Roman Catholicism has room for votaries all the way from the garlic-and-babushka style of the vestigial Catholic ghetto to the social sophistication of the brothers Berrigan; Protestantism allows for everything from tent revivals to incense-shrouded ritual. Similarly, civil religion is perceived differently down at the friendly Veterans of Foreign Wars or American Legion and up at the halls of ivy where the designation was reborn and revivified.

What makes civil religion different is that at this stage it functions chiefly as what Peter Berger and Thomas Luckmann call "a social construction of reality." So far it remains chiefly the product of the scholars' world; the man on the street would be surprised to learn of its existence or to know that he is one of its professors. Gradually it is being worked into the vocabulary; in the winter of 1973 at a presidential prayer breakfast Senator Mark Hatfield urged a probably noncomprehending clientele that America should not worship the captive tribal god of civil religion but should be open to the God of biblical faith.

If sociologists would call it a social construction of reality, historians might say it is the result of the endeavor which creates "symbolic history"—much as the Renaissance, industrial revolution, Reformation, and Middle Ages did not "occur"; they are, Page Smith says, "symbolic names that depend for their power, not on specific, clearly defined episodes, but on their ability to evoke broad generalized movements, long-range trends and developments." They are "the creation of the historian. . . . Events in this category are not given names by those involved in them; they are named, and thus called to life, by historians." Civil religion is a kind of cluster of episodes which come and go, recede back to invisibility after making their appearance; only gradually are they institutionalized and articulated in organizational form.

If civil religion as a designation of scholars points to an otherwise overlooked reality, it is valid to ask what void it fills. It serves the function of giving a name to incidents or phenomena which the namer ordinarily likes or does not like; it refers to some skein of objective realities. How does it arise? We have noted that while people in society may be merely or utterly secular, godless, or religionless, yet in practice in a complex culture their lives cohere around certain symbols and myths. If they did not, there could be spiritual anarchy and anomie. The churches and synagogues, it is said, do not fulfill the old function of providing enough coherence for enough people. The sectarian, particular, private faiths tend to divide people.

They therefore naturally cohere around national symbols. William Butler Yeats once said that "one can only reach out to the universe with a gloved hand—that glove is one's nation; the only thing one knows even a little of." The nation provides many with a source of identity and power. The nation thus becomes more than the locus of political decision; it provides some context for meaning and belonging.

A construct as loose as civil religion is can be used to fill different needs at different times. It can be seen, for example, that liberal intellectuals in the academy favor it when the nation's chief executive represents broadly their school or style of politics. Thus the modern round of talk about civil religion reflected the late stage of Kennedy-Johnson Camelotism. In such a period these intellectuals will tend to deride those critics in various particular or prophetic traditions who have taken civil religion apart from some normative (e.g., Hebrew prophetic or biblical religionist) point of view. Thus Sidney E. Mead[5] in the middle of the 1960s attacked Will Herberg, who had criticized civil religion of the Eisenhower era, for having possessed those very features which Ernest Gellner has said commend civil religion to a society.

When a Richard M. Nixon fills the chief sacerdotal role and sets the style for the nation's civil religion for a period of years, those same intellectual designators and appreciators tend to flee for cover. They strike out in rage against the Nixonian interpretation or heresy and point to the existence of a *true* civil religion somewhere else. Having criticized the Herbergs of the world for measuring the best in their historic faith over against the worst in civil religion, they turn docetic and move away from incarnationalism to contend, for example, that civil religion hardly ever touched ground. While adherents of church and synagogue religion slosh around in inauthentic faith, civil religion at least existed once in a speech or two of Abraham Lincoln.

Why in the positive or affirmative moments did the liberal advocates of civil religion criticize the critics? For one thing, they had overlooked the positive values of a civic religion. They underestimate the needs for social cement. They do tend to use a double standard for measurement. They may fear competition for the sects. Defenders of civil religion in the academy during the moments when they can cheer current manifestations of this faith are often social realists.

If civil religion is episodic, a creation of historians' symbol-making functions or sociologists' ability to perceive how people socially construct reality, it might be observed or concluded that there are an infinite number of apprehensions of civil religion. In these terms, there would be as many civil religions as there are citizens. Because they are present to a world, they are condemned to meaning (Merleau-Ponty), and in this condemnation they reach for the state. On these terms not much passion is associated with civil religion. Citizens are enraged when the national anthem cannot be played at an athletic event, but do not sing it when it is. They favor by a four to one majority a constitutional amendment which would allow for prayer in schools, but did not pray there when the option was licit.

In practice, there are not 208 million civil religions in America; more passion is gathered around several subspecies. But before these are noticed, it is important to regard for a moment the particularist survivals which work against the idea or practice of civil religion. In the American past these were often denominations in Christianity and the like. In the 1950s Will Herberg detected a trend wherein Americans resisted anomie on one hand and yet reached further than to specific denominations through three large symbolic pools: Protestant, Catholic, Jew.[6] In the 1970s resistance often comes in the form of various ethnic retreats from homogeneity. Black militant scholars, among them Vincent Harding, have argued that civil religion is a repressive WASP construct, used to locate the black outside the approved realm. The Black Muslim has to reach for Islamic symbols because so much white Christianity is fused with the approved civil religion. Many Jews stand back from prayer in public institutions because this expression of civic religion has such a Christian undertone. Non-WASPS like to point out[7] that most civil religion, at least the current academic version of it, is not so netural as its designators would have it; it is a reflection of a WASP apprehension of a world.

Denominational, tri-faith, or ethnic particularist alternatives tend to be accidents. Are there different conceptions? I believe there are four clarifying elements. The differences between them are not clear-cut, but it is useful and it will minimize confusion in terminology and argument if these are outlined with some care. When that care is taken, civil religion can be judged in the context of what it set out to do and not what scholars think it should. When Will Herberg lumps all expressions of civil religion together, he will be able to note that it is universal and idolatrous. When Sidney E. Mead is allowed to do the designating, civil religion will be superior to particular faiths; when those who share his point of view criticize Richard Nixon, Nixon will come out on the short end of analyses—when, it may be argued—he is only doing what his kind of civil religionist ought to be doing, when he fulfills his stated intentions and serves in a role which the electorate has chosen.

In this reading, there are two kinds of two kinds of civil religion. I shall eschew neologisms—let me disappoint those who are seeking novel designations. The stress is here on common sense and traditionally approved terms.

One kind of civil religion sees the nation "under God." Somehow a transcendent deity is seen as the pusher or puller of the social process. He or it may be conceived variously personally or impersonally, as intensely involved or aloof, as providence or progress or process. But somehow there is a transcendent objective reference of a kind which has traditionally been associated with deity. The other main kind stresses "national self-transcendence." It does not see people, left to themselves, automatically given to self-worship. But either references to deity disappear entirely or "God" is drained of earlier cognitive imports and may appear terminologically only out of habitual reference.

Within each of these two kinds there are two kinds of approaches or analyses. With due apology to those Old Testament scholars who do not like to see the line drawn too severely; but with due appreciation to those sociologists who keep drawing the line anyhow, with common-sense application of the terms, let us speak of these as "priestly" and "prophetic." The priestly will normally be celebrative, affirmative, culture-building. The prophetic will tend to be dialectical about civil religion, but with a predisposition toward the judgmental. The two are translations of Joseph Pulitzer's definition of the compleat journalist or, in my application, of the fulfilled religionist: one comforts the afflicted; the other afflicts the comfortable. Needless to say, no adherent need always express only one side or kind; in traditional faiths the priestly and prophetic interact and overlap, though probably most spokesmen or leaders are associated more with one approach than with the other. Thus a priest may judge and a prophet may and often does integrate people into a system of meaning and belonging. But the priest is always alert to the occasions when such integration can occur and the prophet is always sensitive to the fact that he may have to be critical of existing modes of such integration.

The Nation under God: The Priestly Mode

The phrase "under God" appears in Abraham Lincoln's addresses and after the middle of the twentieth century was smuggled into the pledge of allegiance to the flag (by a secular Congress, after the minister-author of the original pledge had neglected to include it). No doubt a content analysis of historic civil religious assertions in the American past would show what the overwhelming majority of references would stress the reality "under God." Civil religion would normally exist, similarly, for priestly reasons. The prophet Joel speaks for Yahweh when he says, "Sanctify a fast, call a solemn assembly" (Joel 1:14). So would a president of the local chapter of a veterans' group or of the United States.

The God under whom the nation lives will probably be pictured and symbolized in terms similar to those used by the particular religions within a nation. This deity gives identity, meaning, and purpose to the nation and its citizens. He or it exists prior to and independently of the state and may be expected to outlive and outlast the civil society. He may be the Trinity, or God the Father of Jesus Christ, or the Supreme Architect, or a Benign Providence. In any case, he or it represents a promissor to the nation; in this terminological reference one speaks of "the promise *to* American life" more readily than of the "promise *of*" America.

While this may be the conventional pattern of the majority of civil religionists, it is likely to be that of the critical liberal intellectuals who are wont to use the term. The God of a nation "under God," it has been implied in the quotation from Ernest Gellner, may and probably will undergo constant transformations. But, then, so does the God of historic faiths, as any student of the history of Christian (or Buddhist, or Hindu, or Muslim) thought and "doctrine" will know.

For example, at one time the nation was said to be "under God" of a kind of deist reality, the center of power and meaning for most of the national founding fathers. They were usually members of historic Christian churches, but their effectual symbolic references had become deist. This is the case of Benjamin Franklin, George Washington, and Thomas Jefferson, to name just a few obvious examples.

More Americans probably draw their reference to life "under God" from Puritan, evangelical, Catholic, or Jewish forebears than from the deist few who were successful at introducing some of the ethos of the Enlightenment into the political sphere. In these latter readings, an addressable God created, guided, and led a nation toward its destiny. This God mandated a mission, demanded loyalty that went beyond loyalty extended to the state—though a conflict of loyalties was rarely pictured. Thus the churches could give enthusiastic support to this version of civil religion.

Civil religion "under God," in its priestly form, normally appears as a fusion, then, of historic faith (as in Jewish or Christian traditions) with autochthonous national sentiments. Usually it will have as its main priest the president, since he alone stands at the head of all the people—and civil religion would be inclusive—and he has greatest potential for invoking symbols of power. Dwight D. Eisenhower was a particularly gifted priest, who appeared in a decade of cold war when the nation needed its anxieties ministered to and when it needed divine sanction for its adventures. For many critics of civil religion, Eisenhower's carrying out of his priestly roles acquired almost normative status.[8] The strength of this approach lay in the fact that it did bring a nation together in a sort of "era of good feeling"; its liability: it may have contributed to moral pretension in support of American participation in the cold war as a *jihad,* a holy war.

Critics who were shocked at the Eisenhower role would, if they engaged in structural and functional analysis, find reason for their surprise and shock to disappear. The president is normally expected to play a priestly role. Even Abraham Lincoln, everyone's favorite civil religionist-as-prophet, normally was the priest. Edmund Wilson said he regarded the union with an awe usually associated with religious mysticism. But at one or two crucial turns he remarkably moved to a prophetic vocation, and for this he is remembered.[9] But presidents could not be presidents if their main function was to call God down in judgment on his nation's policies.

In the priestly spirit, Eisenhower could say that "America is the mightiest power which God has yet seen fit to put upon his footstool. America is great because she is good."

> *Gott strafe England*, and God save the king,
> God this, God that, and God the other thing.
> "Good God!" said God, "I've got my work cut out for me."

The Nation under God: The Prophetic Mode

Mention has just been made of the way that in rare occasions the nation's chief priest may step into the prophetic role. Historically such a passage is rare, but extremely potent. Just as Christians measure their faith by the cross of Christ in self-giving love, or by the quality of witness of the Hebrew prophets in their canon, so civil religionists measure their faith by central and epochal statements of national faith in the prophetic style.

If Joel, speaking for Yahweh, could "call a solemn assembly," Amos could speak in the same name and say, "I despise the noise of your solemn assemblies." We have seen something of the dialectical-judgmental potential at several important turns in American history. The men whom many regard as the two greatest native-born theologians, Jonathan Edwards in colonial times and Reinhold Niebuhr in the recent past, gave voice to the two kinds of witness that are in tension with each other. Jonathan Edwards can be remembered both as the angry prophet of God against all the works of men and as a postmillennialist who thought that in his community, colony, or in what was to become the American nation, the "latter-day glory" would appear. The "nation" was clearly under God; but God expected more of chosen people than of others.[10]

Lincoln regarded the nation with a sense of religious mysticism. But he then could remind the people that the Almighty has his own purposes. In the classic texts of prophetic civil religion "under God," he reminded both sides in the Civil War that both sides prayed to the same God, read the same Bible, and the like—but both could not win. Both liked to claim God on their side; Lincoln said they should instead try to conform their wills to his own mysterious will, so far as it could be known.[11]

In the middle of the twentieth century, Reinhold Niebuhr affirmed the civil society and participated in it, as consultant to national figures like George Kennan, Dean Acheson, Arthur Schlesinger, Jr., and Hans Morgenthau and as participant in partisan politics. But when he found a prideful nation acting in the name of God, he would speak in the words of the psalmist: "He that sitteth in the heavens shall laugh." His favorite category in civil religion was "The Irony of American History."[12]

Perhaps these three figures should be thought of as critical public theologians as opposed to votaries of civil religion. It may be unrealistic to picture most adherents using their religion over against their own identity, integration, or power—just as one would not be likely to picture most Christians remaining in range of a pulpit simply to be put in their place. In all three cases, however, these public theologians are prophets from within the tradition. The outsider never has the same kind of credentials.

The employment of, say, biblical prophetic motifs over against national pretensions, is potent. When Protestant evangelicals scored their hero Billy Graham for remaining silent in the face of bombing of civilians in Vietnam, they came with better credentials and more power than would those who did not see the life of the nation under the judgment of an angry God. (They had little effect on Graham, but they did speak to many in his clientele. Graham at this time found it necessary to dissociate himself from the prophetic tradition, saying that he really conceived his vocation to be that of a New Testament evangelist, not an Old Testament prophet.)

The prophetic mode has to be dialectical. If it comes unilaterally from outside or is totally rejective from within, it does not belong to the civil religion, which is an expression of a somehow-covenanted group of insiders. The dialectician says "both/and": God both shapes a nation and judges it, because he is transcendent in both circumstances. The main critics of civil religion from both the left and the right are those who come in the name of a transcendent deity. Thus Senator Mark Hatfield in the comment that has already been mentioned:

> If we as leaders appeal to the god of civil religion, our faith is in a small and exclusive deity, a loyal spiritual adviser to power and prestige, a defender of only the American nation, the object of a national folk religion devoid of moral content. But if we pray to the biblical God of justice and righteousness, we fall under God's judgment for calling upon his name but failing to obey his commands.[13]

The classic picture of the prophets of God vs. the prophets of Baal comes to mind in this interpretation of civil religion "under God"!

In order to introduce the other kinds of civil religion it is necessary to set a stage. We picture some secularization; that is, that spheres of life which were once interpreted in the light of a transcendent reference now are construed simply "as they are," so much as possible. This secularization is accompanied by a new openness to religious transformation, particularly to the intrusion of religions of the East. They are full-bodied religions, but they lack objective reference to a transcendent deity. To a lesser extent, the Afro-American movement has shown how alternative ways of interpreting reality have been present in African religion.

When Bishop Ian Ramsey said that we have a "spirituality devoid of God," he was doing some Christian complaining about styles of being spiritual but not "under God." Yet many today would say that "spirituality devoid of God" is a legitimate and positive expression in our day. In the Christian world some radical theologians spoke of this as "this-worldly transcendence." Some of the theological language associated with "process" uses divine references in these contexts. God symbols are not necessarily purged, but they play a lesser role. Terminological neatness is not possible. When the Gallup people poll Americans, between 95 percent and 98 percent of them say that they believe in God. But to interviewers they display a broader range of options. And it is possible to believe in a transcendent deity and be among the 95 percent majority, and at the same time see the possibilities of a self-transcendent nation as being not necessarily the object of worship but the locale of power and meaning or spirit.

In a sociological essay that stands in the Meadian historical tradition of affirmation of civil religion, Robert N. Bellah in 1966 noted this transformation, first in negative terms (just as in a later essay he saw the positive side of this-worldly transcendence).

> The civil religion . . . is . . . caught in another kind of crisis, theoretical and theological, of which it [sic] is at the moment largely unaware. "God" has clearly been a central symbol in the civil religion from the beginning and remains so today. . . . But today . . . the meaning of the word *God* is by no means . . . clear or . . . obvious. There is no formal creed in the civil religion. We have had a Catholic president; it is conceivable that we could have a Jewish one. But could we have an agnostic president? Could a man with conscientious scruples about using the word *God* the way Kennedy and Johnson have used it be elected chief magistrate of our country? If the whole God symbolism requires reformulation, there will be obvious consequences for civil religion, consequences perhaps of liberal alienation and of fundamentalist ossification that have not so far been prominent in this realm. The civil religion has been a point of articulation between the profoundest commitments of the Western religious and philosophical tradition and the common beliefs of ordinary Americans. It is not too soon to consider how the deepening theological crisis may affect the future of this articulation.[14]

In the intervening years there has been considerable talk about transcendence which may or may not go on "under God." New models are being sought. The Marxians, Sartreans, Marcuseans join spokesmen of Eastern and African religions to speak of transcendence without deity, or at least without seeing deity integral to the process. This is transcendence "from below," as it were, what philosopher Ernst Bloch calls "transcending without transcendence." This is something held open for a possible and as yet undecided future in this vacant place—or, as French poets of the symbolist school called it, "empty transcendence." Something of Martin Heidegger's "the understanding of being" is implied here. Most seekers along this path, it may be noted, may not need civil religion as the focus, but some do.

The Nation as Self-Transcendent: The Priestly Style

When the language of civil religion shifts from talk about the promise *to* America (from a transcendent deity) to the promise *of* America, and national self-transcendence, the signal of priestly civil religion, is raised. Usually this has occurred at the margins of American life. Thus Robert Welch, the author of the *Blue Book* of the John Birch Society, fused an evolutionary cosmic vision with national purpose to produce a priestly "this-worldly transcendent" civil religion. Modern fascisms have this element, and should a version of these become strong in the American future, it would probably be an expression of priestly civil religion.

While marginal priestly civil religion is rare and relatively impotent, there are moderate versions of the same expressed occasionally on higher levels and in more responsible circles. In John F. Kennedy there were occasional references to the nation which saw it in the place where God had once been. Kennedy either by instinct or with the aid of sophisticated speech-writing *periti* reminded a nation that here on earth God's work must truly be our own. There was here almost a Teilhardian sense of co-creatorship; but the reference to deity seemed to be more than nominal.

In Richard M. Nixon's vocabulary, the nominal reference remains, but a subtle shift has occurred. Advocates of prophetic biblical religion are nervous about such a shift, but it is not universally railed against. Thus Gerald Strober and Lowell Streiker, in an apologia for the religion of middle America, write—in terms abhorrent to prophetic religionists:

> Henderson, Fiske, and Gary Wills have all criticized the President for his "lack of a sense of transcendence." But the America of American civil religion is scarcely less "transcendent" than is the God of the Judaeo-Christian tradition.[15]

The Henderson referred to in that positive reference is Charles B. Henderson, Jr., who wrote a full-length dissection of Nixon's view of the nation as self-transcendent or even as the object of transcendent reference. He concluded:

> Nixon systematically appropriates the vocabulary of the church—faith, trust, hope, belief, spirit—and applies these words not to a transcendent God but to his own nation, and worse, to his personal vision of what that nation should be. . . . Lacking a transcendent God, he seems to make patriotism his religion, the American dream his deity.[16]

Given the president's willingness to make reference to deity and Graham's assurance that the president does believe in a transcendent God, it may be a bit unfair to say, "lacking a transcendent God. . . . " But it is not unfair to say, as Henderson does, that he takes the vocabulary of transcendence and applies it chiefly to his personal vision of the nation. His is talk about the "promise *of* American life" as a religious ultimate. This does not mean that he never uses the language of prophecy. At the presidental prayer breakfast in 1972 his speech even quoted Abraham Lincoln's dialectical references.

Mention might here be made in passing, at least, to a "left-wing" alternative to the views of the Welches at the right and the Nixons at the center. In my own writing on civil religion in 1959 I stressed both the Eisenhowerian version "under God" and the religion-in-general or religion of the American Way of Life as expressed in the tradition of A. Powell Davies, John Dewey, Horace Kallen, Agnes Meyer, and J. Paul Williams. In the liberal intellectual tradition of John Dewey's *A Common Faith* or Walter Lippmann's *A Public Philosophy* there has been room for a quasi-transcendent set of values which emerge from the social process itself. This is a democratic humanism with overtones of religious ultimacy. Rarely, however, has explicitly religious language been associated comprehensively with this point of view.

An exception was J. Paul Williams in *What Americans Believe and How They Worship*. If Williams did not exist, we should probably have had to devise him for this category, because he is an "ideal type" who shows that the priestly approach to national self-transcendence in civil religion does not always belong to the political right and center. Williams said that "democracy must become an object of religious dedication." "Systematic and universal indoctrination is essential." There must be what Williams himself called metaphysical sanctions, "open indoctrination of the faith that the democratic ideal accords with ultimate reality . . . that democracy is the very law of life." And there will be ceremonial reinforcement, a "devotion to democratic ideals like the devotion given by ardent believers in every age to the traditional religions." "Ignoring the lack of spiritual integration invites disaster. Relying on the haphazard methods of the past will not meet the need. . . . Governmental agencies must teach the democratic ideal *as religion*."[17]

In the years since that was written, the democratic left has suffered many setbacks and for the moment, at least, lacks the potency to give voice to such appeals. Should that form of humanism return to power, we may expect similar expressions again.

The Nation as Self-Transcendent: The Prophetic Style

The second kind of the second kind of civil religion has to be matched with the Lincolnian dialectical version. It is ecumenical, unwilling to see civil religion exhausted by one nation's purposes. Usually it is advocated by people with strong monistic and integrative impulses. The spokesmen are tolerant and allow for many particularities and demonstrate awareness of the rights of peculiar sects to propagate. But they are impatient with them and uneasy about too much pluralism. At the same time, they are cautious lest civil religion be seen as idolatry, as worship of the nation. Thus, for Sidney Mead,

> to be committed to an ideal world beyond the present world and to the incarnating of that ideal world in actuality [is an element in what he calls the "religion of the Republic"]. Seen thus the religion of the Republic is essentially prophetic, which is to say that its ideals and aspirations stand in constant judgment over the passing shenanigans of the people, reminding them of the standards by which their current practices and those of their nation are ever being judged and found wanting.[18]

The religion of the Republic does *not* mean worship of state or nation, says Mead. He blames people under European theological influence for hinting that it does or might. In the older language, "one most constant strand in its theology has been the assertion of the primacy of God over all human insitutions." But this God-reference has been attenuated symbolically, intellectualized and spiritualized beyond recognition, toward a "cosmopolitan, universal theology."

"Our final concern . . . is to assure ourselves that our attitude toward the nation does not become idolatrous; that the state does not become God; that the Republic does not become heteronomous vis-a-vis other nations." In this succession, Robert N. Bellah was to argue that "the civil religion at its best is a genuine apprehension of universal and transcendent religious reality as seen in or, one could almost say, as revealed through the experience of the American people."

He concludes with a "since" that assumes that something has been established:

> Since the American civil religion is not the worship of the American nation but an understanding of the American experience in the light of ultimate and universal reality, the reorganization entailed by . . . a new situation need not disrupt the American civil religion's continuity.

With more sensitivity to the ecumenical and nonidolatrous idea of national self-transcendence than to the problem of the faiths of other men in other nations who do not share much of the American way of looking at reality, he continues:

> A world civil religion could be accepted as a fulfillment and not a denial of American civil religion. Indeed such an outcome has been the eschatological hope of American civil religion from the beginning. To deny such an outcome would be to deny the meaning of America itself.[19]

By the time reference to a "world civil religion" is made, God-talk has been thinned out; the question of "the meaning of America itself" is a heavy-laden theological term (since one cannot know the meaning of America until the end of its history); problems abound in these two paragraphs. But they do illustrate that the intention of dialectical-prophetic civil religionists is not only to affirm what is, but to avoid idolatry and move toward an *oikoumene*. "Our nation stands under higher judgment." In a later essay, Bellah went on: "Every society is forced to appeal to some higher jurisdiction and to justify itself not entirely on its actual performance but through its commitment to unrealized goals or values."[20]

Such language is possible to those for whom the idea of the "nation under God" is no longer satisfactory. Thus Roger Garaudy, French Marxist who participates in dialogues with Christians:

> As far as faith is concerned, whether faith in God or faith in our task and whatever our differences regarding its source—for some, assent to a call from God; for others, purely human creation—faith imposes on us the duty of seeing to it that every man becomes a man, a flaming hearth of initiative, a poet in the deepest sense of the word: one who has experienced, day by day, the creative surpassing of himself—what Christians call his transcendence and we call his authentic humanity.[21]

In the future it is possible that this kind of language will be refined and propagated with more comprehension in the American environment.

So far as the future is concerned, it may be that culture will be ever more sensate and secular or it may turn newly religious. Perhaps a new style of consciousness will emerge. In the latter instances, public theologians in the civil religious traditions will probably look for what Tillich denominated "Catholic substance and Protestant principle," not in any denominational sense but as priestly and prophetic realities in tension with each other. If the two elements can be built into civil religion, it will not be so ominous to its critics, nor so simply enjoyable and utilizable by its priests. In the meantime, some creative apathy against its claims—some foot-dragging, finger-crossing, thumbing-gestures, and puckish good humor—are in order. The tradition of Mark Twain, Mr. Dooley, Will Rogers, and Mort Sahl should be involved to prevent people from taking the claims and counterclaims of civil religion so seriously. Maybe some division of labor is in order. We are told that when Harold Macmillan was criticized for not giving his people a sense of purpose, he replied that if the people wanted a sense of purpose they should go to their archbishops. The particular communities—be they religious, ethnic, or oriented around interest groups—can creatively refract generalized civil religion through specific prisms. They can contribute to peoples' identity and power, their search for meaning and belonging. We shall probably continue to hear advocacies both of a "world civil religion" and for the reformation of the existing centers of value which are now embodied and contended for apart from the civil realm. The future belongs, no doubt, to neither but only to both.

NOTES

1. Luckmann's position is defined in *The Invisible Religion* (New York: The Macmillan Co., 1967), chap. IV, pp. 50ff.

2. A sample basis for such inclusive definitions of religion appears in what strikes me as an admirable approach to symbolization in Clifford Geertz, "Religion as a Cultural System," in Donald R. Cutler (ed.), *The Religious Situation: 1968* (Boston: Beacon Press, 1968), pp. 639ff.

3. See Carlton J. H. Hayes, *Nationalism: A Religion* (New York: The Macmillan Co., 1960), chap. XII, 164ff.

4. Ernest Gellner, *Thought and Change* (Chicago: University of Chicago Press, 1965), p. 123.

5. Sidney Mead, "The Post-Protestant Concept and America's Two Religions," in *Religion in Life*, Vol. XXXIII (Spring 1964), pp. 191-204.

6. Will Herberg, *Protestant, Catholic, Jew: An Essay in American Religious Sociology* (New York: Doubleday, 1955).

7. Thus D. W. Brogan in his essay in Cutler, *op. cit.*, pp. 356ff.

8. William L. Miller, *Piety Along the Potomac: Notes on Politics and Morals in the Fifties* (Boston: Houghton Mifflin Co., 1964) is the most detailed account of Eisenhower-era civil religion.

9. Edmund Wilson, *Eight Essays* (New York: Doubleday, 1964).

10. This approach to Jonathan Edwards is taken in Alan Heimert,

Religion and the American Mind (Cambridge, Mass.: Harvard University Press, 1966), pp. 96ff.

11. See William J. Wolf, *The Almost Chosen People: A Study of the Religion of Abraham Lincoln* (Garden City: Doubleday, 1959), chaps. 8 and 9.

12. *The Irony of American History* (New York: Charles Scribner's Sons, 1952).

13. Mark Hatfield is quoted in *The Christian Century,* February 21, 1973, p. 221.

14. "Civil Religion in America," in *Daedalus* (Winter 1967), pp. 15f.

15. Lowell D. Streiker and Gerald S. Strober, *Religion and the New Majority* (New York: Association Press, 1972), p. 179.

16. Charles B. Henderson, Jr., *The Nixon Theology* (New York: Harper & Row, 1972), p. 193.

17. For reference to J. Paul Williams and his colleagues, see my *The New Shape of American Religion* (New York: Harper & Row, 1959), chap. IV, and "The Status of Societal Religion," in *Concordia Theological Monthly* Vol. XXXVI, No. 10 (November 1965), pp. 687ff.

18. Sidney E. Mead, "The Nation with the Soul of a Church," in *Church History,* Vol. XXXVI, No. 3 (September, 1967), pp. 275-283.

19. Robert N. Bellah, "Civil Religion in America," in *Daedalus* (Winter, 1967), pp. 12, 18.

20. See also Robert N. Bellah, "Transcendence in Contemporary Piety," in Herbert W. Richardson and Donald R. Cutler (eds.), *Transcendence* (Boston: Beacon Press, 1969), p. 91.

21. Roger Garaudy, *From Anathema to Dialogue* (New York: Herder and Herder, 1966), p. 123.

III

Criticism

HERBERT RICHARDSON

8 Civil Religion in Theological Perspective

1

THE CONCEPT "civil religion" unites two terms: the civil order and the religious order. The civil order is not the only term with which religion can be linked. There can be a "nature religion," an "ecclesial religion," a "mystical religion," and so forth. In such concepts, religion is linked with nature, the church, and special psychological experiences, respectively. In fact, any aspect of human life can be linked with religion and made an object of ultimate concern in this way.

Two things happen when we link religion with some other thing. First, we ascribe to that thing some ultimate value or transcendent meaning. For example, Robert Bellah points out that civil religion "provides a transcendent goal for the political process."[1] In civil religion, the political process is related through symbols and rituals to ideals concerning man's ultimate fulfillment. When a person or group links up religion with some aspects of its life, therefore, we can learn from this fact something about their own orientation to the world: namely, what is important to them and what concerns them ultimately.

The second thing that happens when we link up religion with some other aspect of life is that we conceive ultimate reality as if it resembled this thing. We can, for example, use the game of chess as a model for ultimate reality—and think of the universe as a "cosmic chess game."[2] Or we can use the city (Greek: *polis*) as a model of the universe—and think of ultimate reality as a cosmic-polis. We affirm, in this way, a relevant analogy between two things. In the same way, we can link nature and religion, thereby thinking of ultimate reality as a "life process" and the meaning of life as "birth, life, death, and rebirth." Or we can take art or dance as the model of all reality and analogize from these to "life is creativity" or the "dancing God."

We see, then, that linking religion with any other term effects two things: one is sociological and the other is theological. On the sociological side, this linking is a way of constructing, through appropriate symbols and rituals, an ultimate meaning and direction for a particular human activity. On the theological side, this linking is a way of affirming an analogy, or special relation, between something in this world and ultimate reality; a way of "modeling" or picturing what God is and our relation to him. So, for example, a person who identifies with a political group and its civil religion not only thereby affirms that this group has a transcendent goal and some ultimate value (the sociological aspect), but he will also tend to think that the categories of politics—sovereignty, law, justice, the state—are especially appropriate for describing ultimate reality (the theological aspect). To relate anything to a transcendent and ideal dimension is also to affirm that it is, in some way, "true."

In this essay we shall be analyzing civil religion from both these points of view: the sociological and the theological. We shall first analyze what it means sociologically and historically that Americans have developed a unique civil religion through which they express their faith that politics is a matter of ultimate concern. Then we shall analyze what it means to use the civil, or political, order as a model for conceiving reality and God's relation to man. That is, we shall ask what it means to think of God in political terms as, for example, a "king" who "rules" through "law" which requires "obedience." And we shall consider alternative models of God and their implications for civil religion.

Just as our social images can have theological relevance, so our theological judgments can have social and political relevance. When we think of God as a "sovereign" or imagine the world as ordered by a "law," we are not only using political categories to describe God; we are also using theological symbols to describe politics. For example, when we think of God as *like a king*, it shows that we think kings are very very important; and when we think that the cosmos is like a *civitas* (a "city" or political realm), it shows that we think politics is a fairly ultimate activity. We see, therefore, that in analogizing we not only ascribe finite characteristics to what is infinite, we also claim infinite characteristics for what is finite. It is this reciprocal relation between social and religious imagery that makes an analysis of civil religion so urgent in our time.

One of the functions of civil religion is to legitimate and control the use of political power in a society. To explore this theme is the main focus of the present essay. The questions we must ask are: how are the institutions of the political order to be valued and controlled? Do we have a better *civitas* when we regard political institutions and activities as having an ultimate value (i.e. when we take them with religious seriousness)? Or do we have a better *polis* when we refuse to take politics with religious seriousness and reject the notion that any nation has special responsibilities "under God"? The very ultimacy, or unconditionedness, with which many Americans approach politics, could well be destructive of the civil order rather than truly constructive. Just as a person who plays chess or football with "religious seriousness" has lost so much sense of proportion that he actually ruins the game, so people who approach politics as if ultimate moral and religious issues were at stake may also be destroying the political process itself. Some things go better if we value them less.

But, someone might protest, how can we control human politics and law if we value them less? How can we order the life of a nation unless we relate it to higher, transcendent norms? How can we limit man's pretensions to absolute power unless we bring those pretensions under the higher sovereignty of God? How can we maintain human freedom unless we believe it to be a divine gift? What better way is there to limit the institutions and activities of the *civitas* than in the light of its own highest ideals, its civil religion? These are some questions that must be answered.

Robert Bellah's 1967 essay, "Civil Religion in America," has provoked lively discussion; and it should be noted that Bellah has considerably developed his own thinking on this subject over the past seven years.[3] His 1967 essay will serve, however, as a conversation partner to my own discussion, primarily because Bellah's concern there is also with the way political power can be effectively limited and rightly used.

In his essay Bellah affirms that the persisting thrust within American civil religion has been to affirm that civil power stands under the sovereignty of God and that the nation must judge its own acts in the light of divine righteousness. American civil religion, Bellah affirms, is America's attempt to bring its own life under a higher ideal, and it functions to make "any form of political absolutism illegitimate."[4] I believe Bellah has correctly described the essential thrust of American civil religion. At its best it limits the misuse of power by affirming that there is an analogy between political categories and religious-moral ones—criticizing political life from the vantage point of these higher ideals. Our nation does not claim that it is God, but that it stands "under God" and his judgment.

Bellah sees, too, that American civil religion can be idolatrous. This occurs, he argues, when the gap between the nation and its ideals is closed, so that the dimension of transcendence is lost and America falls into laudatory self-congratulation. When this occurs, he argues, it is a *misuse* of civil religion. Richard Nixon, for example, misuses civil religion; but Abraham Lincoln and John Kennedy used it properly.[5]

However, we should consider the possibility that the misuse of civil religion does not arise merely because some men use it improperly. It may be that such misuse is generated by the very structure of civil religion itself so that it is inevitable. The misuse may arise not from the way people use civil religion, but from the way that civil religion operates. We have already seen that every model of God has a built-in doubleness. That is, whenever we "ascribe finite characteristics to what is infinite," we also "claim infinite characteristics for what is finite." Whenever, therefore, we seek to relate American politics to God's sovereignty, we are also relating God's sovereignty to American politics. In attempting to be pious, we can also become proud.

It is structurally inevitable that if we seek to limit human power by requiring that it imitate a divine exemplar, we actually generate the very state of affairs we are seeking to avoid. Here is how the mechanism works.[6] If a person really tries to will what God wants and do what God wills, then the more he struggles and succeeds, the more he will interpret his strivings and achievements as approximations of "the will of God." He might begin by seeing a gap between where he is and where he ought to be, but as soon as he starts trying to be better, he also starts closing that gap and removing the grounds for bringing himself under criticism. The better he becomes, therefore, the less reason he feels there is for limiting his exercise of power. In the same way, when any political party identifies its program with a utopian vision and the kingdom of God, the more justified it feels in pursuing this program with unqualified zeal and the less likely it will be to accept criticism or compromise. Hence, the more earnestly anyone strives to attain a transcendent and divine ideal, the more likely he will be to regard himself and his strivings as righteous.

Is it not true that Americans have experienced this structural anomaly throughout their history? It is, ironically, the "best" politics in America that always becomes idolatrous, for it is through its best and highest aspirations that American politics most reduces the discrepancy between the "is" and the "ought," thereby identifying its strivings with what it believes should be and making itself the norm of judgment on itself. In this way American civil religion always tends to generate the very situation it seeks to prevent. It may be the case that such idealizing civil religion and the identification of political activity with moral striving is inevitable, but it would seem to be a very precarious thing to try to control political power by invoking civil ideals and moral principles.

2

Given the structural ambivalence of civil religion, the question must be raised whether there is any other way of limiting and controlling political power. Even if there were some other way, it would not, of course, abolish civil religion, for civil religion is an inevitable social structure. It is because he regards civil religion as inevitable that Bellah seeks to discover within it limits and norms for controlling the use of political power.[7] There is, however, another alternative: one might grant that civil religion is inevitable and yet look for some other way to limit and steer the power of the state. That other way might involve an opposition to the very civil religion with which the state inevitably clothes its aspirations to power.

There can be, I concede, no serious disagreement with Bellah's sociological descriptions of civil religion in America. But serious opposition has been raised against his assertion that American civil religion is an inevitable social structure. To these critics, Bellah has replied as follows:

> Why something so obvious [as civil religion] should have escaped serious analytical attention is in itself an interesting problem. . . . But part of the reason this issue has been left in obscurity is certainly due to the peculiarly Western concept of religion as denoting a single type of collectivity of which an individual can be a member of one and only one at a time. The Durkheimian notion that every group has a religious dimension . . . is foreign to us. This obscures the recognition of such dimensions within our society.[8]

Bellah's reply to those who criticize civil religion is, therefore, that it is inevitable because "every group has a religious dimension." To say that civil religion should not exist is to say that the *civitas*, the civil order itself, should not exist—for one cannot exist without the other. Every group generates idealizing symbols and communal rituals that guide it and hold it together. These are the "religion" of the group.

This notion of religion is not unique to sociology. A usual explanation of the Latin root *re-ligere* is "to bind together." Religion is those feelings, symbols, and acts that bind a group together; and since there are many groups, there are many "religions." A person can be a member of many at one and the same time. With regard to this argument I believe there can be no serious misunderstanding or disagreement.

The place where Bellah's proposal becomes more problematic, I suggest, is in his conception of the American civic "group." Rather than sharply differentiating such units as "people," "nation," and "state," Bellah tends to speak of them as one. For example, he writes: "Every nation and every people come to some form of religious self-understanding, whether the critics like it or not. Rather than simply denounce what seems in any case inevitable, it seems more responsible to seek within the civil religious tradition for those political principles which undercut the everpresent danger of national self-idolization."[9] In this statement, we see that Bellah has lumped together—as if they were one group—"people," "nation," the "civil" or "political" order, and, implicitly, the national state. That is, he has not maintained sharp distinctions among various groups and their functions. In this way his argument slips from a valid assumption to an invalid one: from the valid assumption that every civil group inevitably generates a civil religion to the invalid assumption that a civil group is a nation-state. But civil groups are not always nation-states. Nation-states originate from the uncommon fusion of two quite different groups: the cultural unit (the "nation") and the civil unit (the "state").

It is at this point, I believe, that the confusion about Bellah's argument arises. For while it is true that every group generates its own symbols and rituals, and while it is true that every civil group will generate its own civil religion, it is not true that every civil group will be the unity of both a nation and a state, or that every civil religion will be a *national civil religion*. Nations and states are distinguishable social entities and they can generate not simply different, but even opposed, religions. When we find a nation and a state combined in a single complex social group, that unity is not inevitable nor is the religion it generates. Rather, when a nation and a state become one unit, it is a contingent historical development—and such a development may certainly be judged as "wrong." While, therefore, civil religion may be inevitable, the national form of civil religion in America is not inevitable—and it is certainly wrong.

What Bellah has done is to generalize the form that the civil order has taken in America, i.e., to generalize the nation-state and its kind of civil religion. Had he maintained a distinction between the civil religion that is inevitable and the identification of the nation with the state that is not, then his account of American civil religion might have been very different. For example, rather than interpreting the Civil War as a vindication of the unity of the American nation "conceived in liberty," he might have interpreted it as the event in which the original bi-national character of the state (no less written into the Constitution than the affirmation of liberty) was finally destroyed. On this view of the matter, Abraham Lincoln might appear less as a Christ-figure than as a tragic Caesar-figure, namely, as the one through whom the state (in collaboration with its majority nation) destroyed multi-nationalism within its own borders and became a modern nation-state. American civil religion has been, since that time, primarily a justification of that historical development.

Since nations are cultural groups that generate idealizing symbols and binding rituals, they possess extraordinary social power. They have been, traditionally, the major limitation on the power of the state and its efforts to centralize control. They have performed this function because, traditionally, a state is made up of several nations, or cultural groupings—each of which has an interest in maintaining a degree of autonomy and pursuing its own goals. In the conflict of a state's nations with one another, as well as in their opposition to the state itself, nations compete for power against the state and weaken the state's effective sovereignty. They do so by generating loyalties that qualify people's commitment to the state's ideals and its civil religion.

The dramatic increase in the power of modern states has come about through the process of "nationalism," that is, through the identification of the state's interests with the interests of one of its more powerful constituent nations: the German state with Prussia, the Soviet state with Russia, and the United States with the "north." Through this identification, the power of two previously separate and competing social groups is fused and this merger is ratified by the creation of a complex national-political ideology, or national civil religion. In this civil religion the state appropriates the history and culture of one nation as its own. While this process is going on, the state's other nations and cultural groups must be vigorously suppressed and the culture of the dominant nation diffused throughout the land.[10] This is what occurred in the American Civil War. In this war the American state identified its interests with those of its northern nation and, following the war, the Yankees were able to impose their culture and commercial interests not only on the south, but also on all incoming immigrants. Yankee schoolmarms spread throughout the land and "universal education" was imposed on all the young in order to socialize them into the values of the official culture. The attempts of Catholics and other groups to establish separate schools that would allow them to resist assimilation into the Yankee nation was persistently undermined by the state. And America created an ideological history and language that rendered invisible blacks, nisei, chicanos, and other peoples who were unlikely candidates for Puritan forefathers.[11]

Through its identification with the symbols and interests of one of its national cultures, the American state overcame its major competitors for social power. This is the method of nationalism, no different in America from elsewhere. In the first moment nationalism is domestic policy and the state turns inward in the attempt to destroy its multi-national cultures. In the next moment nationalism becomes foreign policy and the state turns outward in the effort to incorporate other states within the web of its culture and commerce. Hence it is not mere coincidence that the American Civil War was followed by the American imperial age, as the United States raced to join European nation-states in foreign expansion and, finally, in two world wars.

It is difficult for Americans to realize that, even today, most states are not nation-states but embrace a variety of nations and other groups that do not share a common history or values. Moreover, most nations do not exist merely within the borders of a single state, but are dispersed through many. The German nation exists in many states; so do the French, English, Ukrainian, Armenian, Indian, and others. The fact that nations are not co-extensive with one state and the range of its power is what limits its sovereignty and contains its ambitions. A person may be loyal to his national group and also loyal to his civic group. When these are not one and the same, but two different groups, then the symbols and power of each put a limitation on the symbols and power of the other. In such cases the power of the *civitas* is not limited by judging it in terms of its own ideals, but by confronting it with the ideals and social power of another group.

In its civil war America became a nation-state and created a national civil religion, a religion which both justified the fact that it had become a nation-state and removed from the state the traditional restraint on its exercise of power. When Bellah proposes that we should seek criteria for limiting the idolatrous ten-

dencies of the state within the tradition and among the ideals of
American civil religion, he is seeking criteria where they are no
longer easily found. Rather, to limit civil power we must begin
by rejecting our civil religion and its canonical history of America.
We must seek to reinstitute, at the very least, the principle of
multiple nationhoods and multiple loyalties. Only as its separate
cultures and regions begin to affirm their own specific identity
and ideals in opposition to American civil religion will the power
of the American state be reduced to an appropriate size.

3

We come now to a second set of questions about civil religion:
specifically theological ones. We have already seen that complex
terms such as "civil religion" or "nature religion" provide categories
that can be used in our conceiving God and man's fulfillment. We
have seen, too, that every social group generates an idealized
vision of itself that can be accepted as a model of man's relation
to ultimate reality. The theological question is: which of these
models of ultimate reality is most adequate, if any?

One might, of course, reply that they are all equally valid (or
invalid). But this reply is specious because it overlooks the fact
that what is here sought is an answer to the question how man
should proportion out his time and energies and to which groups
he should give greater loyalties. Although every group generates
a religious symbolism and although any aspect of human life can
become an object of ultimate concern, it is clear that most persons
and societies regard some as more important than others. This
practical decision about investment of feeling and energy reveals
their implicit theological judgment about which aspects of life are
most important to human fulfillment.

Historians and sociologists have observed that Americans tend
to believe that political groups and their symbolisms and values
are more important than other groups and their symbolisms.[12]
Americans tend to regard political loyalty as much more important
than other loyalties. This means that the activities of other groups
tend to be subordinated to the political sphere. Americans talk and
act as if the *ultimate* questions of human life were being decided in

the realm of the *polis*; and Americans also believe that political categories have a special appropriateness for symbolizing ultimate reality and man's fulfillment. Such a conviction is intrinsic, of course, to the emergence of political nationalism. And it is striking that this conviction unites America's seventeenth-century Puritans, her eighteenth-century deist revolutionaries, and her nineteenth-century nationalists. All these men believed in the primary importance of the political realm of life. The ultimate concern of all these men was cast in the imagery of the *civitas*.

For Puritans, as for American nationalists, the political-legal order provided the model of God. John Calvin, the inspiration behind Puritanism, recast the Christian religion into a book of "Institutes," that is, made it into a law code patterned after the "Institutes" of the Roman emperor Justinian. Calvin also proposed that the highest of human vocations is law—for the lawyer's work most resembles the essential divine activity: legislation. This Puritan tradition has continued in America as a movement primarily concerned with the reformation of the civil order: e.g. the Great Awakening, benevolence societies, the social gospel, abolition, and the civil rights movement.

What the Puritans believed was also believed by Enlightenment thinkers. Thomas Jefferson described his own vision of the greatest possible beatitude, or happiness, in political terms: as sitting in Congress with the most illustrious of his colleagues.[13] Hannah Arendt has further documented the extraordinary fact that in America a new notion of ultimate beatitude, or salvation, appears: the idea of "civil happiness," the happiness that comes only through being involved in politics.[14] So Calvin and Jefferson (and Nixon and McGovern) agree on one thing: that the *political order* is where the drama of human salvation is being worked out. In regard to this faith, the American right and the American left are in full communion with one another.

Precisely because Americans tend to accept the primacy of the civil model of God, they have also identified closely with the Old Testament. Historians have frequently observed the pervasive influence of the Old Testament on American life. America thinks of itself as a "new Zion," "a city set on a hill," "a chosen people," and "a promised land." Her mission is to be "a light to the

nations," "a holy people," and seekers after "the kingdom of
God." American towns have biblical names: Hebron, Salem,
Bethel, Nazareth, New Canaan. In that the Old Testament is so
vivid to many Americans, they acquiesce easily in the notion that
true religion must be civil religion—and American Christians tend
to have an Old Testament type of Christianity. They believe that
religion must have, first of all, *political relevance*. To suggest to
them that Christianity is radically opposed to civil religion is to be
met with incredulity. For example, consider this second argument
by Robert Bellah in behalf of his view:

> Whatever the case may be with Christianity, and it is a complicated
> one, it is clear that both Judaism and Islam over most of their
> history and in several forms have been civil religions. What
> Christians call the Old Testament is precisely the religious interpreta-
> tion of the history of Israel. Is it so clear that American analogizing
> from the Old (or New) Testament is necessarily religiously il-
> legitimate? Why should the history of a people living two or three
> thousand years ago be religiously meaningful, but the history of a
> people in the last two hundred years be religiously meaningless?
> Again it is a case of how it is done, not whether it is done.[15]

What is striking here is Bellah's characterization of and identification with Old Testament religion (and the complexities he
acknowledges in squaring his advocacy of civil religion with
Christianity). First, it is striking that Bellah gives centrality to
those aspects of the Old Testament that affirm civil religion, for
there are parts of the Old Testament that oppose it altogether.
Second, it is striking that Bellah seeks to justify America's attempt
to develop a civil religion by pointing out that Israel has done the
same thing. What Israel has done is accepted by Bellah as his
norm. If Israel has done this, why can't America? What is wrong
with trying to do what is done in the Old Testament? This is the
question that shall now be answered.

We can begin by recalling that the Old Testament was itself
at one time relatively "new." The Old Testament political model
of God as a king who creates by his command and governs
through his law replaced an older idea of God. That older idea
of God utilized biological categories rather than political ones. It
grew out of a nature religion, out of a preoccupation with fertility

and fecundity, the kind of concerns that would be foremost in the life of pastoral-nomadic peoples.[16] Throughout the Old Testament one sees nature religion as the background against which the new idea of God as lawgiver and king is being developed. There is, for example, constant conflict between the cult of Yahweh and fertility cults; there is the exaggerated patriarchalism that develops in opposition to the more equal balance between male and female that is associated with agricultural life.

The conflict between the biological and the political models of God was not (and is not) without practical implications for social life. When Israel chose to use the law rather than nature as the primary model of ultimate reality, she was just beginning a transition from pastoral-nomadic to urban-national life. She was shifting from an agricultural economy that was dependent on the cycle of natural fertility to an artifactual-trading economy that was primarily dependent on urban organization, law, and contracts.[17] When, therefore, Israel used civil institutions as the prime analogue of man's relation to God and as the best model of fulfilled human life, she facilitated her transition from pastoral-nomadic to urban-national life. To think of God as a "monarch" ruling by a "law" in a cosmic "kingdom" provided the ideological justification for this transition. It was a way of suggesting that urban-national life was "closer" to ultimate reality, more like the life of God himself. Moreover, by developing this political model of reality, Israel not only upgraded the importance of the civil order, she also downgraded the importance of pastoral-nomadic life and weakened its social power. She denied that its religion was true by opposing her new gods to its old ones. She limited its power by articulating an alternative theo-social symbolism.

To fail to see the ideological character of the civil model of God in the Old Testament is to fail to understand the practical social power of Israelite theology. Moreover, to fail to see that Old Testament theology functioned to facilitate the urbanization of Israel and the dissolution of her various pastoral-nomadic traditions into a centralized state and national ideology is to fail to see why the Old Testament has been so important for Americans. Americans are fascinated by the Old Testament precisely because its symbols are congruent with what has also been going on in

America. Once we see this ideological bias of the Old Testament model of God and see how Old Testament civil religion has also been implicated in the emergence of the American nation-state, then we can see why these things are so questionable, even dangerous, today. When America analogizes from the Old Testament —with its paradigm of the entire universe as an emerging *civitas* under the sovereignty of God—she "discovers" a divine ratification of her own aspiration to establish a holy nation-state: one people, one government, one faith, one God. Such analogizing from the Old Testament involves America in an ideology that gives a religious sanction to the most destructive aspects of modern nationalism.

The point can be further dramatized by recalling the crucial cultic importance of war in the creation of the city-nation—an importance no less today than in ancient times. Political power is usually centralized and increased in conjunction with war. A king establishes his power and increases his authority through war and its necessities. In fact, it has been concluded that war creates kingship; the institution of centralized personal sovereignty arises as a part of war itself. This is as true in modern America as it was in the ancient Near East. The American presidency has increased its power in conjunction with war and the needs of "national security." In modern states, as in ancient Israel, war is a civil ritual ("holy war").[18] Through war the state demonstrates its ultimacy by demanding that men sacrifice their lives for it. This explains why the basic cultic rite of civil religion is human sacrifice in warfare and why the major holidays of the state are remembrances of great battles and its valorous dead. It also explains why (since great kings must also be great warriors) the great American leaders have been generals and "war presidents." Today we no longer sacrifice our children to nature, but we feed them to the state.

It is urgent that America understand this ideological bias within her traditional identification with Israel's history and religion— and repudiate it. It is urgent, too, that America oppose to her civil religion an alternative faith. For this to take place, however, requires another model of reality and the replacement of the Old Testament with something new.

4

Just as the Old Testament displaced an earlier nature religion by substituting political categories for biological-natural ones, so the New Testament seeks to displace the political-legal model of ultimate reality by proposing an alternative picture of man's relation to God.[19] Whatever else this new model may be, the historical circumstances of its origin require that it present itself as an alternative to civil and political categories. Hence in the New Testament the "gospel" is that which liberates us from the "law," the virtue of "agape" is higher than "justice," and "the crucified Christ" is raised above all "principalities and powers." In these formulae we see the efforts of early Christianity to articulate a new model of ultimate reality.

The religion of Christianity seeks to be not merely an effective critic of civil religion, but also an alternative to it. But it can be this only by rejecting two claims: (1) the claim of every earthly Caesar and *civitas* to be ultimate and (2) the claim that *civil categories* are adequate for conceiving the relation of man to God. This is why Christianity rejects not merely the worship of an earthly king, but also the claim that God is *like a king*. Christianity affirms that what is higher than all earthly kings is not some heavenly king, but the suffering crucified Christ. In this affirmation we see that Christianity is opposing not only Rome's demand that a political ruler should be venerated, but also Israel's affirmation that God is like a political ruler. Because it refused to conceive God's relation to the world in terms of the civil-legal model, Christianity also rejected the idea that the highest value in life is justice or that man is saved by obedience to a law.

This does *not* mean that Christianity rejects justice as a value or denies the importance of political life. Quite the contrary. The history of Christian thought has repeatedly affirmed that justice is the most important value in the *purely historical, or natural, sphere*. It is, however, not the most important value of all. In the same way Christianity's rejection of the *civitas* as the most appropriate model of ultimate reality does not imply that Christianity rejects the importance of political life in *this* world and age. It simply means that Christianity knows that life already has a transhistorical and supernatural possibility that surpasses the very best that can take place in this world and age. Christianity does not repudiate the law as such, but the claim that the law any longer continues as the mediator of man's relation to God.

Christianity replaces the legal model of man's relation to God with the "evangelical" or "gospel" model. It replaces the idea that ultimate reality is like the *civitas* with the idea that ultimate reality is an *ecclesia*, or church. It affirms that God is known not in glory, but in suffering. This is the "New Testament," and we shall show how it differs from the "Old Testament" in three ways.

First, membership in the *civitas* presupposes functional and hierarchical difference of persons: ruler-ruled, just-unjust, young-old, managers-workers. Civil *justice* presupposes and orders this difference. It seeks to have each do that for which he is fitted or to render unto each according to his needs or deeds. Assuming that people are different and act differently, it tries to deal with these difference "fairly." In this way the justice of the *civitas* tends to reify these differences and identify persons with their civil roles. Membership in the *ecclesia*, on the other hand, presupposes the fundamental identification of persons: the ruler with the ruled, the guiltless with the guilty, the old with the young, the Greek with the Jew. The experience of identification is not merely an act of sympathetic imagination—that also exists in a good *civitas*. Rather, the identification of persons with one another within the *ecclesia* arises out of the shared experience of union with Christ. The union of each person with Christ is his bond of communion with others. To become one with Christ—through faith or sacramental union—is to become someone else: Christ and my brothers. Such an experience of communion is not produced by the melting down of differences, but by the act of spiritually indwelling one another. It is an experience of polyconsciousness, of being many persons, of being the *communio sanctorum*: the church. To become one with Christ is to become one with the church. Hence the Christian experiences not that he is a *part* of a plurality, but that this plurality is what he *is*.[20] In this way man exists in the church through identification, whereas he exists in the *civitas* through difference.

A second contrast between the New and the Old Testaments is

that the gospel brings the law under a higher principle of social order. How does this work? Christianity, beginning with the experience of the identity of persons in Christ, now brings the operations of justice under this higher norm. That is, Christianity points out—on the basis of its experience of man's unity in Christ —the *inequity* of all civil equity. Justice assumes the difference of persons and pays each according to his work. The gospel affirms their identity in Christ and proposes—as in the parable of the laborers in the vineyard—that all should be paid identically. Justice assumes the difference of persons and judges some men guilty. The gospel sees their identity in Christ and knows that the guilty are forgiven and the innocent have sinned. The Christian knows that the perfection of our union in Christ belongs to another age and is not yet; but he also knows that this identification of men with one another has already begun in this age and even now stands as the norm by which we must reform justice. The law we still have with us, but we must measure the law by love and by our union with Christ. When we do this, we see that we must introduce a general institutional bias in the law in favor of the oppressed and rejected. We do this as a way of beginning to affirm our unity with all men. To measure justice by the gospel means to reject even-handed equity and protest the injustice that justice always does to the poor and guilty. In this way the law of the state is subordinated to a higher ecclesial reality: the unity of all men in Christ.

A third difference between the *civitas* and the *ecclesia* is that whereas the former belongs to this world and age, the latter belongs to and already lives in a world and age to come. The *ecclesia*, through its communion with the risen Christ, experiences itself as already participating in an order that continues beyond death and the end of history. While already present in this temporal order, the *ecclesia* already lives eternally; while being in this natural realm, it is a supernatural reality.

It is not the idea of being in contact with an eternal, or transhistorical, order that is novel in Christianity. That idea is found in many religions. What is novel is the idea that the spiritual, or supernatural, realm of life has entered history and is already beginning to take on a concrete spatio-temporal form. It is the idea that what comes "after" all time and space has already come and started to exist "in" time and space. This is the meaning of the Christian claim that the Messiah who will come at the end of time *has already come*. History is not over yet, but the trans-historical is already in our midst. The concrete form of its presence and the way we have communion with Christ is the church. In Christianity, therefore, the *ecclesia* replaces the *civitas* as the prime model of ultimate reality; and communion with Christ now displaces "civil happiness" as the highest end of human life.

In all these ways, the civil order is brought under a higher norm. This relativization of the civil order constitutes a special difficulty for the state: it calls into question the theoretical justi-fication of its sovereignty. Let us turn to a fuller discussion of this problem.

According to Aristotle the state differs from other institutions in that its task is to establish a general order with respect to the whole of society.[21] The state is to be the context within which all other special institutions are to be ordered. In modern theories of government the state (now representing the "general will" or the "people") is further claimed to be the source of sovereignty—the sovereignty of other institutions being derived from or subordinate to it. The reason for this argument is that modern theories derive authority from "the people" and it is the state that is assumed to be their representative.

Since modern democratic theories of sovereignty can imagine no alternative institution possessing sufficient universality to claim a general authority to order the whole of society, the state estab-lishes its sovereignty over space, time, property, and persons—increasingly making other institutions appendages to the civil order. Effective limitation of the state's tendency to absolutism must in-volve not merely the affirmation of inviolable human rights and the countersovereignty of *special* groups (such as the nation, uni-versity, family, business, and professions), but also an institutional competitor to the state's claims to have a general oversight over the whole of life and the right to determine the things relating to human fulfillment. This institutional competitor is the church.

Over against the claims of the modern nation-state, the church affirms (1) that there exists a higher dimension of life that ab-solutely exceeds the state's capacity to order and (2) that the church has been established directly by God for the sake of bearing witness to, and establishing an order in the world with respect to this higher end. The first claim calls into question the assumption that the civil order and its institutions (e.g., justice) possess the highest degree of universality or value, and hence opposes the state's claim that it is an autonomous authority, possessing a general authority over the whole of human life. The second claim calls into question the tendency of the state to reduce all other institutions to appendages of the civil order and to treat them as if their activities were, in the last analysis, subordinate to the *civitas*. The church knows that it does not exist as an appendage of the *civitas* and knows that its sovereignty is not derived from it. The church has and exercises its authority by direct "divine institution." This phrase must be understood symbolically, of course, and with close attention to its functional meaning, that is, its meaning in relation to the state.

In America it is frequently suggested that the church is a "congregation" or a "voluntary association," i.e., a group established through the activity of its own members. From this point of view, the church is like a tennis club or a political party. Its authority is not greater than the weight of its members who (in a day of "national churches") are always but a fraction of the total citizenry, the "people." Therefore, they cannot claim to speak with a voice equal in authority to the state's, since the state claims to speak for *all* the people and to act with *their* sovereignty. In this situation, then, no group is able to oppose the claim of the state to an authority over the whole order of society; the best that it can do is to argue that the state is acting wrongly (which still implies, of course, that the *state* should act).

If Christian groups are only voluntary associations within a state, then they leave unchallenged the pretense of the state to possess the authority to order all society. If Christian groups are only voluntary associations, then the state can argue that they speak with the authority of a fraction of the people while it acts in the name of them "all." For this reason, the church cannot acquiesce in the notion that it is a mere congregation or voluntary association established by the authority of its members. The church affirms, rather, that it has been established by God and invested with a general competence with respect to the highest ends of all life. For this reason it rejects the notion that the state possesses a general authority, and questions not merely the decrees of the state, but its *right* to decree. This is how the existence of the church limits the state's claims for itself.

When we think of recent German history, we see the relevance of the church's effort to establish its own realm of authority outside the state's sovereignty. In Nazi Germany the state sought to reduce the church to an appendage of its political program, to make the church an instrument of its own civil religion. When it could not fully accomplish this, the state then demanded that the church be a "pure spiritual reality," that is, that the church not seek to give its teaching regarding the unity of all men in Christ any historical and institutional embodiment. Several aspects of the Nazi state's attack on the church are revealing in this respect.[22]

1. It sought to "unify" the church by establishing an isomorphism between ecclesiastical and political units, so that ecclesiastical membership and political citizenship would always be correlated. It sought to create a "German Christianity." To accomplish this would have destroyed interest groups that overlapped political boundaries and were not susceptible to state control. (It should be noted that the creation of a congruence between political and ecclesiastical boundaries occurred in American Protestantism during the nineteenth century as part of the "nationalizing" of religion. Moreover, it is still fashionable for many Americans to criticize Roman Catholics for their loyalty to a "foreign" group that is not isomorphic with, or wholly contained within, the American nation-state.)

2. In Nazi Germany the state sought to control the church by claiming the right to determine the qualifications of clergy and by appointing Nazi sympathizers to theological professorships, a relatively easy enterprise in state-supported universities. It was the attempt of Nazis to eliminate clergy of Jewish origin from the evangelical church that led to the synod of Barmen—the beginning of ecclesiastical resistance. This was a replay of the eleventh century investiture controversy.

3. The state sought to undermine religious assemblies by a *de facto* abolition of the Sabbath, that is, by scheduling alternative activities so that they would conflict with the time of religious meetings.

4. The state confiscated, or demanded control over, the use of church property—for without property no institution can exist or carry out its functions. For this reason, in part, the church claims for itself and others the right to possess some property absolutely and tax free.

5. The state declared that certain ecclesiastical activities were criminal and arrested church leaders for carrying out ecclesiastical assignments. Reflecting on this power of the state to interfere with human life merely by its power of legal harassment should give us a better understanding of the reason why the church has in the past claimed the right to "try" its own clergy in its own "courts."

In these and other concrete cases, we see exactly how a totalistic state experiences the church as representing a threat to its political aspirations; and we see the methods it uses to limit the church's activities. What a totalistic state opposes is not the church's doctrine. It opposes the church's efforts to establish its autonomous existence outside the state's jurisdiction. This calls into question the state's theory of its own competence and authority, and this is what no state can risk without also risking a general loss of sovereignty. (Perhaps these considerations explain the disproportionate fury of the state in the face of the refusal of a few Amish to send their children to school or the refusal of a few religious pacifists to register for the draft. Such acts in themselves do not interfere with the *operations* of the state. Rather, they challenge its general *right* to legislate compulsory education or military service.)

It is *institutionalized ecclesiastical religion* that is the real limitation on the state's claim to a general sovereignty over society, not mere individual beliefs. The Nazi state tolerated, even encouraged, "freedom of religion." It allowed every individual to believe what he wished as long as that belief did not seek an institutional expression that might interfere with the state's ordering of time and space. In fact, in modern states it is frequently suggested that such individualistic religious beliefs are superior to institutional religion, that somehow it is only the unperceptive who express their beliefs through loyalty to a church.

The sociological considerations with which we began this essay should here be recalled. Just as we saw that every group generates its own religious symbols and rituals, so we should also see that no religious symbols can have any social meaning or power unless they are embodied in a concrete group. The church is the social embodiment of the Christian faith, and it is the alternative to civil religion. The alternative to civil religion is not mere Christian belief or faith in transcendence, but *ecclesiastical Christianity*. This is because mere beliefs and faith in transcendence can be absorbed into a civil cult. There is nothing the church (or any one else) believes that cannot be woven into the state's mythology.

What constitutes the real limitation on civil religion and the tendencies of the state to absolutize itself is not mere doctrine or sheer belief. The real limitation on the power of the state is its citizens' loyalty to and participation in groups whose membership, goals, and procedures are not isomorphic or consistent with the membership, goals, and procedures of the state. We, as citizens, affirm that civil religion is idolatry and limit the power of the state only when we affirm and act on the basis of alternative allegiances that restrict our participation in its cult and values.

I pledge allegiance	*I believe*
to the flag	*in God*
of the United States	*the Father almighty*
of America	*Creator of heaven and earth*
and to the Republic	*and in Jesus Christ, his only son, our lord*
for which it stands:	*who was conceived by the Holy Spirit*
	born of the virgin Mary
One Nation	*suffered under Pontius Pilate*
under God	*was crucified, dead, and buried*
Indivisible	*the third day he rose again from the dead*
with Liberty	*he ascended into heaven*
and Justice	*and sits at the right hand of the Father*
for all.	*from whence he shall come to judge*
	the living and the dead
	and I believe in the Holy Spirit
	the Holy Catholic Church
	the Communion of Saints
	the Forgiveness of Sins
	the Resurrection of the Body
	and the Life Everlasting.

NOTES

1. Robert Bellah, *Beyond Belief* (New York, 1970), p. 172.
2. For example, Herman Hesse's *The Glass Bead Game.*
3. See especially "American Civil Religion in the 1970s," Bellah's second essay in this volume.
4. Bellah, *Beyond Belief,* p. 172.
5. Bellah, "American Civil Religion in the 1970s."
6. Following St. Augustine's analysis in the *Confessions,* Book VII, 9-21.
7. Bellah, *Beyond Belief,* especially pp. 183-186.
8. *Ibid.,* p. 187.
9. *Ibid.,* p. 168.
10. See Leo Marx's essay in this volume for the way in which a dominant culture tries to impose its language-style on minority cultures.
11. See Charles Long's essay in this volume.
12. For example, Alexis de Tocqueville, *Democracy in America,* Part One, XII.
13. Cited by Hannah Arendt, *On Revolution* (New York, 1963), p. 128.
14. *Ibid.,* pp. 115-128.
15. Robert Bellah, "Response," *The Religious Situation 1968* (Boston, 1968), p. 391.
16. Walter Harrelson, *From Fertility Cult to Worship* (New York, 1969).
17. For an analysis of the relation, between religious and social factors in ancient Israel, see my *Nun, Witch, Playmate* (New York, 1971), pp. 4-14.
18. Lewis Mumford, *The City in History* (New York, 1961), pp. 44-46.
19. The Old Testament is not simply the story of monarchy, but the story of the *evolution* of monarchy. The New Testament is not an antithesis to the Old, but the stage where something fully beyond monarchy has appeared. George Riggan in his *Messianic Theology and Christian Faith* (Philadelphia, 1967) distinguishes the following evolutionary stages: Messianic Kingship in ancient Israel, Prophetic critiques of Messianic Kingship, Ecclesiastic Messianism (Zadokite and Maccabean priesthoods), Apocalyptic Messianism, and New

Testament Messianism. Riggan rightly sees that Israelite prophecy is not antimonarchic in principle, which partly explains "the fact that prophecy in its classical form did not long survive the loss of Hebrew political independence" (p. 47).

20. John Meagher, *The Gathering of the Ungifted* (New York, 1972), pp. 141-146.

21. "But, if all communities aim at some good, the state or political community, which is the highest of all, and which embraces the best, aims at a good in a greater degree than any other, and at *the highest good*" (Aristotle, *Politics,* I, 1; Jowett translation, italics added).

22. The best study is J. Conway, *The Nazi Persecution of the Churches, 1933-1945* (New York, 1968). Also Arthur Cochrane, *The Church's Confession under Hitler* (Philadelphia, 1962).

DAVID LITTLE

9 The Origins of Perplexity: Civil Religion and Moral Belief in the Thought of Thomas Jefferson

ROBERT BELLAH and Sidney Mead have argued that the religious, moral, and political beliefs of the founding fathers were formative as well as normative in the development of American civil religion.[1] Whether the civil religious tradition is quite so consistent and uniform as Bellah and Mead suggest, the founding fathers did share beliefs which undoubtedly "shaped the form and tone" (in Bellah's words) of at least one version of the civil or political role of religion in America. Whether that version ought now to be regarded as in any way normative by contemporary Americans, as both Bellah and Mead urge,[2] depends first of all on a careful examination and evaluation of precisely what the founding fathers held to be the proper understanding of the relation of religion and morality to politics.

To carry out such an examination is to make some unsettling discoveries. The founding fathers held a view of the role of religion and morality in politics that, with all its power, served to obscure certain perplexities and difficulties, and to discourage developing the ability to confront and cope with them. Our main task, therefore, is to characterize these perplexities and to show how they

---

I should like to express my gratitude to my colleague, Baird Tipson, for many helpful reactions and suggestions.

were produced, as well as obscured, by a set of convictions close to the hearts of the founding fathers, particularly of Thomas Jefferson.[3]

The perplexities to which I allude can all be traced to a cluster of three basic disparities that inhere in the notion of "civil religion," as Rousseau first employed it, and as it applies to the thought of Jefferson.[4] A crucial passage in Rousseau's discussion of civil religion enables us to identify and sort out the three disparities:

> It is of considerable concern to the State whether a citizen profess a religion which leads him to love his duties. But the dogmas of that religion are of no interest to the State or to its members except as they have a bearing on the morals and duties which the citizen professing it should hold and perform in dealing with others. That consideration apart, it is open to each to entertain what opinions he pleases, and it is no part of the business of the State to have cognizance of them, since, not being competent in the affairs of the other world, . . . it has no sort of concern with such matters, provided the citizen fulfils his duties in this one.[5]

The First Disparity: Tension between Religious Beliefs and Civic Responsibility

Rousseau perceived a deep strain between religious convictions, such as those of Christianity, and the demands of civic life. "So far from attaching the hearts of the citizens to the State, [true Christianity] weans them from it. . . ."[6] Rousseau may not have been sensitive to the variations in viewpoint within the tradition regarding a Christian's relation to the state, but he correctly comprehended both that religious beliefs do under some conditions guide actions, and that religiously guided actions do not necessarily conform to the requirements of civic responsibility.

Rousseau recognized that, because of this potential conflict, *hard choices would have to be made.* He leaves no doubt as to his final standard of judgment for deciding between competing religious and civic claims: "Everything that disrupts the social bond of unity is valueless. All institutions which set man in contradiction to himself are of no worth."[7] Where religious beliefs inspire actions in any way contradictory to civic responsibility, the religious beliefs *ought* to give way and fall into line with the claims of civic unity.

But more than that, it is not enough that religious convictions be politically innocuous; they must to some degree positively quicken the civic devotion of the citizen; they must lead him "to love his [civic] duties." So long as a set of beliefs does not undermine religion's affirmatively instrumental role in relation to the state, then to that extent the rule of tolerance among all religious beliefs should prevail.

The Second Disparity: The Tension between Moral Beliefs and Civil Responsibility

Rousseau's entire discussion in *The Social Contract*, which terminates in his remarks on civil religion, may be taken as the exposition and defense of a *moral* position. The nub of his position is that "the social order is a sacred right which serves as the foundation for all other rights."[8] In other words, so far as those actions go which a person "should hold and perform in dealing with others" in this world, the absolutely overriding determinant is "public utility," or civil unity.[9]

While Rousseau himself comes to a conclusion which effectively equates moral beliefs and civic responsibility, he realizes that that is not the only conceivable position to take, and that reasons have to be supplied in support of it. Rousseau acknowledges other possible moral positions, such as the liberal or individualistic versions of the natural rights tradition. But he believes that these views invariably run up against an irresolvable and therefore intolerable conflict between the claims of civic unity and those of personal moral conscience. He therefore sets out to demonstrate the superiority of his moral position against his liberal competitors, and to proclaim with ruthless consistency the "complete power" of the body politic over its members and their individual rights.[10]

Once again, then, Rousseau gives evidence that he is aware that hard choices must be made among a variety of possible views, and he endeavors in his various treatises to justify his proposal for solving the potential disparity between moral beliefs and civic responsibility.

The Third Disparity: The Tension between Religious and Moral Beliefs

On the basis of the foregoing, Rousseau can be said to take for granted that moral and religious claims vary independently of each other, and, therefore, that the problem of which one takes priority over the other must be specifically worked out as a part of having a system of practical beliefs. As we have seen, Rousseau clearly advocates his own solution to the potential tension between religious and moral beliefs by arguing the superiority of his "morality of civic unity" over any competing religious claims. Again, Rousseau leaves room for the practice of religious duties, but only insofar as they are subordinate to, and do not interfere with, his moral position. The danger of Christianity is that it aspires to total jurisdiction over a believer's life and thus threatens the supremacy of Rousseau's basic moral prescription: Do nothing that is "at variance with the duties of the citizen."

The point of identifying and elaborating briefly these three disparities that inhere in Rousseau's use of the concept of civil religion is to suggest three "stress points" that will need to be attended to by anyone who advocates one or another version of a civil religion.

I have implied that one virtue of Rousseau's position is that he is more or less aware of these stress points and addresses them head-on in his writings. He gives explicit reasons why one should resolve the various potential tensions among religion, morality, and civic responsibility in one way rather than another. It is not necessary to agree with Rousseau's particular position, or with his reasons for adopting that position (as I do not), to admire his ability to see the issues, and to argue a presentable case in response to them.

In fact, one's admiration increases when Rousseau's approach is contrasted with that of Jefferson. The basic difficulty with his approach and, as we shall show, the origin of much of the perplexity that surrounds it, is that, rather than first identifying the stress points, then making the necessary hard choices, and, finally, defending those choices, he attempts to wish away the tensions by means of what I shall call, with restraint, hasty reasoning.

Daniel Boorstin strikes at the heart of the matter: underlying the mood of thinking characteristic of the founding fathers, he says, "was a belief that the reasons men give for their actions are much less important than the actions themselves. . . ."[11] In his later writings, Boorstin makes a virtue of this antitheoretical bias,[12] but his earlier criticisms, in a book he aptly calls *The Lost World of Thomas Jefferson,*[13] are more to the point.[14] The antitheoretical or "pragmatic frame of mind," he comments, "may save us some of the unhappiness and doubt which come from seeing the inadequacies of our own thought; it cannot free us from the necessity of being thinkers."[15]

It is clear that human beings do not turn to reflection, to deliberation, to thinking about the reasons they act as they do, so long as they are self-confident in what they are doing, convinced that "everything is working out for the best." On the other hand, to perceive conflicts among duties, tensions among responsibilities, is to be thrown back on the deliberative process; it is to become sensitive to justifications for and against taking one course rather than another, and it is to gain a new attentiveness, a new respect for the reasons others provide in support of making one or another decision.

My contention is that Jefferson, as a founding father representative of the pragmatic frame of mind, manifested a spirit of supreme self-confidence, particularly in practical matters, that was quite misplaced. He was living at a time when he should have had an eye for crucial disparities and tensions, for what we called the stress points, among the claims of religious, moral, and political action, and he should have led the way in enabling people to face up to the stress points, and to deal with them. His efforts to avoid doing that make up most of our remaining story.

With respect to the first disparity—the tension between religious beliefs and civic responsibility—one reads far and wide in the writings of Jefferson without encountering any evidence that he perceived the slightest strain, within the Christian tradition, for example, between serving God and serving the state. So far as I can determine, there is no attention given to the historic tensions among Christians over the question of pacifism. Does the duty of the citizen to take up arms in defense of the state conflict with the Christian's duty to love his enemy and to turn the other cheek? Many Christians have thought so, and most Christians have had, at least, to face up to this question, and to try to resolve it one way or another. We noted that Rousseau, in his own way, grasped the problem, and explicitly proposed a solution in favor of the duty of the citizen.

But Jefferson has an ingenious way of avoiding the issue, and all similar issues that have exercised Christians over the centuries. By a flick of the pen, he depreciates the significance of religious belief as a determinant of any kind of action, including civic action. With customary finality, Jefferson asserts: "[O]ur civil rights have no dependence on our religious opinions, more than [on] our opinions in physics or geometry."[16]

Statements like this one have become so much a part of our accepted wisdom that we are able, only with the greatest effort, to grasp what Jefferson had in mind in uttering it.[17] When Jefferson states that civil rights have "no dependence" on religious opinions, he means to say that religious beliefs and opinions belong to a residual category that bears very little significance for what really guides and propels human action. In other words, he is providing us—more by assertion than by argument—with a theory of human motivation. Because he holds the theory he does, he sees no issue at all between religious beliefs and civic action.

What is this theory of human motivation? It begins by assuming a frame of reference Jefferson unrigorously but persistently calls "materialistic."[18] Responding to John Adams, he writes:

> I was obliged to recur ultimately to my habitual anodyne, "I feel therefore I exist." I feel bodies which are not myself: there are other existences then. I call them *matter*. I feel them changing place. This gives me *motion*. . . . On the basis of sensation, of matter and motion, we may erect the fabric of all the certainties we can have or need. I can conceive *thought* to be an action of a particular organization of matter, formed for that purpose by its Creator. . . . Rejecting all organs of information, therefore, but my senses, I rid myself of the pyrrhonisms with which an indulgence in speculations hyperphysical and antiphysical, so uselessly occupy and disquiet the mind.[19]

It follows for Jefferson that the "facts" of motion and matter, which underlie all reality, explain the direction of human action, as they explain all other occurrences. Moreover, men properly perceive these facts about the sources of motivation by means of their senses, or their "common sense," as Jefferson calls it in company with the English and Scottish Common-Sense philosophers of the eighteenth century.[20]

Accordingly, things like thoughts, beliefs, opinions, and theories are, for Jefferson, very much "after the fact" of what can be known self-evidently through the senses. That means two things: first, ideas or beliefs do not motivate and direct human action as the Idealists erroneously aver, but rather, the laws of motion and matter account for the course of human action; second, it is not primarily the mind, not the reason, that grasps what actually motivates men, but the senses. "When once we quit the basis of sensation, all is in the wind,"[21] writes Jefferson, and he is saying something important with respect to his theory of motivation: when we depart from what the senses tell us about human action, then all else is beside the point.

Next, what the senses do tell us about the direction of human action is that "man was created for social intercourse,"[22] or "sociability," and that he is motivated by the laws of motion and matter to achieve the "peace and good order" of proper social harmony.[23] Furthermore, the senses apparently indicate that "the rightful purposes of civil government," as well as the point of all civic responsibilities, is to promote and protect proper sociability or civic harmony. Thus the government rightly interferes only to the extent necessary to prevent "overt acts against peace and good order."

However, since, by hypothesis, things like thoughts, beliefs and opinions, including religious thoughts, beliefs and opinions, play almost no role in motivating and directing actions, civil rights *for that reason* "have no dependence on . . . religious opinions." "The legitimate powers of government," writes Jefferson, "extend to such acts only as are injurious to others. But it does me no injury for my neighbor to say there are twenty gods, or no God. It neither picks my pocket nor breaks my leg."[24] What is more, should a religious sect arise that attempted to subvert public order, then, Jefferson assures us, "good sense has fair play, . . . and laughs it out of doors, without suffering the State to be troubled with it."[25]

There is no tension between religious belief and civic responsibility because, in reality, religious beliefs, like all thoughts, are not very significant when it comes to inspiring and directing action. They are basically irrelevant to human affairs, and therefore need not be taken seriously by the government, let alone supported by it.

Contrary to the conventional impression, the original spirit of the American doctrine of the separation of church and state was heavily informed by this condescending attitude toward religious belief, rather than by an attitude of deep respect for the importance and centrality of religious convictions, or by a concern for the agony of those involved in resolving dilemmas caused by conflicts between religious faith and civic responsibility. To the founding fathers, such dilemmas are illusory. They do not exist at all for those in their right senses.

This condescending attitude is well illustrated in the way Jefferson and others regarded the general practice of argumentation, including, of course, religious disputation and discussion.

> [I]n stating prudential rules for our government in society, I must not omit the important one of never entering into dispute or argument with another. I never saw an instance of one of two disputants convincing the other by argument. . . . When I hear another express an opinion which is not mine, I say to myself, he has a right to his opinion, as I to mine; why should I question it? His error does me no injury, and shall I become a Don Quixote, to bring all men by force of argument to one opinion? If a fact be misstated, it is probable he is gratified by a belief of it, and I have no right to deprive him of the gratification?[26]

In this context Jefferson refers to Benjamin Franklin, who put the same point more sharply: "Disputes," he said, "are apt to sour one's temper, and disturb one's quiet. . . ." It is better, Franklin counseled, to settle differences by resorting to the scientific procedures of experiment and observation, rather than by theoretical dispute, for "the Multitude are more effectually set right by Experience, than kept from going wrong by Reasoning with them."[27]

The basic point Jefferson and Franklin are making is that

theoretical arguments, whether in physics, medicine, or religion, are futile distractions. The truth about man and his environment is obtained by experience, by sense perception, by appeals to what the founding fathers loved to call "self-evidence." Differences of opinion and belief there are, but since opinion and belief have no real significance for directing action, conflicts in thought need in no way produce conflicts in action. The road to the natural, self-evident state of sociability is clear and common enough to all in their right senses, so as to remain unaffected by extraneous theoretical arguments.

"Differences of opinion," Jefferson remarked, are "like differences of face . . . , and should be viewed accordingly."[28] In fact, like physical differences, varieties in belief are the result of the same laws of motion and matter that underlie everything that happens. Therefore, the differences that exist serve not to undermine human sociability, but if properly understood, to enrich and ornament it by a pleasing diversity. "Why should we be dissocialized by mere differences of opinion in politics, in religion, in philosophy, or anything else? [Another's] opinions are as honestly formed as my own. Our different views of the same subject are the result of a difference in our organization and experience."[29] That is to say, divergent views are, like other physical variations among men, inconsequential with respect to the central pragmatic purposes of human life.

On occasion Jefferson does appear to take sides in idle theoretical controversies among various political and religious beliefs, as though settling these disputes made some difference in the way people acted. But Jefferson is not an ordinary disputant. He is not interested in reasoning and in exchanging arguments, as though that exercise meant something in itself. Rather, he believed himself capable of resolving disputes, to the extent that was necessary, simply by referring to their ready standard of common sense and scientific observation.

For example, Jefferson decided between the positions of Tory and Whig not—heaven forbid!—by examining and assessing their reasons and arguments, but by making scientific observations, "on the basis of sensation," about the personal and physical characteristics of the two types of people involved: "The sickly, weakly, timid man, fears the people, and is a Tory by nature. The healthy strong and bold, cherishes them, and is formed a Whig by nature."[30] Enabled by their sure standard to perceive the truth with such clarity and simplicity, what need was there to assess reasons and to take arguments seriously?

Similarly, Jefferson applied his standard to religious matters, and, not surprisingly, came once again to conclusions of great simplicity and clarity. He was certain that all conventional theological disputes, particularly those making appeals to revelation, were nothing but the "charlatanry of the mind."[31] "On the contrary," he wrote,

> I hold, (without appeal to revelation) that when we take a view of the universe, in its parts, general or particular, *it is impossible for the human mind not to perceive and feel a conviction* of design, consummate skill, and indefinite power in every atom of its composition. . . . We see, too, evident proofs of the necessity of a superintending power, to maintain the universe in its course and order.[32]

Because Jefferson's version of natural religion was authenticated by sense perception or feeling, he was excused, he believed, from providing any supporting arguments, and he would, presumably, remain impervious to any counterarguments, had he known of them, such as those advanced some years earlier by Immanuel Kant. Kant's attack on natural religion was, after all, but an example of one of those idle, theoretical exercises that, if allowed to get out of hand, distract us from the sure, simple guide of common sense.

There is no doubt that Jefferson took his own Unitarian position as normative, and, therefore, as superior to all competitors. He fully expected, he said, "that the present generation will see Unitarianism become the general religion of the United States."[33] He expected this inevitable upsurge of right religion because, as Americans became liberated from the foolish distractions of theological controversy and, accordingly, more eligible for guidance by sense perceptions, competing religious views would wither away.

Finally, the religion of Jefferson should properly be called a "civil religion." The reason is obvious: the same common sense which directs the civil order to regulate life in keeping with man's natural and self-evident inclination to sociability and civic unity also provides warrant for affirming nature's God as the promoter and protector of civil "peace and good order." Man's drive for civic order and his perception of God naturally come to the same thing. For this reason, there can be no real tension within the civil religion of Jefferson and Madison between religious belief and civic responsibility. Properly understood, they are all of a piece.

Incidentally, Bellah's claim that the founding fathers, in general, never saw their religion as a substitute for Christianity, and always allowed for a "clear division of function between civil religion and Christianity,"[34] is overstated and somewhat misleading. As we have seen, Jefferson did favor tolerating religious views other than his own, but only because he believed these views were quite irrelevant to the conduct of political affairs, and they would eventually wither away, anyway. But more important, he certainly regarded his religion as the obvious (and inevitable) substitute for all traditional versions of Christianity and, by implication, for all other religions.[35]

We turn, next, to the second disparity: the tension between moral beliefs and civic responsibility. As we noted, Rousseau perceived, first, the possibility of conflict between the dictates of conscience, or moral beliefs, and civic responsibility; second, he undertook to provide extended arguments in favor of overcoming the conflict by adopting his standard of civic unity as the overriding moral standard. Whether his position was adequate or not, he comprehended the issue.

Jefferson did not comprehend the issue, nor did he comprehend a number of related problems in the field of morality. As in the matter of religion and political order, there is the same sublime self-confidence that, in the light of common sense, many traditional intellectual complexities and difficulties would be dispelled, and shown up to be the result of thinking too much.

In 1787 Jefferson outlined a course of study to his young friend Peter Carr. When he came to the section on "Moral Philosophy," he gave the following advice:

> I think it lost time to attend lectures on this branch. He who made us would have been a pitiful bungler, if he had made the rules of

our moral conduct a matter of [theory].[36]. . . Man was destined for society. His morality, therefore, was to be formed to his object. He was endowed with a sense of right and wrong merely relative to this. This sense is as much a part of his nature, as the sense of hearing, seeing, feeling; it is the true foundation of morality. . . . The moral sense is as much a part of man as his leg or arm. . . . This sense is submitted, indeed, in some degree, to the guidance of reason; *but it is a small stock indeed which is required for this. . . .*[37]

And Jefferson returns to this theme again and again throughout his life:

Morals were too essential to the happiness of man, to be risked on the uncertain combinations of the head. She laid their foundation, therefore, in sentiment, not in [theory].[38]

Or, again, Jefferson appeals to "the care of the Creator in making the moral principle so much a part of our constitution that no errors of reasoning or of speculation might lead us astray from its observation in practice."[39]

For Jefferson, the moral imperatives, which are dictated so clearly by sentiment, conform completely with the proper purposes of government. There is no better example than Jefferson's famous words in the Declaration of Independence:

We hold these truths to be self-evident: that all men are created equal; that they are endowed by their Creator with inherent and unalienable rights; that among these are life, liberty, and the pursuit of happiness; that *to secure these rights, governments are instituted among men,* deriving their just powers from the consent of the governed. . . .[40]

In Jefferson's world, the end of morality and the end of government is the selfsame happiness of man, and happiness is understood very much, as we would expect, in "materialistic" terms—that is, in terms of "good health" and "material prosperity."[41] One's "own greatest happiness," wrote Jefferson, "is always the result of a good conscience, good health, occupation, and freedom in all just pursuits."[42]

While under ideal circumstances men might be left completely free to pursue their happiness in keeping with the directives of the moral sense, it is often the case in the real world that there exists "a want or imperfection of the moral sense in some men, like the want or imperfection of the senses of sight and hearing in others. . . ."[43] The remedying of such imperfections is the role of the government (along with education). "The rewards and penalties established by the laws" are therapeutic measures designed to restrain arbitrary, egocentric actions on the part of those who are deficient in "social dispositions."

Jefferson has implicit faith in the clarity and reliability of the moral sense of each individual, once its full powers are restored by government (among others), to direct men consistently and harmoniously to everyone's "greatest happiness." Consequently, he shows no concern, from the point of view of either the individual or government, for the problem of possible conflicts or tensions among different views of happiness, nor among different readings of the moral sense. He does allude to these problems in passing, but his comments only highlight his incapacity to see the issues.

In a letter to Thomas Law in 1814, Jefferson refers to the argument of some that the existence of a common moral sense is in doubt because "we find, in fact, that the same actions are deemed virtuous in one country and vicious in another."[44] However, the problem for Jefferson is really not serious;

> The answer is, that nature has constituted *utility* to man, *the standard and test of virtue.* Men living in different countries, under different circumstances, different habits and regimens, *may have different utilities; the same act, therefore, may be useful, and consequently virtuous* in one country which is injurious and vicious in another differently circumstanced. *I sincerely, then, believe with you in the general existence of a moral instinct.* I think it the brightest gem with which the human character is studded, and the want of it as more degrading than the most hideous of the bodily deformities[45]

This passage is entirely baffling. It appears to mean that "the general existence of a moral instinct" amounts to nothing more than the proposition that virtue is everywhere defined with reference to some prevailing view of happiness, so that conflicting views of happiness allow for conflicting moral imperatives. But if that is what the statement means, then we must wonder what has become of the clear, harmonizing directives of a common moral sense! After all, the point of morality, or so Jefferson has told us up to now, is to produce sociability, and it is hard to see how sociability can be the result of conflicting moral imperatives.[46]

Perhaps he would emphasize that he is referring to conflicting ideas of utility as among different countries, so that, on his view, sociability is limited to life within individual societies—with each society, such as the United States, having its own regnant idea of happiness. But that maneuver won't work, for at least two reasons. First, Jefferson more than once speaks of the existence of *universal* human rights, and of the "moral law" of nations,[47] that are based upon the self-evident perceptions of common sense. These universal moral restrictions do not permit of the radical moral variations that Jefferson makes room for in the above passage.

Second, what is it logically that would prevent individuals and groups *within* a country from drawing the conclusion, from Jefferson's assertion above, that conflicting views of utility may provide moral authority for conflicting courses of action? Such a conclusion must follow if we take seriously Jefferson's claim that "nature has constituted utility to man the standard and test of virtue," so long as the parties involved are convinced they are "differently circumstanced." But what then becomes of the natural drift toward sociability and harmony within the civil order?

Of course, the questions we are raising with respect to Jefferson's views help to focus some of the central disparities or tensions often perceived between the demands of moral conscience and the demands of civic responsibility. In the first place, a debate continues to rage in our society between those who defend the overriding duty of every nation (and presumably all citizens within each nation) to pursue "national interest," or "national utility," as Jefferson might call it, as over against those who would impose international moral restrictions on the pursuit of national self-interest.

This debate over the question of whether or not civic duties take precedence over moral duties in international affairs goes back at least to the argument between Hamilton and Jefferson himself regarding the obligation or lack thereof of the United States to support France under a 1778 treaty of alliance. Jefferson advocated the strength of "moral obligation" in this case against

Hamilton's emphasis on the "essential interests" of the United States as being determinative. But the difficulty is that Jefferson's defense of international morality does not square with his assertion about utility as the standard and test of virtue. That he experienced no intellectual curiosity in face of this discrepancy is probably best explained by his impatience with, and indifference to, the processes of ratiocination, particularly in moral matters. Indeed, Jefferson says as much: ". . . so invariably do the laws of nature create our duties and interests, that when they seem to be at variance, we ought to suspect some fallacy in our reasonings."[48]

In the second place, the tension between moral duties and civic responsibility is often specified precisely at the point of conflict between the inclination of individuals and groups to pursue what they conceive to be their happiness, on the one side, and, on the other, their responsibility to the society at large to restrain themselves, and therefore compromise part of their happiness, in the interests of civic unity. Just where the balance should be struck between the pursuit of happiness by individuals or by specialized groups within a society and the requirements of the "common good" continues to be a burning problem. How Jefferson's vague and contradictory comments about the foundations of morality are likely to help is not clear.

We turn, at last, to the third disparity, or the tension between religious and moral beliefs. There is no question that Jefferson drew a distinction between religion and morality. If we were to take the love of God as the ground of moral action, he asks, "whence arises the morality of the Atheist?"[49] However, as we would expect, though there is a clear difference between religious and moral convictions, there is no disparity or tension possible between them. That is true for two reasons: first, because of Jefferson's predictable view that matters of theory and doctrine, such as religious beliefs, are basically irrelevant to action; second, the "heart" of all religion is equivalent to the clear dictates of the common moral sense.

In other words, religion in Jefferson's mind is subdivided into two categories: one category consists of "those moral precepts" "in which all religions agree"—namely, in their moral prohibitions against murder, stealing, plundering, or bearing false witness;

the other category consists of religion as dogma "in which all religions differ." Jefferson explicitly emphasizes that "we should not intermeddle" the two categories, for religious dogmas are, in his words, "*totally unconnected with morality.*"[50]

As in everything else, the sure standard of the moral sense is the only norm for evaluating what is useful and what is beside the point in all religious traditions. By that standard, naturally, the only aspect of religion worth salvaging is the common moral core. The leftover dogmas and superstitions may safely be humored by an enlightened society until they blow away in the wind, with the rest of the theories.

Jefferson never tires of applying his sure standard to religious people and traditions. For example, the Jews can be quickly evaluated: "[The Jews'] system was deism; that is, the belief in only one God. But their ideas of him were degrading and injurious."[51] By contrast, Christianity fares better, but only because it provides us with "a system of morals," which, if filled out, would be "the most perfect and sublime that has ever been taught by man."[52]

In fact, Jefferson goes to great lengths to "pick out the diamonds from the dunghills" in the text of the New Testament. While president, he compiled his *Life and Morals of Jesus of Nazareth*,[53] which was a piecing together of the "genuine" portions of the Gospels—namely, those that reveal the morals of Jesus, without any of the "inferior" theological accretions. As usual, Jefferson's freedom from the incumbrances of doubt or uncertainty about his ability to separate the "genuine" from "inferior" is remarkable, but his confidence does nothing to detract from the dubiousness of his approach to the New Testament, or of his judgments about the similarities among all the world's religions on moral matters.

It is true that for Jefferson religion appears to add what Bellah might call a "transcendent dimension" to his moral beliefs. In fact, at one point Jefferson concedes that "a consciousness that you are acting under [God's] eye . . . will be a vast additional incitement" to act morally, although he emphasizes that such an incitement is not necessary.[54] This seems to come close to a "religious feeling" that is in some way distinct from moral feelings. But to wander into the subtleties of distinguishing types of feeling and their relation to morality is obviously to be drawn into a thicket of theorizing that Jefferson avoids at all costs. Above all, Jefferson nowhere suggests that this religious consciousness might in any way conflict with moral sensibilities. It is therefore fair to conclude that essential religion for Jefferson is virtually identical with essential morality.

Conclusion

As the result of this investigation, we should be doubly perplexed. We should be perplexed, in the first place, because of the three stress points and the problems they inevitably pose for us when we think about the notion of civil religion. We should be perplexed, in the second place, because Jefferson was *not* perplexed about these problems! For there is some evidence that the failure of Jefferson to face up to the stress points has taken its toll in American life.

I am not suggesting that great benefits did not result from the ingenious institutional arrangements constructed by the founding fathers for overcoming religious strife and for making "freedom of conscience" at least a partial reality. Nor am I challenging Bellah's claim that it is an advantage to have developed, as Jefferson did, a concept of civil religion which contains moral standards by which to stand in judgment on the policies and institutions of the United States. If there is any doubt that Jefferson held such a "prophetic" view of civil religion, his comments on the necessity of "a little rebellion now and then" should be consulted.[55] Moreover, many of the basic moral principles espoused by Jefferson strike me as relevant to modern life, and very much worth defending (though on grounds different from his).

But these many advantages cannot quiet our perplexity. We are, as a country, being driven to face up to the stress points, which are there, whether we like it or not. In the process, we are coming to see that Jefferson's way of handling these questions is of doubtful utility.

First, it is obvious that Jefferson's position on the relation of religion and civic responsibility, as well as the relation of religion to morality, has turned our attention away from some important realities. For example, it is difficult to agree with Jefferson that religious beliefs play no important role in inspiring and directing action, or that the actions that religious beliefs do support cannot conflict seriously with prevailing conceptions of moral or civic responsibility. What of the Mormons and their convictions regarding polygamy?[56] What of the Christian Scientists and their resistance to medical treatment for themselves and their children?[57] What of the Old Order Amish, and their refusal, on religious grounds, to send their children to public school beyond the eighth grade?[58] What of pacifists who give some form of religious warrant for resisting the call of civic responsibility?

It is not only implausible to deny the connection between religious belief and specific courses of action, as Jefferson does, but it is an insult to conscientious people to regard their convictions as trivial and beside the point so far as the central pragmatic concerns of human life are concerned. Surely it ought to be a part of the rights of conscience to have one's reasons for action taken seriously, even if they include references to religious doctrine, and even if they conflict sharply with accepted civil practice. Jefferson's automatic disdain toward any religious group that in one way or another substantially challenges the established civic order is repugnant. There is a connection between religion and civic behavior, and that connection ought to be honored.

By our examples we recognize that because conflicting courses of action result from conflicting religious interpretations, hard choices will often have to be made both by society as well as by the dissenting religious groups and individuals. The society may see fit to make certain compromises in the interests of the "free exercise of religion," and the dissenters may also see reason, on their side, to modify their religiously prescribed actions in some ways. The history of Christianity, to mention one religion, is the history of a shifting process of this sort of compromise.[59]

In the matter of compromising, it is important that all parties grasp just what they are doing when they attempt to work out their agreements, and that they understand *the reasons why* they come to the agreements they do. This is part of what it means to face up to the hard choices that often obtain between the demands of God or conscience and the state. If a notion of civil religion, such as the one put forward by the founding fathers, diverts attention from these choice points, then so much the worse for that view of civil religion.

Of course, to advocate giving attention to such matters is to run counter to the Jeffersonian belief that "the reasons men give for their actions are much less important than the actions themselves." But note carefully that if we dismiss the reasons people give for their actions—religious or otherwise—as mere distractions, we ourselves are likely to become inattentive to the discrepancies, hasty conclusions, and contradictory beliefs in our own position. This was, I believe, the price Jefferson paid for his brand of pragmatism.[60]

It is also, I venture impressionistically to suggest, a price we have all paid as descendants of Jeffersonian pragmatism. The energetic public debates of the 1960s and of the recent presidential campaign have revealed (to me, at least) that Americans do not care a great deal about attending to reasons and justifications for policies, particularly where "moral" issues are at stake. Morality, it appears, is at bottom a matter of immediate "feeling," or "sentiment." Deliberating, reflecting, "theorizing" about moral questions are little more than delaying tactics, or "distractions," as Thomas Jefferson would heartily add.

But if Jefferson's method represents the alternative to hard thinking about morality and civic responsibility, then I hope I have demonstrated why we might want to approach all references to "moral feeling" in public discourse with a certain amount of skepticism. It does seem clear that appeals to "moral feeling" or "moral sense," without clarifying and defending the terms, will not provide much guidance in the public policy problems that confront this country at home and abroad.

That is not to say that there is some ready substitute for Jefferson's moral sense, able to provide the sure guidance he promised. On the contrary, it is a gain to admit that the sort of moral certainty on specific questions that Jefferson expected is a rare commodity in a complex civil order that is filled with an array of conflicting value-choices.

Bellah concludes his essay, "Civil Religion in America," by suggesting that the American civil religion "is a heritage of moral and religious experience from which we still have much to learn as we formulate the decisions that lie ahead."[61] That proposition may be true with respect to other representatives of American civil religion. However, if the thought of Thomas Jefferson is any clue, the lessons in moral and religious matters to be learned from the founding fathers are mostly negative.

NOTES

1. Robert N. Bellah, "Civil Religion in America," the first essay in this volume, and Sidney E. Mead, "The Post-Protestant Concept and America's Two Religions," *Religion in Life,* Vol. 33 (Spring 1964); cf. *The Lively Experiment* (New York: Harper & Row, 1963), chaps. 2, 3, 4, and "The Fact of Pluralism and the Persistence of Sectarianism," in *Religion of the Republic,* ed. Elwyn A. Smith (Philadelphia: Fortress Press, 1971).

2. One must infer from the essay, "Civil Religion in America," that Bellah considers the civil religious tradition, as shaped by the founding fathers, to be normative to some extent. The inference is justified, since Bellah credits the founding fathers with originating a tradition he clearly favors. For his part, Mead admires Jefferson and others for providing Americans with "bonds of affection," which, so far as religion is concerned, are "more cosmopolitan, more universal, more general" than the loyalties of particularistic churches. See, for example, "The Fact of Pluralism and the Persistence of Sectarianism."

3. Because of the limits of space, I deal solely with Jefferson. One can only speak of the "founding fathers" in general when he has analyzed them one by one. My intuition is that Jefferson is fairly representative, but such a conclusion would have to be carefully documented.

4. See Jean-Jacques Rousseau, "Of Civil Religion," Book IV, chap. 8 in *The Social Contract,* ed. Ernest Barker (New York: Oxford University Press, 1960). The disparities I have in mind are those points of tension between religious beliefs and civic responsibility, between moral beliefs and civic responsibility, and between religious and moral beliefs. Diagrammatically, the disparities can be identified as the sides of the following triangle:

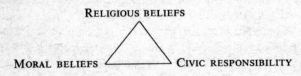

RELIGIOUS BELIEFS

MORAL BELIEFS   CIVIC RESPONSIBILITY

5. *Ibid.*, p. 305.

6. *Ibid.*, p. 302.

7. *Ibid.*, p. 301.

8. *Ibid.*, p. 170.

9. *Ibid.*, p. 301.

10. *Ibid.*, p. 195.

11. Daniel J. Boorstin, *The Americans: The Colonial Experience* (New York: Vintage Books, 1958), p. 151.

12. See *ibid.*, pp. 149-152; cf. *The Genius of American Politics* (Chicago: University of Chicago Press, 1953), especially chap. 1: "Why a Theory Seems Needless."

13. Boston: Beacon Press, 1960. I am indebted to this volume for several ideas.

14. It is hard to understand how Boorstin, having seen so acutely the difficulties with the Jeffersonian point of view in the earlier book, could then lapse into an unseemly glorification of "Jeffersonian pragmatism."

15. Daniel J. Boorstin, *The Lost World of Thomas Jefferson*, p. 170.

16. *The Life and Selected Writings of Thomas Jefferson,* ed. Adrienne Koch and William Peden (New York: Random House, 1944), p. 312. Hereafter cited as LWTJ.

17. Since such statements from "An Act for Establishing Religious Freedom" are by now second nature to most Americans, no one pauses any longer to think critically about them. The sentence, "our civil rights have no dependence on our religious opinions," actually contradicts the point of the context in which it appears: "Well aware that Almighty God hath created the mind free; that all attempts to influence it by temporal punishments or burdens, or by civil incapacitations, tend only to beget habits of hypocrisy and meanness, and *are a departure from the plan of the Holy Author of our religion,* who being Lord both of body and mind, yet chose not to propagate it by coercions on either, as was in his Almighty power to do; that the impious presumption of legislators and rulers, civil as well as ecclesiastical, who, being themselves but fallible and uninspired men have assumed dominion over the faith of others, setting up their own opinions and modes of thinking as the only true and infallible, and as such endeavoring to impose them on others, hath established and maintained false religions over the greatest part of the world, and through all time; that to compel a man to furnish contributions of money for the propagation of opinions which he disbelieves, is sinful and tyrannical . . ." (italics added).

In this passage, Jefferson has obviously adopted *a particular interpretation of religion,* which he calls "the plan of the Holy Author of our religion." From that Jefferson has then deduced a particular conclusion regarding "our civil rights" with respect to the free exercise of religion. In other words, according to the argument of this passage, the expressed view of civil rights *is* dependent on Jefferson's religious opinions! If one did not happen to share those opinions, as many in the history of religions have not, then a quite different view of civil rights could presumably follow. However, neither here nor anywhere else does Jefferson give the slightest indication he is aware of the self-contradictory character of this part of his argument. The explanation for this lapse is, as I shall make clear below, that Jefferson would never have accepted the proposition that his religious interpretation is simply another religious opinion or belief, subject to the same sort of challenge as conventional opinions. His beliefs were, he believed, authenticated in such a way as to set them above ordinary religious convictions.

It is true that Jefferson proceeds in "An Act for Establishing Religious Freedom" to muster a second sort of argument, one that is logically distinct from the first. This is an appeal to "the natural rights of mankind." As Jefferson puts it, ". . . we are free to declare, and do declare, that the rights hereby asserted are of the natural rights of mankind, and that if any act shall be hereafter passed to repeal the present or to narrow its operation, such act will be an infringement of natural right." While this argument is different from the one analyzed above, Jefferson frequently confuses them for reasons we shall explore below.

18. *The Writings of Thomas Jefferson,* ed. Andrew A. Lipscomb (Washington, D.C.: The Thomas Jefferson Memorial Association, 1903), Vol. XV, pp. 240-241, 266. See also, Boorstin, *The Lost World of Thomas Jefferson,* pp. 111-139.

19. LWTJ, p. 700.

20. See Adrienne Koch, *The Philosophy of Thomas Jefferson* (Chicago: Quadrangle Books, 1964), especially chaps. 3 and 6. With respect to the philosophical fashions of the period, Jefferson's loyalties clearly lie with the "sentimentalist" or "moral sense" brand of intuition as opposed to the "intellectualist" or "rationalist" forms of intuition. His heroes were people like Lord Kames, Dugald Stewart, and Frances Hutcheson. (See L. A. Selby-Bigge, *British Moralists* [New York: Bobbs-Merrill, 1964], Introduction, for an excellent discussion of the intellectual context out of which Jefferson came.) As William C.

Lehmann points out in *Henry Home, Lord Kames, and the Scottish Enlightenment* (The Hague: M. Nijhoff, 1971), the Scottish Common Sense philosophers "were essentially empiricists rather than rationalists. Their appeal was always to experience rather than to reason in the abstract, to observation, even if at times introspective, and to experimentation, rather than to first principles" (p. 163; cf. pp. 168-169). For examples of Jefferson's references to the influence of people like Kames and Seward upon him, see LWTJ, pp. 640, 700.

21. LWTJ, p. 701. By no stretch of the imagination may the term "rationalist" be applied to the thought of Jefferson. In this respect Sidney Mead gives voice to a common but very serious mistake in describing Jefferson, Franklin, and Madison as members of a group he calls "the American colonial rationalists" (see *Lively Experiment,* pp. 41-52).

22. *The Writings of Thomas Jefferson,* Vol. XV, p. 25.

23. LWTJ, p. 313.

24. LWTJ, p. 275.

25. LWTJ, p. 277.

26. LWTJ, pp. 591-592.

27. Quoted in Boorstin, *The Americans: The Colonial Experience,* p. 153.

28. Quoted in Boorstin, *Lost World of Thomas Jefferson,* p. 120.

29. *Loc. cit.*

30. *The Writings of Thomas Jefferson,* Vol. XV, p. 492. It is of interest that the same sense of certainty about his political convictions led Jefferson to seek to control books and professors, particularly at the University of Virginia Law School, according to their political persuasion. This point, among Jefferson's other lapses, is brought out in Leonard Levy's *Jefferson and Civil Liberties: The Darker Side* (Cambridge: The Belknap Press, 1963): "When, therefore, Jefferson spoke of the law school of the University of Virginia as a seedbed of future political leaders of Whig persuasion, he meant the school to be an arm of his own party. He was seeking to proscribe the teaching of ideas antithetical to his own views of the federal system. The school was not to teach both Federalist and Republican views objectively or to avoid altogether a study of the American party system; it was to indoctrinate loyalty to Republicanism" (pp. 152-153).

31. *The Writings of Thomas Jefferson,* Vol. XV, p. 492.

32. LWTJ, pp. 706-707 (italics added).

33. LWTJ, p. 704. While Jefferson uses the term "Unitarianism," it is employed in a very broad sense as more or less synonymous with

"Deism." It does not imply a specific denominational view of religion.

34. Bellah, *op. cit.*, p. 8.

35. See below at our discussion of the third disparity, the tension between religious and moral beliefs, where Jefferson's specific views on religion are elaborated.

36. Though Jefferson uses the term "science" in this context (and also in fn. 40), it is clear that what he has in mind is closer to our notion of "theory."

37. LWTJ, pp. 430-431 (italics added).

38. LWTJ, p. 404.

39. LWTJ, p. 636.

40. LWTJ, p. 22 (italics added).

41. Boorstin, *The Lost World of Thomas Jefferson*, p. 53. cf., especially pp. 41-56 for an excellent discussion of these matters.

42. LWTJ, p. 264.

43. LWTJ, p. 639.

44. *Loc. cit.*

45. LWTJ, pp. 639-640 (italics added).

46. Adrienne Koch, in *The Philosophy of Thomas Jefferson*, attempts to argue that the passage cited above "is evidence that Jefferson had moved away, in his mature ethical thought, from a simple belief in moral rules, divinely inspired and innately ingrained in man. The subtler notion, of a moral principle like social utility, conceived to be sufficiently flexible to accommodate the inevitable changes of environment, completed the moral picture" (p. 42). This statement is very misleading. It obfuscates a fundamental ambiguity in the ethical thought of Jefferson between a notion of a clear, universal, invariant "moral sense," on the one hand, and a culturally relative, variable notion of utility as the standard of virtue, on the other. In his early life, as well as later on, Jefferson links the moral sense to social utility, so that we may not speak of any development in that respect. What does happen toward the end of his life is that Jefferson begins to be aware of "cultural relativity," without ever facing up to the strain this problem puts upon his belief in a universal, absolute "moral law." (For evidence of this growing awareness, in addition to the above passage, see *The Writings of Thomas Jefferson,* Vol. XV, pp. 76-77). Virtually at the time he, is beginning to write about the cultural variability of morals (*ca.* 1814), Jefferson is also reasserting his conviction regarding a universal, invariant standard of morality (during the War of 1812): "We believe that the just standing of all nations is the health and security of all. We consider the overwhelming power

of England on the ocean, and of France on the land, as destructive of the prosperity and happiness of the world, and *wish both to be reduced only to the necessity of observing moral duties . . .*" (LWTJ, p. 620; italics added). This passage is interesting on two counts: first, because it speaks *not* of varying utilities among nations which make the same act right in one set of circumstances and wrong in another, but of *one* universal notion of "prosperity and happiness of the world." If there is, after all, one common standard, then it follows that acts are *not* morally relative; second, Jefferson speaks here of a set of "moral duties" which apparently serve to restrict the self-seeking of nations. Such an idea is in complete harmony with comments he makes at various points in his life about an absolute, universal "law of nations" (see note 47, below).

47. See LWTJ, pp. 318-319; cf. LWTJ, p. 565, and *The Writings of Thomas Jefferson*, Vol. XIII, pp. 202-3. "The moral duties which exist between individual and individual in a state of nature, accompany them into a state of society, and the aggregate of the duties of all the individuals composing the society constitutes the duties of that society towards any other; so that between society and society the same moral duties exist as did between the individuals composing them. . . . Of these, it is true, that nations are to be judges for themselves; since no one nation has a right to sit in judgment over another, but *the tribunal of conscience remains,* and that also of the opinion of the world. *These will revise the sentence we pass in our own case,* and as we respect these, we must see that in judging ourselves we have honestly done the part of impartial and rigorous judges. . . . *Questions of natural right are triable by their conformity with the moral sense and reason of man . . .*" (LWTJ, pp. 318-319; italics added). Cf. Adrienne Koch, *Power, Morals, and the Founding Fathers* (Ithaca: Cornell University Press, 1961), especially chap. 3.

48. LWTJ, p. 575.

49. LWTJ, p. 637.

50. *The Writings of Thomas Jefferson*, Vol. XII, pp. 315-316 (italics added).

51. LWTJ, p. 569.

52. *Ibid.*, p. 570.

53. Reprinted in part in *In God We Trust: The Religious Beliefs and Ideas of the American Founding Fathers,* ed. Norman Cousins (New York: Harper & Row, 1958), pp. 173-216.

54. LWTJ, pp. 432-433.

55. LWTJ, p. 436.

56. *Reynolds v. United States,* 1878. See Milton R. Konvitz, *Fundamental Liberties of a Free People* (Ithaca: Cornell University Press, 1957), pp. 44, 396, for a brief, but useful discussion of the ruling against the Mormons' right to practice polygamy on religious grounds.

57. *Ibid.,* pp. 46-47, for a similar discussion of the legal situation of the Christian Scientist.

58. *Wisconsin* v. *Yoder,* 1972.

59. Ernst Troeltsch's *Social Teachings of the Christian Churches* (London: George Allen and Unwin, 1956, 2 vols.), trans. Olive Wyon, elaborates this theme in a classic way.

60. Levy, *op. cit.,* p. 172, makes the following appropriate observation: "Regret and remorse are conspicuously absent from Jefferson's writings, as is reflective reconsideration of a problem. Something in his make-up, more than likely a stupendous ego, inhibited second thoughts. Whether he would deny the plain facts or stubbornly reiterate his original position, he failed to work out fresh guidelines for future conduct. Restatement, not re-evaluation, marked his thinking, and beneath an eloquently turned phrase there lurked a weary, problem-begging cliché. That it was commonplace rarely deprived it of its profundity as a libertarian principle. The 'self-evident truths' of the Declaration of Independence will continue to survive all scorn of being 'glittering generalities.' They tend, however, to overarch real cases."

61. Bellah, *op. cit.,* p. 19.

CHARLES H. LONG

10 Civil Rights—Civil Religion: Visible People and Invisible Religion

AMERICAN RELIGION is usually understood as the religion of European immigrants transplanted into the American soil. Most general
texts dealing with this area begin with the coming of the Puritans
and continue through to the breakdown of the Puritan theocratic
ideal on to the new light, old light debate of the Presbyterians. We
are then treated to a description of the great awakenings and the
religion of the pioneers as they move across the American land-
scape.

Other texts pay equal attention to the different religious communities of the thirteen original colonies and their histories. More
precise and detailed work in the area of American religious history
has shown how certain themes tend to run through much of this
history, becoming the threads on which the fabric of American
religious life weaves its meanings. Thus the notions of wilderness,
new land, errand, etc., form the symbolic threads of the American
religious tradition.

In this same vein, some historians have more recently become
interested in what is now called American civil religion. "Civil
religion" is an exceedingly vague phrase and attempts at definitions have often led to more ambiguity. There are, however, some
basic notions involved in the phrase. One might do well if he

placed the phrase in the context of the French sociological tradition extending from Denis Fustel Coulanges's *The Ancient City* to Émile Durkheim's *The Elementary Forms of the Religious Life*. In these works religion is defined as either a correlate of the structure of a society or as a projection of the image of society into objective and sacred symbols. If we apply this notion to American religion, the emphasis would fall on the religious meanings inherent in the founding documents of the American Republic: the Declaration of Independence and the Constitution. As such the religious vision stemming from this orientation differs from that of the revealed religion, Christianity; for the revealed religion offers salvation to all human beings regardless of circumstance, whereas in the civil religion salvation is seen within the context of belonging to the American national community.

Civil religion emerges as a parallel structure alongside revealed religion and its institutions, or it may find expression through revealed religion, or again it may borrow symbols from the revealed religion. Issues of this kind are discussed exhaustively in H. Richard Niebuhr's *Christ and Culture* where a typology of the possible range of relationship is described in detail.

If American religion is dealt with in either of these two ways or in a combination of these two ways, we must note some glaring omissions. Let me raise the issue by asking a simple question, the answer to which will raise a serious methodological issue. What is meant by "American" and "religion" in the phrase "American religion"? If by "American" we mean the Christian European immigrants and their progeny, then we have overlooked American Indians and American blacks. And if religion is defined as revealed Christianity and its institutions, we have again overlooked much of the religion of American blacks, Amerindians, and the Jewish communities. Even from the point of view of civil religion, it is not clear that from the perspective of the various national and ethnic communities that there has ever been a consistent meaning of the national symbols and meanings. In short, a great deal of the writings and discussions on the topic of American religion has been consciously or unconsciously ideological, serving to enhance, justify, and render sacred the history of European immigrants in this land.

Indeed, this approach to American religion has rendered the

religious reality of non-Europeans to a state of invisibility, and thus the invisibility of the non-Europeans in America arises as a fundamental issue of American religious history at this juncture. How are we to understand this invisibility and how are we to deal with it as a creative methodological issue? It is no longer possible for us to add the "invisible ones" as addenda to a European dominated historical method, for such a procedure fails to take into account the relationships of the omitted ones to the Europeans throughout American religious history. Nor is it possible for us, simply in imitation of the historical method we are criticizing, to begin the project of writing history in which the ideological values of blacks and Amerindians dominate. This procedure has no merit, for it could not make sense of that problem of invisibility which allowed us to raise the issue of our discussion. The issue raised here is a subtle one and questions must be asked concerning the very nature of historical method.

Our first task, it seems to me, is to ask how certain groups were rendered "invisible" in the historical narrative and cultural symbols of the American majority.

Sidney Mead states that

> Americans during their formative years were a people in movement through space—a people exploring the obvious highways and many unexplored byways of practically unlimited geographical and social space. *The quality of their minds and hearts and spirits was formed in that great crucible—and in a short time.* Their great and obvious achievement was the mastery of a vast, stubborn and oft-times brutal continent. This is the "epic of America" written with cosmic quill dipped in the blood, sweat and tears of innumerable little men and women. . . . This is the mighty saga of the outward acts, told and retold until it has overshadowed and suppressed the equally vital but more somber story of the inner experience. *Americans have so presented to view and celebrate the external and material side of their pilgrim's progress that they have tended to conceal even from themselves the inner experience with its more subtle dimensions and profound depths.*[1]

Ralph Ellison, in the prologue to his novel *Invisible Man*, writes:

> I am an invisible man. No, I am not a spook like those who haunted Edgar Allan Poe; nor am I one of your Hollywood-movie ectoplasms. I am a man of substance, of flesh and bone, fiber, and liquids—

and I might even be said to possess a mind. I am invisible understand, simply because people refuse to see me. Like the bodiless
heads you sometimes see in circus side-shows, it is as though I have
been surrounded by mirrors of hard distorting glass. When they
approach me they see only my surroundings, themselves, or figments
of their imagination—indeed, everything and anything except me.

Nor is my invisibility exactly a matter of a biochemical accident
of my epidermis. That invisibility to which I refer occurs because
of a peculiar disposition of the eyes of those with whom I come in
contact. A matter of construction of the *inner* eyes, those eyes with
which they look through their physical eyes upon reality. . . . You
wonder whether you aren't simply a phantom in other people's
minds.

These two statements deal with the issue of concealment and
invisibility. From the point of view of a religious historian, these
statements carry great import, for they refer to definitive and fundamental modes of orientation of the American people. The statements
have to do with the American cultural language, the American mode of perception, and the American religion. "The mighty
saga of the outward acts" is a description of the American language, a language rooted not simply in the physical conquest of
space, but equally a language which is the expression of a hermeneutics of conquest and suppression. It is a cultural language that
conceals the inner depths, the archaic dimensions of the dominant
peoples in the country, while at the same time it renders invisible
all those who fail to partake of this language and its underlying
cultural experiences. The religion of the American people centers
around the telling and retelling of the mighty deeds of the white
conquerors. This hermeneutic mask thus conceals the true experience of Americans from their very eyes. The invisibility of Indians
and blacks is matched by a void or a deeper invisibility within the
consciousness of white Americans. The inordinate fear they have
of minorities is the expression of the fear they have when they contemplate the possibility of seeing themselves as they really are.

This American cultural language is not a recent creation. It is
a cosmogonic language, a language of the beginnings; it structures
the American myth of the beginnings, and has continued to express
the synchronic dimensions of American cultural life since that
time. It is a language forged by the Puritans and Jeffersonians and

carried on by the succeeding generations. The Puritan "errand into the wilderness" was undertaken in the name of religious freedom, a freedom which would allow the colonists from Europe to divine the Word of God in a manner appropriate to their dispositions and knowledge, and a freedom to show this light of the gospel to all humans far and near. This wilderness was, in following the biblical paradigm, a place of knowledge, a place of retreat from the world for prayer and reflection upon divine meanings. And again this wilderness was a paradise, a kind of Eden, a space overflowing with the bounty of creation. These meanings of the wilderness are undercut when they confront the American aborigines. The aborigines do not partake of these later meanings. Even when they are the teachers of the Puritans, the Puritan cultural language fails to take cognizance through an alteration of their own language; or even when they are greeted benignly by the aborigines, the shift in language and thus in cultural perception fails to take place. The aboriginal is a wilderness creature, a wilderness creature who, like the wilderness itself, must now be conquered. The conquest of the aboriginal began in the seventeenth century and continues to the present time. The linking of the aboriginal with the wilderness and the subsequent conquest of both is the issue of race and ecology. It is an issue that points up the hermeneutical structure of the American cultural language.

The Jeffersonian language is equally ambiguous and this ambiguity is made more intense by the factor of self-consciousness. Unlike the Puritans who wished to be a light unto Europe, the Jeffersonians were thrilled by the possibility of creating a free society in a new land. They were enlightened men who had thought about the meaning of freedom as an essential ingredient of human societies. Around the issue of the existence of slavery was to be played the poignant and commiserating drama of the Jeffersonian conscience. Jefferson is the archetype of the sophisticated liberal. But this issue is much deeper than the biography of Jefferson; Jefferson is the hand behind the Declaration of Independence and the moving spirit of the Constitution. These are the founding, the cosmogonic documents. Through these documents the character of the Jeffersonians and the structure of American societal language gains a definitive form.

The compromise over slavery at the beginning is the first of a long series of compromises; this first compromise sets the tone for what is almost a ritual of language concerning the nature of black freedom and, consequently, the meaning of freedom in the American Republic. Indeed, we are able to discern almost precisely the one-hundred-year periods in which the Jeffersonian cultural and linguistic compromise rises to an intense and violent level in the history of the United States. From 1776 to the 1860s is almost a hundred years, and from the end of the Civil War to the present is already more than a hundred years. The uproars of the 1960s were another dramatic ritual of the archetypes of American religion.

At each of these mythical cycles the opportunity is given for a change of the ritual, for a break in the repetition of this kind of eternal return. It was first present in 1776, and then again in the bloody Civil War, and then again in the 1960s with the Kennedys, Martin Luther King, Jr., and Malcolm X; but at each of these junctures the American revolution is aborted and the clever priests skillful in the ways of ritual purity and manipulation come upon the scene to ensure the repetition of the American ritual.

It is from this perspective that we must understand the meaning of religion in America from a black point of view. In this sense, the distinction between civil religion and church religion is not one that would loom very large for us. In the first place, it is the overwhelming reality of the white presence in any of its various forms that becomes the crucial issue. Whether this presence was legitimated by power executed illegally, or whether in institution or custom, its reality, as far as blacks were concerned, carried the force and power of legal sanction enforced by power. The black response to this cultural reality is a part of the civil rights struggle in the history of American blacks.

Joseph Washington in his book of a few years ago, *Black Religion*, accused the black church of being too much concerned with civil rights and not concerned enough with theology. Conversely, he accused the white church of being too much concerned with theology and not concerned enough with civil rights. This judgment is too neat and it furthermore does not understand the elements of black religion involved in the civil rights struggle. The fact that the black churches have been the locus of the civil rights struggle is not incidental, for the civil rights battle represented the black confrontation with an American myth that dehumanized the black person's being. It was a mode of affirmation on the part of blacks and a protest in the name of human rights and freedom. The location of this struggle in the church enabled the civil rights movement to take on the resources of black cultural life in the forms of organization, music, and artistic expression, and in the gathering of the limited economic resources. The civil rights movement has been one of protest and exposition. A protest in the name of freedom and an exposition of the hypocrisy of the American language. But more than just hypocrisy was being exposed in this movement, for at points the American system itself was seen as a gross irrationality or a rationalized demonism. The vicissitudes of the black struggle against the American myth can be traced from recalcitrant slaves through the Nat Turners, Denmark Veseys, David Walkers, Du Boises, Marcus Garveys, Malcolm Xs, and Martin Luther Kings to the present day.

To the extent that the struggle for black freedom was carried on through the seeking of legal redress and petition, it was a part of the American cultural language; for in this manner there is the tacit acceptance of the possibility of the American language as an adequate language for the expression of human freedom for all the American peoples. But something more subtle was always at work in the black communities. First of all the very organization of black people meant that they were not invisible to each other; their humanity was affirmed in each other. Second, they came to know the American cultural language, or to use the colloquial form, they came to "know the man." Third, and probably more importantly, they learned to know *another* reality, a reality not created or given by the man. This otherness is expressed in the black spirituals as God, or as a mode of perception of the world which is not under the judgment of the oppressor. It is equally expressed in the practical and concrete proposals that speak of *another* place. For example, after the passage of the fugitive slave law, many black abolitionists discerned that blacks could never be free in this land and they began to contemplate the possibility of another land, another place—sometimes the islands of the Caribbean, but more often Africa. So from Blyden and Delaney to Du Bois and Garvey, the image and reality of Africa has continued to weave itself into the black religious consciousness as a religious and historical structure. It is an archaic form in the black consciousness; it is at the same time a reminder of historical origins, an eschatological hope, an affirmation of a vague homeland, and a gesture of solidarity with those who also "came to know the man." This sense of otherness, or the sense of the other which has arisen out of the black experience, is equally present when the black thinks of America as a free society; for if blacks are to be free persons in American society, this society will indeed have to be a radically different society; it will indeed be an-*other* society.

Let us now in light of a black perspective on American religion ask our second question: how is it possible to do justice to the facts of American religious history, and at the same time overcome the concealment of peoples and meanings from the majority group in America, and still further, give visibility to those who were rendered invisible through the concealment? The problem has to do with the pattern, the network, the nexus onto which the facts of this history are interpreted. I am raising a question that is very close to the problem of myth.

If we take myth as defined by Mircea Eliade, namely, that myth is the *true* story, then it is the question of a true rendering of American religion, a story of American religion that does justice to the inner life meanings and vitalities of those who were made invisible in the old interpretive schema, and it should be a true story that would halt the repressive concealment of the white Americans.

As in all hermeneutical procedures we must begin with the misinterpretations, for it is precisely the misinterpretations which raise the problem of hermeneutics, and it is only by going through the misinterpretations that a new awareness of the problem will take shape. I have already alluded to the misinterpretations and the symbols of American reality that flow from them. Allow me to sketch out the basis for a new interpretation of American religion.

I have cited before that I wish to be faithful to the facts of American religion; my problem, or better, the problematic issue, centers around the matrix or pattern on which the facts are spread. I am here interested in the issue of authenticity or truth as something more than simply factual knowledge. Myth emerges as a category at this point because I am at this point interested in telling the *true story* of the American peoples—a true story which moves beyond concealment and invisibility.

In the telling of the story of America and American cultural reality we have been dominated by one tradition, the tradition of the "mighty saga of the outward acts, told and retold," in such a manner, "until it overshadowed and suppressed the equally vital, but more somber story of *the inner experience*."

The telling and retelling of the American experience in this mode has created a normative historical judgment and ideology of the American experience. The *historical* telling of this story has in the form of historiography relegated itself to a position of objectivity, and this objectivity, in terms of the canons of scholarship, becomes identified with truth. But what this mode of awareness has not realized is that, in the terms of contemporary French phenomenology, it is still at the stage of the first naïveté. Those who take this approach have not yet raised the question of why they wish the facts to conform to this conception of the truth, or better, why they have selected only these facts as the sinew of the truth.

All interpretations of American religion, whether from the point of view of the revealed tradition or the civil tradition, have been involved with a subjective concealment of the inner dynamics of their own religious-cultural psychic reality and a correlative repression and concealment of the reality of the *others*. This procedure has been undertaken to give American reality a normative and centered mode of interpretation. This methodological procedure has a hallowed position in Western culture. It constitutes the problematic and the resolution of the issue of *episteme*. The notion of the *episteme* constitutes the problem of any form of coherence, and as understood in American cultural history it raises the question of a normative center of interpretation.

The invocation of the notion of *episteme* is an indication of the seriousness of this methodological problem. While the idea of *episteme* as a pre-methodological concept allowed for an organizing principle of coherence and gave a normative center for the organization of data, it simultaneously operated as a center, a presence, making impossible the permutation or transformation of the other data. The "mighty saga of the outward acts" as the center of American religion and reality meant that all the *other* peoples and cultures had to remain *in their places*—places allotted to them by this centered reality of the European tradition of immigrants.

The concealment and correlative invisibility of various and sundry American peoples results from this methodological centeredness of the American *episteme*. But this concealment and invisibility, once it has been revealed as a contradiction, constitutes a coherence encompassed within a contradiction, and from a hermeneutical point of view this is a misinterpretation of American reality that issues in the problem of desire—a desire documented by the cultural, political, and scholarly pursuit of the society to raise another hermeneutical issue. This new hermeneutical issue on the practical level must deal with the religious reality of all the peoples called American, and on the theoretical level it must question the hallowed tradition of a historical *episteme*.

From this new position all history must be seen as chronology and to the extent that this chronology seems normative, such norms must be understood as heuristic, simply devices for the generation of new data. The notion of equality which is part and parcel of the American cultural language must express itself in purely theoretical terms; we must work for a meaning of equality in historical methodology, for it is only in this way that we simultaneously combat the racist and the moralistic liberals. The question of the meaning of American religion in its revealed or civil forms calls for new theoretical considerations. Are we ready and prepared to face this radical revolution?

I have in this short essay attempted to raise certain theoretical problems in relationship to historical method and historiography of American religion. New understanding of this history will be forthcoming with a change of consciousness, but my emphasis on consciousness is not moral but intellectual and theoretical.[2]

NOTES

1. Sidney Mead, *The Lively Experiment* (New York: Harper & Row, 1963), p. 11.

2. I am indebted to works which have come from the history of

religions methods and from what has come to be known as the "structuralist schools." In the former, Mircea Eliade's *The Myth of the Eternal Return*, Bollingen Series XLVI (New York: Pantheon Books, 1954), and in the latter Lévi-Strauss's *The Savage Mind* (London: Weidenfeld and Nicolson, 1966), and Jacques Derrida's programmatic essay, "Structure, Sign, and Play in the Discourse of the Human Sciences," in *The Structuralist Controversy*, ed. Richard Macksey and Eugenio Donato (Baltimore: Johns Hopkins Press, 1970), are important.

Over the last ten years I have been doing quite extensive research in black and Amerindian religious traditions. The evidence of this research in this essay is minimal, but the research has led to the methodological position put forth. Until there are new methodological insights in American religion, it is somewhat unimportant to make too much of the research. As one may see I have valued the hints of Sidney Mead, especially in his *The Lively Experiment*.

LEO MARX

11 The Uncivil Response of American Writers to Civil Religion in America

"I used the word," said Tristram brutally, "as a gesture of defiance. It's just a dirty word, that's all."

"Exactly," said the unfrocked with quiet joy. "All dirty words are fundamentally religious. They are all concerned with fertility and the processes of fertility and the organs of fertility. God, we are taught, is love."

Anthony Burgess, *The Wanting Seed*

Let me begin by acknowledging a debt to Norman Mailer for the argument that follows. It was inspired by a story he tells in *The Armies of the Night* (1968) where he is reflecting upon the uses of obscenity in saving whatever may be worth saving in our democratic ethos. To be even more specific, it was inspired by the scatological epithet "noble shit" upon which the story turns. It is important to add, however, that Mailer does not claim to have invented this vigorous oxymoron. He gives all the credit to an anonymous G.I. in World War II. I take pleasure in this fact because anonymity is a distinguishing mark of my subject here: the vigor, poetry, and truth so many of our writers have found in that anonymous work of the collective imagination called the American vernacular. Obscene language, to be sure, is a special kind of vernacular, but a distinctive and especially potent kind. Here is the way Mailer describes its power and its virtues:

> There was no villainy in obscenity for him, just—paradoxically, characteristically—his love for America: he had first come to love America when he served in the U.S. Army, not the America of course of the flag, the patriotic unendurable fix of the television programs and the newspapers, no, long before he was ever aware of the institutional oleo of the most suffocating American ideas he had come to love what editorial writers were fond of calling the democratic principle with its faith in the common man. He found that principle and that man in the Army, but what none of the editorial writers ever mentioned was that that noble common man was obscene as an old goat, and his obscenity was what saved him. The sanity of said common democratic man was in his humor, his humor was in his obscenity. And his philosophy as well—a reductive philosophy which looked to restore the hard edge of proportion to the overblown values overhanging each small military existence— viz: being forced to salute an overconscientious officer with your back stiffened into an exaggerated posture. "That Lieutenant is chickenshit," would be the platoon verdict, and a blow had some- how been struck for democracy and the sanity of good temper.[1]

For all his playfulness, Mailer is making a serious claim for obscenity here. He regards it as a weapon in a continuing struggle for egalitarian rights and principles—a kind of class struggle, en- listed men against officers, dirty words against the pretentious vo- cabulary of domination. When confronted with the "institutional oleo of the most suffocating American ideas," obscene language can be extremely effective. It is an appropriate and salutary response to expressions of what we lately have been instructed to call "civil religion"—that is, the effort to invest the highest political authority with religious legitimacy. In what follows, I propose to endorse—or at least partially endorse—Mailer's claim, not on my own behalf, but rather, by demonstrating that it has the tacit support of a long line of gifted American writers. Beginning at least as far back as Emerson's time, they prepared the way, both in theory and in practice, for the use of *un*civil language as a natural and proper means of coping with the rhetoric of a spurious civil religion.

But first, a further word about the concept of civil religion. The term initially was introduced by Rousseau, in *The Social Contract* (1762), and so far as I know it never had been applied to American thought until Robert Bellah's controversial essay, "Civil Religion in America" (1966).[2] There Bellah argues that in the United States we have had, alongside, and rather clearly differentiated from, the churches, an elaborate and well-institutionalized civil religion—one that possesses "its own seriousness and integrity." It is a body of beliefs, symbols, and rituals which provides a religious dimension for the whole fabric of American life, including the political realm. In defining the actual content of this national religion, Bellah relies heavily upon the rhetoric of American presidents, and particularly their inaugural addresses—all but one of which, he notes, mentions or refers to God.

But unfortunately Bellah does not explain why we should take the sentiments contained in the inaugural addresses as a genuine expression of collective religious motives. Although he admits that what people say in solemn occasions need not be taken at face value, he proceeds to use John F. Kennedy's inaugural address as a major exhibit of America's deep-seated religious values and commitments. After citing the beginning and the end of Kennedy's speech, both of which invoke the name of God, he quotes the following sentence as having a "distinctly biblical ring" and as being indicative of a national commitment to a "transcendent goal for the political process."

> Now the trumpet summons us again—not as a call to bear arms, though arms we need—not as a call to battle, though embattled we are—but a call to bear the burden of a long twilight struggle year in and year out, "rejoicing in hope, patient in tribulation"—a struggle against the common enemies of man: tyranny, poverty, disease and war itself.

In context it is evident that Bellah would have us believe that President Kennedy and his supporters really were committed, above all else, to a global struggle against tyranny, poverty, disease, and war. For it is on the basis of this sort of rhetoric that he invites us to concur in his astonishingly credulous endorsement of the seriousness and integrity of American civil religion. However, my chief purpose is not to quarrel with Bellah's argument or the evidence he brings to its support, but rather, to indicate how differently certain of our most distinguished writers have reacted to this strain of nationalistic religiosity.

Returning now to Norman Mailer, I must add that his claim for obscenity is not confined to the efficacy of dirty words in deflating overblown official pieties. It also serves, he says, as a therapeutic and regenerative medium. It helps to restore a sense of proportion, self-regard, even sanity. To speak religiously, Mailer imputes to the use of obscenity a kind of redemptive power, and not merely for individuals. It is capable of redeeming basic cultural resources. Obscenity, he seems to be saying, may be the key to another, more authentic, truly democratic, if as yet inchoate and unrealized form of civil religion. A close look at the way obscene words actually come into ordinary speech suggests to Mailer a possible method of salvaging certain traditional, lofty, if now moribund democratic ideals.

> . . . Mailer never felt more like an American than when he was naturally obscene—all the gifts of the American language came out in the happy play of obscenity upon concept, which enabled one to go back to concept again. What was magnificent about the word shit is that it enabled you to use the word noble: a skinny Southern cracker with a beatific smile on his face saying in the dawn in a Filipino rice paddy, "Man, I just managed to take me a noble shit." Yeah, that was Mailer's America. If he was going to love something in the country, he would love that.[3]

Quirky and faddish though it may sound, this notion of the saving power of obscenity has a long background in American literary history. In 1911, for example, George Santayana also had called attention to the discrepancy in America between an earthy native viewpoint, grounded in particulars, and another mode of thought characterized by abstract, largely imported ideals. "America," he said, in his influential lecture on the genteel tradition, "is a young country with an old mentality."[4] It had inherited a traditional, essentially religious outlook from Europe, but while that genteel mode of thought was becoming increasingly attenuated, Americans also were developing a fresh and, as it were, underground mentality of their own out of their distinctive firsthand experiences. In fact, Santayana says, correcting himself, America really is "a country with two mentalities, one a survival of the beliefs and standards of the fathers, the other an expression of the instincts, practice and discoveries of the younger generations." In all the "higher things of the mind," by which he meant religious, literary, and moral activity, the hereditary spirit prevails, but in the realm of practical affairs—inventions, industry, social organization—the new mentality, grounded in the observations and instincts of the mass of people, has taken over. Had Santayana ventured to give this fresh, native outlook a name, it might well have been "vernacular." For the great divide he had discovered in American culture was exemplified by the obvious gulf between two languages. One was polite, upper-class, bookish, conventional, churchly, and associated with what now would be called the Eastern Establishment. The other was cruder, more colloquial, closer to the raw, often profane particularities of everyday life in the West.

Whether Santayana was correct about the continuing dominion of the genteel tradition in American writing as late as 1911 need not concern us here. (He seems not to have been aware of the radical innovations of writers like Crane, Norris, and Dreiser.) Later in the essay, when he asks whether there had been any successful efforts to escape from the genteel culture, efforts to express something worth expressing behind its back, he feels obliged to mention Walt Whitman and Mark Twain, to whom I will return.

But the theoretical basis for Norman Mailer's defense of obscenity, its usefulness for cultural therapy, had been laid even earlier—by Ralph Waldo Emerson. It should be said that Santayana does discuss Emerson, but he neglects to mention Emerson's extraordinarily cogent ideas about the way a language—and by implication an entire culture—can lose its efficacy. It becomes corrupt at the same time, and for the same reasons, that civil life becomes corrupt. It is striking, incidentally, to see how much of the argument of George Orwell's influential essay, "Politics and the English Language," Emerson had held forth in 1836.

A man's power to connect his thought with its proper symbol, and so to utter it, depends on the simplicity of his character, that is, upon his love of truth and his desire to communicate it without loss. The corruption of man is followed by the corruption of language. When simplicity of character and the sovereignty of ideas is broken up by the prevalence of secondary desires—the desire of riches, of pleasure, of power, and of praise—and duplicity and falsehood take place of simplicity and truth, the power over nature as an interpreter of the will is in a degree lost; new imagery ceases to be created, and old words are perverted to stand for things which are not; a paper currency is employed, when there is no bullion in the vaults. In due time the fraud is manifest, and words lose all power to stimulate the understanding or the affections. Hundreds of writers may be found in every long-civilized nation who for a short time believe and make others believe that they see and utter truths, who do not of themselves clothe one thought in its natural garment, but who feed unconsciously on the language created by the primary writers of the country, those, namely who hold primarily on nature.[5]

Emerson is describing a psychological process by which words are drained of evocative power and meaning. The crux of the matter is the conflict between the forthright expression of motives and what he calls "secondary desires." When a concern for wealth, power, pleasure, or praise intervenes, the language becomes corrupt. Right here, according to Emerson, we are at a precise point of intersection between literature and politics. As Orwell would put it a century later, "The great enemy of clear language is insincerity. When there is a gap between one's real and one's declared aims, one turns as it were instinctively to long words and exhausted idioms, like a cuttlefish squirting out ink."[6] But the problem, for Emerson, was how a language, once corrupted, could be purified. How was a serious writer to do his work when the medium had been expropriated for fraudulent purposes? The cure, he said, would come from those wise writers who abandoned the moribund language, and renewed the living relation between words and nature—and by "nature" here, it should be said, he meant something much closer to what we nowadays would mean by "experience."[7]

But wise men pierce this rotten diction and fasten words again to visible things; so that picturesque language is at once a commanding certificate that he who employs it is a man in alliance with truth and God. The moment our discourse rises above the ground line of familiar facts and is inflamed with passion or exalted with thought, it clothes itself in images. A man conversing in earnest, if he watch his intellectual processes, will find that a material image more or less luminous arises in the mind, contemporaneous with every thought, which furnishes the vestment of the thought. Hence, good writing and brilliant discourse are perpetual allegories. This imagery is spontaneous. It is the blending of experience with the present action of the mind. It is proper creation.[8]

In "The American Scholar," the following year (1837), Emerson urged the close affinity between radical egalitarianism and the purification of language. In a democratic era, he argued, truth-telling writers would supplant a polite literary language with one that is common, low, even vulgar. Speaking of the "auspicious signs" of an Age of Revolution, he said:

One of these signs is the fact that the same movement which effected the elevation of what is called the lowest class in the state, assumed in literature a very marked and as benign an aspect. Instead of the sublime and the beautiful, the near, the low, the common was explored and poetized.

By now, I realize, it is extremely difficult to attend to the meaning of these too familiar propositions. But they embody a conception of language and of literature in relation to the politics of democracy which points directly toward Mailer's defense, in our time, of obscenity. Whatever we may say about Emerson's failure to practice what he preached, his commitment *in theory* was unequivocal. He was endorsing a literature rooted in the common life, and in a language closer to American speech than to the idiom of Augustan gentility still associated with literature by his educated contemporaries.

The literature of the poor, the feelings of the child, the philosophy of the street, the meaning of household life, are the topics of the time. It is a great stride. It is a sign—is it not?—of new vigor when the extremities are made active, when currents of warm life run into the hands and the feet. I ask not for the great, the remote, the romantic; . . . I embrace the common, I explore and sit at the feet of the familiar, the low. . . . This perception of the worth of the vulgar is fruitful in discoveries.[9]

Later, during the slavery crisis of the 1850s, Emerson had the melancholy opportunity to apply his theory of the homologous corruption of language and of politics to the notorious case of Daniel Webster. For Emerson as for many other New Englanders, the senator was a political hero—a great American statesman whose eloquence was thought to have derived from profound integrity of mind and spirit. No small part of Webster's reputation rested upon an elaborate, Ciceronian oratorical style—the kind of public rhetoric echoed in the periodic sentences of the Kennedy inaugural address, with its trumpeting summons: "not as a call to bear arms, though arms we need—not as a call to battle, though embattled we are." Here is a sentence from the peroration of Webster's famous reply to Hayne (1830), a favorite set piece for declamation by schoolchildren:

> I have not accustomed myself to hang over the precipice of disunion, to see whether, with my short sight, I can fathom the depth of the abyss below; nor could I regard him as a safe counsellor in the affairs of this government, whose thoughts should be mainly bent on considering, not how the Union may best be preserved, but how tolerable might be the condition of the people when it should be broken up and destroyed.[10]

A few sentences later Webster concluded with an apostrophe to the flag, a cardinal symbol of civil religion, that remains one of the purplest passages in the annals of American oratory. "When my eyes shall be turned to behold for the last time the sun in heaven," he says, "may I not see him shining on the broken and dishonored fragments of a once glorious Union. . . ."

> Let their last feeble and lingering glance rather behold the glorious ensign of the republic, now known and honored throughout the earth, still full high advanced, its arms and trophies streaming in their original lustre, not a stripe erased or polluted, nor a single star obscured, bearing for its motto. . . .

And so on and on, rising in the end to the ringing "Liberty *and* Union, now and for ever, one and inseparable!" Many of Emerson's contemporaries equated this orotund style with eloquence, signifying that the speaker had won access to a plane of higher truth.

But then, in 1850, Webster had thrown his whole weight (as Emerson saw it) on the side of slavery, and had helped to ease the passage of the odious Fugitive Slave Law. Emerson's reaction is particularly pertinent here because Webster, one of the high priests of American civil religion, in effect had sacralized the very idea of the Republic. In order to justify his support of compromise with the slave power, he made preservation of the Union his primary commitment, and in the showpiece speech of March 7, 1850, he mobilized all of his rhetorical ingenuity in its behalf. But Emerson did not share the general admiration for Webster's performance, as he explained in his own speech on "The Fugitive Slave Law" in 1854. In Webster's earlier speeches, Emerson said, the senator had earned the nation's gratitude as one "who speaks well for the right—who translates truth into language entirely plain and clear!" But on March 7 Webster evidently had abandoned that standard. As always, he had displayed literary skill, clear logic, even eloquence, but these were relatively unimportant as compared with the fact that he ended up on the wrong side.

> Nobody doubts that Daniel Webster could make a good speech. Nobody doubts that there were good and plausible things to be said on the part of the South. But this is not a question of ingenuity, not a question of syllogisms, but of sides. *How came he there?*[11]

The answer, Emerson suggests, is that he came there because of a defect in character. Webster lacked "what is better than intellect, and the source of its health," namely, the quality of thought which derives from the heart. In his rousing peroration Webster had found it possible to make statements like this: "We have a great, popular, constitutional government, guarded by law and by judicature, and defended by the affections of the whole people. . . . In all its history it has been beneficent; it has trodden down no man's liberty; it has crushed no State. Its daily respiration is liberty and patriotism. . . ."[12] With this sort of passage in view, Emerson argued that Webster had exhibited a lack of "moral sensibility."

> There are always texts and thoughts and arguments. But it is the genius and temper of the man which decides whether he will stand

for right or for might. Who doubts the power of any fluent debater to defend either of our political parties, or any client in our courts? . . . But the question which History will ask is broader. In the final hour, when he was forced by the peremptory necessity of the closing armies to take a side—did he take the part of great principles, the side of humanity and justice, or the side of abuse and oppression and chaos?

Although Emerson's charge against Webster may strike us as well founded, it is not at all clear that the senator had betrayed the principles of civil religion as Professor Bellah defines them. Emerson held Webster to the test of "humanity and justice," but according to Bellah these are not among the first principles of the dominant American form of civil religion. "The God of the civil religion . . . ," he writes, "is . . . much more related to order, law, and right than to salvation and love." Appropriately enough, the God of this nation-state "is actively interested in history, with a special concern for America."[13] The point is that worship of such a God is easily reconciled with a shallow kind of political pragmatism entailing a commitment to law and order, to the imperatives of "history," whatever that means, and to the corporate well-being of the Republic. The question of the "right" for which this God allegedly stands, however, is more ambiguous. The slavery crisis had split the concept of right in America down the middle, separating the right of property from those other rights—life, liberty, and the pursuit of happiness—to which the revolution also had been committed. It seemed to Emerson that Webster had come down on the side of the right to own slaves.

But it is necessary to add that Emerson did not see Webster's defection as a special case. On the contrary, his want of moral sensibility struck Emerson as symptomatic of the condition of many thinking Americans. Webster, in effect, was a representative man, and what he represented is that "prevalence of secondary desires" (for riches, pleasure, power, and praise) over "simplicity of character and the sovereignty of ideas" which marks the simultaneous corruption of language and of politics. Why was this happening to American democracy? Why did educated men so easily relinquish their moral judgment? Emerson's answer to that question is stun-

ningly relevant—and poignant—in the era of the Vietnam war
and the Nixon administration.

> The way in which the country was dragged to consent to this, and
> the disastrous defection (on the miserable cry of Union) of the men
> of letters, of the colleges, of educated men, nay, of some preachers
> of religion—was the darkest passage in the history. It showed that
> our prosperity had hurt us, and that we could not be shocked by
> crime. It showed that the old religion and the sense of right had
> faded and gone out; that while we reckoned ourselves a highly
> cultivated nation, our bellies had run away with out brains, and the
> principles of culture and progress did not exist.[14]

But the following year Emerson was compelled to admit that
the principles of a native culture had not entirely disappeared
into the great American belly. One day in July 1855 he received
an unsolicited package containing the work of an unknown poet
who spoke a language as different from Webster's as could be
imagined. Here are some of the lines Emerson must have read
in the first edition of Walt Whitman's *Leaves of Grass*:

> Walt Whitman, an American, one of the roughs, a kosmos,
> Disorderly fleshy and sensual . . . eating drinking and breeding,
> No sentimentalist . . . no stander above men and women or apart
>   from them . . . no more modest than immodest.

> Unscrew the locks from the doors!
> Unscrew the doors themselves from their jambs!

> Whoever degrades another degrades me . . . and whatever is done
>   or said returns at last to me,
> And whatever I do or say I also return.
> . . . .

> Through me forbidden voices,
> Voices of sexes and lusts . . . voices veiled, and I remove the veil,
> Voices indecent by me clarified and transfigured.

> I do not press my finger across my mouth,
> I keep as delicate around the bowels as around the head and heart,
> Copulation is no more rank to me than death is.

> I believe in the flesh and the appetites,
> Seeing hearing and feeling are miracles, and each part and
>   tag of me is a miracle.

Divine I am inside and out, and I make holy whatever I touch
      or am touched from;
The scent of these arm-pits is aroma finer than prayer,
This head is more than churches or bibles or creeds.[15]

Whitman, as we know, had been inspired by Emerson's conception of the poet and of poetic language. "Thought," Emerson had said, "makes everything fit for use. The vocabulary of an omniscient man would embrace words and images excluded from polite conversation. What would be base, or even obscene, to the obscene, becomes illustrious, spoken in a new connection of thought."[16] But Whitman had carried this principle much further than Emerson had imagined a poet should or could. He had taken a long step toward exemplifying what Mailer was to call the "reductive philosophy" of the common man, a defiant use of forbidden, indecent language which "looked," as Mailer put it, to restore the hard edge of proportion to overblown values.

Yet it cannot be said that Whitman was rejecting the idea of an American civil religion. Rather, he was attempting to relocate it, to identify the vitality and uniqueness in our national life—perhaps even the possibility of transcendence—with the "disorderly fleshy and sensual" as against the refined, polite, and conventional. This symbolic relocation of the sacred is very much like the process Mailer was to employ in our time; its goal was the emergence of a vernacular civil religion capable of supplanting the official creed. Although Whitman celebrated American democracy, his democratic God is not the God usually invoked by our presidents on inauguration day. Whitman's is a populist deity unsympathetic with a hierarchical social order; if he can be said to have a "special concern for America" it is because America is perceived as the embodiment of a universal, international spirit of egalitarian fraternity. So far as the Brooklyn "rough" who speaks for Whitman believes in a civil religion, it has about it a flavor of undiscriminating, irreverent, sans-culottish narcissism:

Who goes there! hankering, gross, mystical, nude?
How is it I extract strength from the beef I eat?

What is a man anyhow? What am I? and what are you?
All I mark as my own you shall offset it with your own,
Else it were time lost listening to me.

I do not snivel that snivel the world over,
That months are vacuums and the ground but wallow
            and filth,
That life is a suck and a sell, and nothing remains at
            the end but threadbare crepe and tears.

Whimpering and truckling fold with powers for invalids
            . . . conformity goes to the fourth-removed,
I cock my hat as I please indoors or out.

Shall I pray? Shall I venerate and be ceremonious?
I have pried through the strata and analyzed to a hair,
And counselled with doctors and calculated close and
            found no sweeter fat than sticks to my own bones.[17]

In 1855 it would have been difficult to imagine a viewpoint (or a tone) better calculated to make Americans think of Walt Whitman, in Santayana's phrase, as "an unpalatable person." Only foreigners seemed to accept the notion, said Santayana, that Whitman's undiscriminating poetry might be lending expression to the spirit and the inarticulate principles really animating American society.[18] But in retrospect it seems more likely that the foreigners, like Whitman himself, had misjudged the majority of Americans. The poet had hoped that his countrymen would absorb him as affectionately as he had absorbed his country, but in fact they preferred the genteel and far more conventional verses of Henry Wadsworth Longfellow. By the same token they preferred the idea of joining the polite middle class to the Whitmanian notion of remaining permanently among the uncouth, free-spirited, unacquisitive "roughs." Perhaps this is only to say that Whitman had ignored, or underestimated, the attractiveness of upward social mobility in an expanding capitalist society.

After the Civil War Whitman experienced a disillusion with the moral sensibility of the nation not unlike Emerson's during the slavery crisis. Whitman's tortured essay "Democratic Vistas" (1871) surely is one of the most searching examinations of civil religion by an American writer. That a "religious element" necessarily lies at the core of democracy, Whitman had no doubt; but in America he was forced to admit that capacity for belief in the potential virtue and good sense of the mass of men had somehow failed to develop. What he found, instead of a democratic faith, comports with Emerson's earlier image of a nation whose bellies had run away with its brains:

> I say we had best look our times and lands searchingly in the face, like a physician diagnosing some deep disease. Never was there, perhaps, more hollowness at heart than at present, and here in the United States. Genuine belief seems to have left us. The underlying principles of the States are not honestly believed in, (for all this hectic glow, and these melo-dramatic screamings,) nor is humanity itself believ'd in. What penetrating eye does not everywhere see through the mask? The spectacle is appalling. We live in an atmosphere of hypocrisy throughout. The men believe not in the women, nor the women in the men. A scornful superciliousness rules in literature. . . . A lot of churches, sects, etc., the most dismal phantoms I know, usurp the name of religion. . . . The depravity of the business classes of our country is not less than has been supposed, but infinitely greater.[19]

The ultimate standard of national well-being invoked by Whitman in "Democratic Vistas" is not the standard implied by the genteel, or presidential, civil religion. It is not the degree of "order, law, and right" achieved by the Republic; nor is it the nation's corporate power or prosperity—though Whitman assumes that a certain modest level of affluence is a prerequisite for civic health. No, for Whitman the real test is the kind of men and women, hence the quality of thought and feeling, the society nurtures. "Are there, indeed," he asks, "*men* here worthy the name? . . . Are there perfect women, to match the generous material luxuriance? . . . Are there arts worthy freedom and a rich people?" And then, with a clear implication that he is asking the crucial question: "Is there a great moral and religious civilization—the only justification of a great material one?" The question merits special emphasis, because it so often is present if unexpressed—veiled behind the contemptuous attitude held by American writers toward the officially sanctioned civil religion. It is a question, moreover, to which the rhetoric of most presidential addresses hardly provides an adequate answer. Whitman's own answer, in the very next sentence, anticipates T. S. Eliot's powerful twentieth-century image of urban-industrial culture as an arid waste land. "Confess," says

Whitman, "that to severe eyes, using the moral microscope upon humanity, a sort of dry and flat Sahara appears, these cities, crowded with petty grotesques, malformations, phantoms, playing meaningless antics. Confess that everywhere, in shop, street, church, theatre, bar-room, official chair, are pervading flippancy and vulgarity, low cunning, infidelity. . . ."[20]

In canvassing possible alternatives to this profane spirit, Whitman did not look to the upper stratum of culture. In the judgment of a poet who had begun his career by boasting, "I too am not a bit tamed . . . / I sound my barbaric yawp over the roofs of the world," the American literary scene in 1870 was contemptible. "Do you call those genteel little creatures American poets?" he asked. At least this much seemed clear: what was needed was not more polish, more cultivation, or more preachment from on high. In our times, he said,

> . . . refinement and delicatesse are not only attended to sufficiently, but threaten to eat us up, like a cancer. Already, the democratic genius watches, ill-pleased, these tendencies. Provision for a little healthy rudeness, savage virtue, justification of what one has in one's self, whatever it is, is demanded.

So far from attributing vulgarity to an excess of democracy, Whitman felt that it derived from too little. "I should demand a program of culture," he said, ". . . not for a single class alone, or for the parlors or lecture-rooms, but with an eye to the practical life, the west, the working-men, the facts of farms and jack-planes and engineers, and of the broad range of women also of the middle and working strata. . . ." Here Whitman seems to recognize that the vernacular, as a medium of expression, can be effective only as part of a larger "program of culture." Literature alone cannot do the job. This is a fact that many of our writers, including Norman Mailer, often have tended to forget. Whitman affirms the need for a "little healthy rudeness," not as an end in itself, but as part of the effort to achieve an essentially classless culture. In effect he is looking for a manifestation of the vernacular spirit that arises from an egalitarian way of life, and he has a pretty good hunch about where it might be found.[21]

> Today, doubtless, the infant genius of American poetic expression, (eluding those highly-refined imported and gilt-edged themes . . .),

lies sleeping far away, happily unrecognized and uninjur'd by the coteries, the art-writers, the talkers and critics of the saloons, or the lecturers in the colleges—lies sleeping, aside, unrecking itself, in some western idiom, or native Michigan or Tennessee repartee, or stump-speech . . . , or in some slang or local song or allusion of the Manhattan, Boston, Philadelphia or Baltimore mechanic. . . . Rude and coarse nursing-beds, these; but only from such beginnings and stocks, indigenous here, may haply arrive, be grafted, and sprout, in time, flowers of genuine American aroma, and fruits truly and fully our own.[22]

In retrospect anyone familiar with American literature may be expected to identify this rude genius of the native idiom. By now Mark Twain's preeminence in shaping the basic colloquial style of modern American writing has been universally acknowledged. But what is less fully appreciated is the extent to which he seized upon the vernacular, and the viewpoint it embodied, as (to use Norman Mailer's term once again) the medium of a "reductive philosophy." What delighted Mark Twain was the opportunity afforded by Huck Finn's speech, like the obscene talk of Mailer's G.I.s, to deflate overblown values. The very essence of Mark Twain's humor derived from the contrast between the boy's rude idiom and the kind of piety and pretension associated with polite civil religion. Consider an example from a decisive episode (chap. 31) in *Huckleberry Finn*. The boy is having one of his periodic spells of anxiety about what might happen when the word got around that he had "helped a nigger to get his freedom." "The more I studied about this," he says, "the more my conscience went to grinding me, and the more wicked and low-down and ornery I got to feeling." Henry Nash Smith has explained what happens next.[23] As the inner dialogue continues, what we hear sounds less and less like the boy's usual voice and more and more like the stock cadence and diction of a preacher. It is as if the dominant religious culture had quite literally invaded his consciousness, supplanting his own sensibility, and transforming the very structure of his sentences.

And at last, when it hit me all of a sudden that here was the plain hand of Providence slapping me in the face and letting me know my wickedness was being watched all the time from up there in heaven, whilst I was stealing a poor old woman's nigger that hadn't

ever done me no harm, and now was showing me there's One that's
always on the lookout, and ain't agoing to allow no such miserable
doings to go only just so fur and no further, I most dropped in my
tracks I was so scared.[24]

Of course it may be objected that the voice we are hearing is
not, strictly speaking, that of the *civil* religion but of the organized
church. In a sense that is true, but the two are not so easily sepa-
rated. As Robert Bellah says, civil religion in America "borrowed
selectively from the religious tradition in such a way that the
average American saw no conflict between the two."[25] In this case,
moreover, the guilt that Huck feels is stirred in part by his violation
of the civil law. In his rudimentary sense of things, obeying the
law and observing the rituals of the church are equally important
prerequisites for social respectability. To be accepted by those he
calls the "quality" one should pray and one should respect the
sanctity of property in slaves.

But Huck's surrender to this conformist impulse is only tempo-
rary. No sooner has he written the note to Miss Watson betraying
Jim than he gets to thinking about their trip down the river, reliv-
ing it in his mind, recalling specific images of their shared life on
the raft, so that he *sees* Jim before him "all the time, in the day,
and in the night-time, sometimes moonlight, sometimes storms,
and we are floating along, talking, singing, and laughing." Here
Mark Twain brings the reductive power of the vernacular into
play, recording the boy's mental process as he discovers the disparity between the learned abstractions of the genteel culture
("there's One that's always on the lookout" etc.) and the sensory
details of the downstream journey with his black companion. As
his feeling of loyalty to Jim revives, he reverts to his native idiom.
What is happening, in Emerson's language, is that Huck now
"pierces" the "rotten diction" of law and order he had adopted
in a spasm of guilt, and he does so in precisely the way Emerson
had recommended: *by fastening words again to visible things.* The
process by which he reverses himself can be described in psychological or linguistic terms, but in the dramatic unfolding of the
episode the crux of the matter is political. At the critical moment
everything depends on Huck's choice of sides. Which side is he

on? "I was a trembling," he says, "because I'd got to decide, forever, betwixt two things, and I knowed it." The famous decision ("All right, then, I'll *go* to hell") is a pointed repudiation of the civil religion of the old South, with its racist God and its continuous hold on the people long after the Civil War.

Like Mark Twain, whose seminal influence he acknowledged, Ernest Hemingway delighted in the specificity and the deflationary power of the vernacular. In a sense his work stands midway between Mark Twain's and Mailer's. By the time he began writing, after World War I, American civil religion was becoming closely identified with the kind of bellicose nationalism so familiar today. In *A Farewell to Arms* (1929) the narrator, Lieutenant Henry, is provoked to a long rumination on the subject by the passing remark of Gino, his patriotic Italian comrade. "What has been done this summer," Gino says, "cannot have been done in vain."

> I did not say anything. I was always embarrassed by the words sacred, glorious, and sacrifice and the expression in vain. We had heard them, sometimes standing in the rain almost out of earshot, so that only the shouted words came through, and had read them, on proclamations that were slapped up by bill-posters over other proclamations, now for a long time, and I had seen nothing sacred, and the things that were glorious had no glory and the sacrifices were like the stockyards at Chicago if nothing was done with the meat except to bury it. There were many words that you could not stand to hear and finally only the names of places had dignity. Certain numbers were the same way and certain dates and these with the names of the places were all you could say and have them mean anything. *Abstract words such as glory, honor, courage or hallow were obscene beside the concrete names of villages, the numbers of roads, the names of rivers, the numbers of regiments and the dates.*[26]

This passage points directly toward Mailer's argument on behalf of obscenity. To Hemingway's Lieutenant Henry the sacralizing abstractions of the civil religion—*glory, hallow, sacrifice,* and *sacred*—are themselves "obscene." In view of his commitment to realistic dialogue, Hemingway obviously would have liked to record the characteristic response of soldiers to such indecent pieties. What makes them indecent, of course, is that they bear so little relation to the facts. Or, to put it more bluntly, they are used to tell lies. They exemplify the simultaneous corruption of language and of politics, hence they call forth the combat soldier's talent for obscenity. But in 1929 it was not yet possible for a writer to get dirty words in print. In theory, to be sure, the vernacular style always had aimed at linguistic verisimilitude, but in practice it never had reached that goal. Only recently John Seelye has demonstrated, by rewriting *Huckleberry Finn*, how much damage the conventional nineteenth-century standards of propriety had done to that great book. By endowing the fourteen-year-old boy with a natural interest in sex, and with an adequately indecent vocabulary, Seelye shows that Mark Twain's narrator is simply too nice to be wholly credible.[27] Yet we know that Mark Twain, according to the standards of his day, was something of a bold innovator. But then we should not forget that as recently as 1940 Ernest Hemingway had to resort to the most outlandish contrivances (" 'Oh, obscenity them,' Primitivo said with an absolute devoutness of blasphemy . . . . 'Oh, God and the Virgin, obscenity them in the milk of their filth.' ") to render the speech of combatants in the Spanish Civil War.[28]

But this is not the place to survey the erosion of restraints upon the printing of hitherto unprintable words since World War II. Suffice it to say that in the United States the virtual disappearance of restrictions, at least with respect to imaginative writing in book form, coincided with the civil crises of the 1960s. The new radical politics and its affiliate, the cultural underground, gave a strong push to the old campaign for linguistic freedom. This minority of the disaffected included, along with young people and blacks, a large segment of the academic and literary communities. Like Hemingway's Lieutenant Henry, moreover, adherents of the civil rights and anti-Vietnam War movements were repelled by the mendacious language used to justify national policies. (This of course included the rhetoric used by presidents of the United States.) They felt that it was obscene, and they responded by increasing the strident vulgarity of their own language. A close study of linguistic patterns in this period would supply abundant evidence, I believe, for the symbiotic relation between the sanctimonious rhetoric of national celebration and obscenity. It is worth recalling that the Berkeley Free Speech movement, which marked an important stage in the emergence of student radicalism, came to an end as a somewhat feckless campaign to legitimate the use of dirty words. According to sociolinguists, every society probably has at least three linguistic style levels: (1) formal or polite; (2) colloquial; and (3) slang or vulgar.[29] During the 1960s the radicals used an increasingly vulgar language to counter what they regarded as an increasingly meretricious (root meaning: whorish) polite language. In the underground press, in slogans displayed on placards carried in demonstrations, and in their everyday speech, many of the militants felt obliged to use words like "shit" and "fuck" as often as possible.

But their promiscuous use of these once forbidden words points to a difficulty with the argument on behalf of obscenity with which I must deal. It seems obvious that in many instances this verbal reflex is of a piece with such other expressions of adolescent rage as trashing, ripping off, and vandalism. It is truly characteristic, though not in the exact sense in which he used it, of what Lenin called "infantile leftism." But then some would say that the use of obscenity is never anything more than a childish, trivial, and ineffectual gesture of defiance. To make a habit of linguistic stridency is always self-defeating. After a barrier of convention has been crossed often enough, the excluded idiom quickly loses its power to shock, as decreed by the law of diminishing returns. The stale, repetitious "pig language" of some sixties' radicals is a good illustration. But there is an even more serious problem here. In a sense this criticism of the use of obscenity is akin to the one that Santayana leveled against other vernacular modes of resistance to the genteel culture. Referring to humorists like Mark Twain, he noted that they were unable to abandon the tradition they mocked. Although they were skillful in pointing to what contradicted the genteel ethos in the facts, he said, they had "nothing solid to put in its place."[30] Cannot the same charge be brought against writers like Norman Mailer, who rely upon obscenity to oppose the vapid idiom of the official American civil religion? Do they have anything more solid than a few dirty words to put in its place?

Let me say at once that my answer is a qualified yes, they do.

They do have something more than a vocabulary to offer, though whether that something can be called "solid" is another question. The point, in any case, is that no serious claim on behalf of the vernacular (or the obscene) can rest solely upon the power of the words in and of themselves. It is not a particular language in itself that matters, but rather, the ethos or system of value it embodies; the vernacular is prized because it represents a tacit alternative to the ethos inherent in the language used by celebrants of the genteel civil religion. The vernacular, in other words, derives a large part of its power from the felt presence of its opposite. As Norman Mailer says, in the anecdote about the Southern cracker in the rice paddy, the common man's use of obscenity is a feature of his humor, and his humor in turn is an expression of his "reductive philosophy." What the G.I. in the story reduces when he exclaims, "Man, I just managed to take me a noble shit," is everything the word "noble" implies about a hierarchical system based upon arbitrary rank. (Once the target had been the feudal system; here it is the military system of the United States.) In the old sense "noble" referred to exalted, lofty ideals detached from the earthy facts of the common life. The humor here consists in the G.I.'s casual, economical transfer of such grandeur as nobility connotes to a physical act as commonplace yet universal as an everyday bowel movement. Incidentally, the idea of making nobility a modifier of excrement is a variant of a device often favored by Mark Twain as, for example, when he named the two scoundrels in *Huckleberry Finn* the King and the Duke.

In each case reduction is merely the first stage in a complicated process. "What was magnificent about the word shit," Mailer says, "is that it enabled you to use the word noble again. . . ." Similarly, the vernacular perspective from which *Huckleberry Finn* is written has the effect of relocating the positive attributes of nobility. It removes the qualities of magnanimity and greatness from people upon whom the title "king" or "duke" formerly had been conferred, and it bestows them upon social riffraff like the illiterate son of the town drunk. It is worth recalling that when *Huckleberry Finn* was published conservative critics were alarmed by its potentially subversive power; they saw it as a threat to values "cherished by accredited spokesmen for American society," and they attacked it for "irreverence" as well as for "coarseness."[31] In spite of such attacks, however, the vernacular style was to become a dominant—probably *the* dominant—style of modern American literature.[32] Far from being idiosyncratic, in fact, Mailer's high estimate of the American vulgate as a literary medium has been endorsed, in practice if not in theory, by many of our most admired twentieth-century writers. It would not be difficult to illustrate this fact by citing passages from the work of, say, Faulkner, Salinger, Ellison, Williams (both Tennessee and William Carlos), O'Connor, or Burroughs. It seems obvious, moreover, that all of them turned to the vernacular partly with a view to locating an alternative to the dominant genteel culture.

In other words, the linguistic process exemplified by Mailer's story about "noble shit" has for its aim regeneration as well as reduction. Obscenity is not merely a linguistic solvent for the old, threadbare national religion, it is a means of generating a new religion. In *The Armies of the Night* Mailer manifestly hoped, by using this method, to renew a feeling for his country akin to what we usually call patriotism. It is surprising to discover that a number of other disaffected or radical writers of the 1960s shared this motive. In the work of Paul Goodman, for example, one can hear (along with the outrage directed against the "organized system") a lament for old-fashioned patriotic feelings.

> Our case is astounding. For the first time in recorded history, the mention of country, community, place has lost its power to animate. Nobody but a scoundrel even tries it. Our rejection of false patriotism is, of course, itself a badge of honor. But the positive loss is tragic and I cannot resign myself to it. A man has only one life and if during it he has no great environment, no community, he has been irreparably robbed of a human right. This loss is especially damaging in growing up. . . .[33]

Susan Sontag was provoked to similar reflections by her discovery, during a trip to Hanoi, of the "essential purity" of Vietnamese patriotism. The contrast with her country was discouraging.

> Ever since World War II, the rhetoric of patriotism in the United States has been in the hands of reactionaries and yahoos; by monopolizing it, they have succeeded in rendering the idea of loving

America synonymous with bigotry, provincialism, and selfishness. But perhaps one shouldn't give up so easily. . . . Probably no serious radical movement has any future in America unless it can revalidate the tarnished idea of patriotism.[34]

And most recently John Schaar, a political theorist who would like to see a revitalization of radical politics in America, took up the same theme.[35] His elaborately wrought "case for patriotism" is particularly relevant here because, in developing his argument, he finds it necessary to draw a sharp line between an acceptable form of national affirmation and the Rousseauian mode of civil religion. The kind of patriotism Schaar advocates derives from Lincoln's idea of America as a covenanted Republic. We are a nation formed by a covenant, that is, by dedication to the libertarian and egalitarian principles of the Declaration of Independence, and those principles comprise the standard by which we must judge ourselves. Lincoln would consider the nation to be righteous and to deserve being honored "only insofar as it honors the covenant." This conception is markedly different from Rousseau's civil religion. It provides a moral standard for judging national behavior, whereas Rousseau designed his religion chiefly in order to induce the citizen to venerate the nation and, in his own words, to make him "love his duties."[36] In America, Schaar believes, the Rousseau-like conception "drove out" Lincoln's, an observation that helps to account for the antipatriotic tone adopted by so many of the writers I have been discussing.[37] What they wanted, it seems evident, was a view of their country which would enable them to judge it as well as to venerate it.

In any event, the desire of writers for a renewal of some form of patriotism is a significant feature of the ambiguous political context in which Mailer formulated his rationale for obscenity. Like Goodman, Sontag, and Schaar, he wanted to "love something in the country," and the most likely thing he could find was the vernacular of the common man—a language as far removed as possible from the language of national celebration. Up to a point, it must be admitted, American politics of the 1960s lent credence to such an identification of uncivil language with radical protest. The conservative backlash at the end of the decade was marked by a new and more stringent effort to stop the outpouring of obscenity associated with long hair, black militants, Whitmanesque lifestyles, unorthodox sexual behavior, and radicalism. The 1973 decision of the Supreme Court, with its provision for a lax form of "local option" in the control of indecent works of art and literature, would seem to belong to this reaction against the radical counter-culture. In rejecting the possibility of any hypothetical definition of obscenity for the nation as a whole, the Court urged juries to apply "contemporary community standards"—a phrase that carries more than a hint of deference toward a "middle American" view-point. From the vantage of the articulate radicals and conservatives of the period, then, the political significance of indecent language would seem to be fairly clear.

But when we extend this line of reflection beyond organized politics to Mailer's "common man," the presumed affinity between users of the vernacular and radicalism quickly evaporates. During the 1960s men like the "skinny Southern cracker" of *The Armies of the Night* were more than likely to be followers of Richard Nixon if not George Wallace. Cannot the same be said of most of the male peer groups, the men in gyms, locker rooms, and bar-racks whose rhetorical virtuosity Mailer admires? Their speech may exhibit the vitality of the American vernacular, but it is unlikely that their political attitudes bear any resemblance to those of Emerson, Whitman, Lincoln, or Mailer. On the contrary, they may be expected to assume, along with today's conservatives, that obscene language is for men only, and that to use it in public (where "ladies" are present) is a badge of political disreputability. Their egalitarianism is vitiated, among other things, by the sexist prejudices that usually accompany the use of obscenity as a short-hand for male bonding. They are a long way from the viewpoint one would associate with a truly democratic culture. To say this is only to repeat the point made earlier about Whitman's failure to win a mass audience. The readers he hoped to reach, so far as they read any poet, preferred Longfellow's work. They had no desire to identify with Whitman's crude working-class heroes; they were willing, if not eager, to adopt genteel values (including polite language) as a necessary condition of upward social and economic mobility. To pretend that today most Americans are free (or ever have been) to espouse a view of language like Mailer's is to ignore the extent to which language behavior, like all other cultural activity, is shaped by social structure.

And yet, having said all this, it is still possible to discern the tacit alternative to the reigning culture, including polite civil religion, embodied in the vernacular strain in American writing. It may not be a "solid" alternative, as Santayana suggested, in the sense that "solid" implies a firm basis in social and political reality, but it is philosophically coherent nevertheless. The first principle of the vernacular ethos is radical egalitarianism. It takes seriously the basic proposition to which the nation, as Lincoln phrased it, had dedicated itself in 1776. What is more (a second principle), the vernacular style tends to associate egalitarian principles of justice and of governmental authority with a forthright recognition of all the physical aspects of human existence. As Whitman said, the person who is "no stander above men and women or apart from them" does not press his fingers across his mouth. He does not deny, he does not avert his attention from, any bodily function, including sexuality and death. Writers have a duty to liberate culture from all the pruderies: "voices indecent *by me* clarified and transfigured." And, finally, the third basic principle may be the most important in distinguishing the vernacular ethos from genteel civil religion and from the dominant tradition in Western theology—the religion of the churches. So far as it lends credence to spiritual experience, to any possibility of transcendence, the vernacular locates that experience in this life, here and now. It recognizes no distinct realm of the spirit, either here or beyond this world.

Whether we regard such an ethos as secular or religious is finally, I suspect, a semantic question. The significant fact, in any case, is that many of our most gifted writers have been committed to it, and in varying degrees they all have been compelled to recognize America's failure to develop a vernacular culture. Their increasingly strident use of colloquial language, including obscenity, is in large measure attributable to that failure. As the gap between the rhetoric of our democratic civil religion and our collective behavior has widened, they have resorted to the forbidden language as a kind of literary shock therapy. Like so many features of American life these days, however, there is something of a desperate, end-of-

the-line quality about the resort to dirty words. Once the obsceni-
ties have made their way into polite letters, what then? What is
to be the next phase in the development of this vernacular strain
in American writing? To ask these questions is to evoke what Frank
Kermode calls a "sense of an ending." It is as if our writers are
rushing, along with the Republic itself, toward that act of judgment
which Lincoln held forth as an indispensable feature of a genuine
civil religion. In conclusion, therefore, I want to cite what is
probably the most affecting, and the most explicitly religious,
evocation of this egalitarian commitment in our literature—one
that forms the basis of a prophetic judgment.

The passage is from chapter 26 of *Moby Dick*. Ishmael, the
narrator, has been commenting upon the fortitude of Starbuck,
the first mate, and about a certain "immaculate manliness" he
associates with him. But he is quick to dissociate that quality from
any conception of rank, hierarchy, or socially defined nobility.
"This august dignity I treat of," the narrator says, "is not the
dignity of kings and robes, but that abounding dignity which has
no robed investiture." The source of this dignity is at once religious
and political. It radiates from God: "The great God absolute! The
centre and circumference of all democracy! His omnipresence, our
divine equality!" Here again a kind of "reductive philosophy" is
at work; divinity is an attribute of equality and not the other way
around. Divine equality! It is an ultimate moral principle, and
although Melville does not write in the vernacular here, a rationale
for what can only be called the vernacular perspective is implicit
in his appeal to the idea of equality as a sanction for writing a
special kind of book. It is a book that imputes high qualities,
hitherto reserved for the nobility, to ordinary seamen.

> If, then, to meanest mariners, and renegades and castaways, I shall
> hereafter ascribe high qualities, though dark; weave round them
> tragic graces; if even the most mournful, perchance the most abased,
> among them all, shall at times lift himself to the exalted mounts; if
> I shall touch that workman's arm with some ethereal light; if I shall
> spread a rainbow over his disastrous set of sun; then against all
> mortal critics bear me out in it, thou just Spirit of Equality, which
> has spread one royal mantle of humanity over all my kind! Bear
> me out in it, thou great democratic God! who didst not refuse to

the swart convict, Bunyan, the pale, poetic pearl; Thou who didst clothe with doubly hammered leaves of finest gold, the stumped and paupered arm of old Cervantes; Thou who didst pick up Andrew Jackson from the pebbles; who didst hurl him upon a warhorse; who didst thunder him higher than a throne! Thou who, in all Thy mighty earthly marchings, ever cullest Thy selectest champions from the kingly commons; bear me out in it, O God!

Melville's fervent apostrophe to the God of equality lends force to both his hope and his fear for American democracy. Not only does it justify him in attributing noble qualities, even a capacity to evoke tragic emotions, to low characters, but it also sustains his conception of the terrible end of their journey. It is a basis for the prophetic judgment implicit in the final destruction of the *Pequod*. So far from respecting the principles of divine equality, Captain Ahab is an arrogant, contemptuous manipulator of his crew. He is driven by irrational motives which stem from a life-time of repression. In *Moby Dick* the defeat of democratic hopes is related directly to the psychic and bodily disharmonies reulting from a way of life compulsively devoted to aggressive, competitive achievement, in this case killing whales for profit. The psychopathology of the Ahabian quest is pertinent here because it comports with the association of egalitarian values and the liberation from sexual taboos that had been implicit in the vernacular perspective since Emerson's time. It therefore helps to place the argument on behalf of obscenity in historical perspective. As Mailer has said, "the obsession of many of us with scatology is attached to a disputed communication within us, within our bodies."[38]

For all of these reasons, therefore, it is not wholly fanciful to think of Melville's apostrophe to the great democratic God as having been delivered on behalf of a long line of American writers from Emerson to Whitman, from Mark Twain to Hemingway to Norman Mailer. Their work does offer us something to put in the place of a genteel culture and a complacent civil religion. It is an unsteady, intermittent apprehension of equality as an ultimate good. Of course Santayana was correct, this alternative is not very solid. How could it be? It is a mere principle, or a vision of an ideal condition, and the job of incorporating it into our institutions, first undertaken in 1776, has scarcely begun.

NOTES

1. *The Armies of the Night* (New York, 1968), p. 47.

2. Bellah's paper was delivered at a *Daedalus* conference on American Religion in May 1966. It is reprinted as the first essay in this volume.

3. *The Armies of the Night*, 48. For an interesting discussion of this passage, in somewhat different terms, see Richard Poirier, *Norman Mailer* (New York, 1972), pp. 92ff.

4. "The Genteel Tradition in American Philosophy," *The Genteel Tradition, Nine Essays by George Santayana*, ed., Douglas L. Wilson, (Cambridge, Mass., 1967), pp. 37-64.

5. "Nature" (1836), in *The Complete Essays . . . of Ralph Waldo Emerson*, ed. Brooks Atkinson (New York, Modern Library Edition, 1940), p. 17.

6. *The Collected Essays . . . of George Orwell*, 4 vols. (New York, 1968), Vol. IV, p. 137.

7. The distinction between a corrupt language used by writers who are under the sway of "secondary desires" and a vital language used by writers who "hold primarily on nature" is grounded in a more basic distinction between two modes of perception that Emerson drew from a variety of sources including the ideas of Wordsworth, Carlyle, Coleridge (all probably traceable to Kantian philosophy), but also (by a kind of osmotic process) from his New England theological forebears. Jonathan Edwards, for example, held that God had made man capable of a "twofold understanding or knowledge of the good," one that was "merely speculative and notional," the other that consisted of "the sense of the heart." The former was an abstract kind of knowledge, whereas the latter was grounded in sense experience and therefore engaged "the will, or inclination, or heart." "There is a difference," Edwards wrote, "between having a rational judgment that honey is sweet, and having a sense of its sweetness. A man may have the former, that knows not how honey tastes; but a man cannot have the latter unless he has an idea of the taste of honey in his mind." For Edwards, like Emerson, the language of redemption had to be a language nurtured by a bond with physical nature, that is, by actual sensory experience. See his 1734 sermon, "A Divine and Supernatural Light," in *Jonathan Edwards, Representative Selections,*

ed. Clarence H. Faust and Thomas A. Johnson (New York, 1935), pp. 106-107).

8. Emerson, *Complete Essays,* p. 17.

9. Emerson, *"The American Scholar,"* pp. 60-61.

10. *Speeches and Documents in American History,* 4 vols., ed. Robert Birley (London, n.d.), Vols. II, p. 77.

11. "The Fugitive Slave Law," pp. 861-876.

12. Birley (ed.), *Speeches and Documents,* p. 182.

13. Bellah, "Civil Religion in America."

14. Emerson, "The Fugitive Slave Law," p. 867.

15. *Leaves of Grass, The First (1855) Edition,* ed. Malcolm Cowley (New York, 1959), pp. 48-49.

16. "The Poet," p. 327.

17. P. 43.

18. *The Genteel Tradition, op. cit.,* pp. 52-53.

19. *Leaves of Grass and Selected Prose* (New York, Modern Library Edition, 1950), p. 467.

20. P. 469.

21. Pp. 75, 483, 487, 489.

22. P. 504.

23. *Mark Twain, The Development of a Writer* (Cambridge, Mass., 1962), p. 121.

24. *Adventures of Huckleberry Finn,* Library of Literature (Indianapolis, 1967), p. 242.

25. "Civil Religion in America."

26. *A Farewell to Arms,* (N.Y., 1949) p. 191 (italics added).

27. *The True Adventures of Huckleberry Finn,* as told by John Seelye (Evanston, Ill., 1970).

28. *For Whom the Bell Tolls* (London, 1955), p. 275.

29. Susan Ervin-Tripp, "On Sociolinguistic Rules: Alternation and Co-occurrence," in John J. Gumperz and Dell Hymes, eds., *Directions in Sociolinguistics* (New York, 1972), pp. 213-250. For many insights into the sociolinguistic implications of obscenity I also am indebted to my colleague, Professor Elizabeth W. Bruss.

30. *The Genteel Tradition, op. cit.,* p. 50.

31. Henry Nash Smith, *Mark Twain,* p. vii. This hostile reaction to the use of the vernacular in the 1880s is not unlike the current hostility to the use of obscenity. Linguists, particularly sociolinguists and psycholinguists, help to account for this fact. To some extent words are considered "obscene" because of their association with a particular group—often one that has a low social status. (Thus "fornication" is

acceptable but "fuck" is obscene.) Words also may fall into this category when they are used to violate a putatively sacred "domain of use." Presumably the meeting ground of religion and government represented by "civil religion" constitutes such a domain. Joshua A. Fishman, "Domains and the Relationship between Micro- and Macrosociolinguistics," in Gumperz and Hymes, eds., *Directions in Sociolinguistics,* (N.Y., 1972) pp. 435-453; Stanley Newman, "Vocabulary Levels: Zuni Sacred and Slang Usage," in Dell Hymes, ed., *Language in Culture and Society* (New York, 1964), pp. 397-406; E. Sagarin, *The Anatomy of Dirty Words* (New York, 1962); Harold J. Vetter, "Language and Taboo," *Language Behavior and Communication* (Itasca, Ill. 1969), pp. 169-187.

32. Richard Bridgman, *The Colloquial Style in America* (New York, 1966); Leo Marx, "The Vernacular Tradition in American Literature," *Studies in American Culture*, Joseph J. Kwiat and Mary C. Turpie, eds. (Minneapolis, 1960), pp. 109-122.

33. *Growing Up Absurd, Problems of Youth in the Organized Society*, (New York, 1962), p. 97.

34. *Trip to Hanoi* (New York, 1968), pp. 81-82.

35. "The Case for Patriotism," *American Review* (May 1973), pp. 59-99.

36. *Rousseau, Political Writings,* ed. and trans. Frederick Watkins; (Edinburgh, 1953), p. 152. Compared with the moral complexity of Lincoln's covenant, Rousseau's civil religion rests upon a blandly reassuring, simple-minded creed. "The dogmas of the civil religion," he writes, "ought to be simple, few, and precisely formulated, without explanations or commentaries. The existence of a powerful, intelligent, benevolent, foreseeing and providential God, the continuance of life after death, the happiness of the just, the punishment of the wicked, the sanctity of the social contract and the laws, these are the positive dogma" (p. 153).

37. Schaar's observation also may help to account for the confusion surrounding Robert Bellah's controversial essay. For Bellah had tried to formulate a theory of civil religion embracing the ideas of both Rousseau and Lincoln. If Schaar is correct, the two are mutually exclusive, and the task Bellah had set for himself was impossible.

38. *Cannibals and Christians* (New York, 1966), p. 281. Cited by Poirier, *Norman Mailer, op. cit.*, p. 55.

IV

Response

ROBERT N. BELLAH

12 American Civil Religion in the 1970s

1

JUST SEVEN YEARS AGO I published in *Daedalus* an article entitled "Civil Religion in America." I used the phrase to describe the religious dimension of American political life that has characterized our Republic since its foundation and whose most central tenet is that the nation is not an ultimate end in itself but stands under transcendent judgment and has value only insofar as it realizes, partially and fragmentarily at best, a "higher law." As far as I know, the phrase "civil religion" had never been used in the American context in quite that way before. The term comes from Rousseau's *Social Contract*, but others concerned with some of the things I was interested in had not used it. Instead they spoke of "the religion of the Republic," "the religion of the American Way of Life," "America's Fourth Major Faith," or "American Shinto." Of course these phrases are not all synonymous, nor do they mean quite what I meant by the American civil religion, but they were referring to similar or related things. Yet it was the phrase "civil religion in America" that took on a life of its own, that has been picked up by *The New York Times* and by the popular news-weeklies, that has inspired books, essays, and symposia.

Yet from the very beginning there have been those who have questioned not only my analysis but the very existence of the American civil religion. Discussions have been proposed under the title "Does the American Civil Religion Exist?" The topic has frequently generated negative reactions ranging from a vague un-

255

easiness to outright hostility. Some have wished to deny categorically that there is anything there worth discussing at all.

Indeed, both the currency of the term and the doubts about it raise issues that I must discuss, however briefly, before embarking on my main subject. Part of the problem is epistemological, but part of it is evaluative. Behind the question "Does the civil religion exist?" lies the much more troubling and profound question, "Should the civil religion exist?" Let me discuss the epistemological question first.

In a sense, and not in a trivial sense, civil religion in America existed from the moment the winter 1967 issue of *Daedalus* was printed. Of course many of the examples I gave existed long before 1967 and, as I have already indicated, other observers had analyzed some of the same things under different terms. By saying civil religion in America came into existence in the winter of 1967 I do not mean that the notion was arbitrary, fanciful, or a myth, in the pejorative sense of that word. But I do mean that it was what Peter Berger would call a social construction of reality. It was an interpretation, to some extent a new interpretation, of various pieces of evidence many of which were themselves first-order interpretations, first-order social constructions of reality. What I am trying to say is said very simply by Wallace Stevens when he wrote, "We live in the description of a place and not in the place itself." The very currency of the notion of civil religion is the earnest of its reality. It is now part of the description of the place in which we live and that at a certain level is that.

What follows is that the notion is both more substantial and less substantial than common sense might indicate. It is more substantial because it is not likely to be "disproved" by showing that there are not things "out there" to which it refers. Its reality depends less on the existence of certain things out there than on a consensus that it is a useful way of talking about things that indubitably are out there. But it has a consequent insubstantiality in that if another interpretation, another social construction of reality in the same general area, replaces the one I have offered, which happens all the time in social discourse, then the civil religion will cease to exist. I myself am far from wedded to the term, though I do think the analysis is a useful one.

To understand why my notion gained greater currency than

some others in the area, insofar as I do understand it, gets us, I think, into the second question, the question of evaluation. Most of the people who previously looked at what I was describing, at least those who looked analytically—intellectuals, scholars, or theologians—did not like what they saw. Their main intent was to deplore what they took to be a misplaced sacredness, a blurring of the necessary boundary between church and state. They either lacked a comparative dimension, believing American patriotic piety to be a peculiarly American aberration, or they placed it in a very negative comparative context in which the chief other member was Nazi Germany. What the notion of civil religion did was to raise the whole discussion to a higher level of generality at which potentially the question of evaluation could for the moment be bracketed. My argument was premised on the sociological idea that all politically organized societies have some sort of civil religion, and that it might be worth trying to understand that phenomenon before attacking or dismissing it. My closest predecessor, Sidney Mead in his notion of the religion of the Republic, was similarly nonpejorative but perhaps lacked just the conceptual generality that made the idea of the civil religion serviceable. Now what has upset some people about my idea and what is, I think, the real source of many of the doubts as to whether civil religion exists, is that, in opposing the negative and pejorative interpretation, I seemed to say and in part did say, that the civil religion is a good thing. From this was drawn the erroneous conclusion that I think civil religion is always and everywhere a good thing or that the American civil religion in all its manifestations is a good thing, and I became the recipient of a certain amount of hostile polemic not least from the distinguished German theologian of hope, Jürgen Moltmann. One cannot avoid the question of evaluation in this area and I will not avoid it here, but I must say at the outset that if there is any utility in the notion of civil religion it is as an analytical tool for the understanding of something that exists, which, like all things human, is sometimes good and sometimes bad, but which in any case is apt to be with us for a very long time. I do not expect universal agreement even with that statement, but I do hope it is clear that it is not my purpose to praise civil religion in general or American civil religion in particular.

One theoretical issue that has plagued the discussion of civil religion in America has to do with the problem of generality vs. particularity. Some have attacked the civil religion as being too vague and general, too lacking in content, to be serviceable as an effective religion. Others have attacked just its specificity, especially its idolatrous exaltation of American particularity, as a weakness. Herbert Richardson argues persuasively for the importance, indeed the indispensability, of a notion of transcendence in a democratic polity. Such a notion provides the highest symbolic expression and legitimation for the openness of a genuinely participational political process. But it is essential that the transcendence which is a constitutive part of the democratic process remain symbolically empty, for particularity of content would operate to prevent precisely the openness it is meant to guarantee. Richardson even argues that the openness of the political process is itself the best symbolization of transcendence in the civil sphere. But perhaps the iconoclastic biblical God who has always been invoked in the civil religious tradition provides just such a symbol of open transcendence, recognizing that there is an inevitable tendency to turn even such a God into a particularistic idol, a tendency which in the civil religion as well as in the church religions, always needs to be combated. Some have raised the question of whether the Mahayana Buddhist conception of *sunyata*, emptiness, might not be a more adequate symbol of the open transcendence legitimating a democratic political order than the biblical God. This question points in the direction of a useful distinction offered by Martin Marty.

Marty proposes to distinguish between civil religion and public theology, a distinction which I view as a major contribution to the discussion of civil religion. The publicly institutionalized civil religion must remain as symbolically open or empty as possible, both for the reasons suggested by Richardson and in order not to exclude significant groups who could not share overspecific symbols. But public theology can speak from particular religious traditions to the national need. Some of the greatest American theologians from Jonathan Edwards to Reinhold Niebuhr have made outstanding contributions to public theology, to the religious understanding of the American experience seen through their own theological concepts. Indirectly they have enriched the civil religion by their interpretations, while never making their interpretations normative for others. Imaginative writers outside any particular church tradition, men like Emerson, Whitman, Hart Crane and Archibald MacLeish, have also made major contributions to public theology, though their conceptions of transcendence have been more pantheistic than biblical. And there is no reason that a major contribution to public theology and thus indirectly to civil religion could not be made from a Mahayana Buddhist position. A variety of interpretations, even a cumulative tradition of interpretation, is not inconsistent with the openness of civil religious transcendence as long as no public theological position is institutionalized as a civil religious orthodoxy. Indeed, a variety of public theologies is a guarantee of the openness of civil religion. In the balance between civil religion and public theology a fruitful tension between generality and particularity may be maintained.

2

My starting point for the discussion of American civil religion in the 1970s is a painful one. My original article on civil religion in America started with the inaugural address of John F. Kennedy. Here I want to start with Richard M. Nixon's second inaugural address. If I had had this document before me seven years ago the tenor of that piece might have been different. I would like to give a sufficient portion of this address so that you will see it in its own texture and content before any analytical comments of my own:

> Above all else, the time has come for us to renew our faith in ourselves and in America.
>
> In recent years, that faith has been challenged.
>
> Our children have been taught to be ashamed of their country, ashamed of their parents, ashamed of America's record at home and its role in the world.
>
> At every turn, we have been beset by those who find everything wrong with America and little that is right. But I am confident that this will not be the judgment of history on these remarkable times in which we are privileged to live.

America's record in this century has been unparalleled in the world's history for its responsibility, for its generosity, for its creativity and for its progress.

Let us be proud that our system has produced and provided more freedom and more abundance, more widely shared, than any other in the history of man.

Let us be proud that in each of the four wars in which we have been engaged in this century, including the one we are now bringing to an end, we have fought not for selfish advantage, but to help others resist aggression.

Let us be proud that by our bold, new initiatives, and by our steadfastness for peace with honor, we have made a breakthrough toward creating in the world what the world has not known before— a structure of peace that can last, not merely for our time, but for generations to come.

We are embarking here today on an era that presents challenges as great as those of any nation, or any generation, has ever faced.

We shall answer to God, to history, and to our conscience for the way in which we use these years.

That is an important expression not only of the soul of Richard Nixon but of the soul of a good portion of the American people in early 1973. Let us note at least one element of complexity— the passage ends on a different note from which it begins. It begins with a call to renew our faith in America; it ends with the assertion that we shall be finally answerable to God. That final statement operates as an obstacle, however fragile, to the argument that the civil religion of Richard Nixon is a form of national self-worship without any element of higher judgment. But except for that final sentence, which refers, after all, not to anything in the past but only to what we may do in the future, the rest of the passage is a remarkably unqualified assertion of American goodness without any sense of a need for judgment at all.

We may contrast Nixon's second inaugural address in this respect with the greatest of all the inaugural addresses, Lincoln's second. The contrast is not entirely arbitrary since, as *The New York Times* reported on the morning of January 20, a "concert work using the text of President Lincoln's Second Inaugural Address was dropped from the official program of President Nixon's Second Inaugural because the Inaugural Committee reportedly considered the words embarrassing in today's context." Let me quote from some of those embarrassing words:

> If we shall suppose that American Slavery is one of those offences which, in the providence of God, must needs come, but which, having continued through His appointed time, He now wills to remove, and that He gives to both North and South, this terrible war, as the woe due to those by whom the offence came, shall we discern therein any departure from those divine attributes which the believers in a Living God always ascribe to Him? Fondly do we hope—fervently do we pray—that this mighty scourge of war may speedily pass away. Yet if God wills that it continue, until all the wealth piled by the bond-man's two hundred and fifty years of unrequited toil be sunk, and until every drop of blood drawn with the lash, shall be paid by another drawn with the sword, as was said three thousand years ago, so still it must be said "the judgments of the Lord, are true and righteous altogether."

Better indeed it would be for us if President Nixon were not congratulating himself on peace with honor but were telling his people that this was America's most criminal war, for which we have already paid a terrible price and for which we will continue to pay the wages of sin for decades and generations to come.

About every generation since 1900 someone or other has written that it saw "the end of American innocence." Yet Richard M. Nixon in 1973 proclaimed an American innocence that is awe-inspiring, stupefying, in its simplicity. Nor is this any late aberration on his part. He has said the same thing many times and in many ways. Let me remind you of his words in his first inaugural address when he said, "I know America. I know the heart of America is good." (What would Jonathan Edwards have said to that?) He went on to spell out this good American heart as follows: "When we listen to 'the better angels of our nature,' we find that they celebrate the simple things, and the basic things—such as goodness, decency, love, kindness." We cannot dismiss those words as insincere or calculating. Charles Henderson has recently argued, and I think persuasively, in his book *The Nixon Theology*, that that view of man, especially of American man, is one of Nixon's most deeply held beliefs. Henderson has even shown how it is related, though tenuously, to Nixon's early Quaker faith and the idea of George Fox, which Nixon himself has quoted, that "there is that of God in every man." Nor can we doubt that what Mr. Nixon says confirms what many millions of Americans at least hope is true. Yet if we find, as I think we must, that Nixon's view is hopelessly inadequate to the understanding of the tragic reality of late twentieth-century America, I think we must necessarily conclude that *the* civil religion is similarly inadequate. Just as Mr. Nixon stands in very considerable tension with his own Quaker denomination, which has perhaps more consistently than any other never failed to produce prophetic voices calling this nation to account, so also he stands in great tension with some of the most central sources of the civil religion itself, as I have suggested in my contrasting quotation from Lincoln. If we can speak of one American civil religion as we can speak of one Christianity, that does not mean in the one case any more than in the other that we will not find the most profoundly varying and indeed conflicting interpretations of even the most basic shared symbols.

Besides its sustained hymn to American innocence, Nixon's second inaugural address made basically only one other point that I want to allude to briefly, though it is just as important: both the nations of the world and our own citizens must learn to give up their dependence on the American government. For a long time, but with increasing insistence at the end of his first term, Mr. Nixon emphasized the need for individual self-reliance and individual independence. This insistence reached a kind of culmination in a sentence in his second inaugural that quite consciously recast one of the most famous passages in John F. Kennedy's inaugural address. Mr. Nixon said, "In our lives, let each of us ask not just what will government do for me, but what can I do for myself?"

The note of individual autonomy and suspicion of the dominance of centralized government is a very deep one in the American tradition. What makes Mr. Nixon's assertions as one-sided in this area as in respect to American innocence is the lack of any counterbalancing concern with the common good, any deeply felt concern for the weaker brother, for these latter concerns are equally a part of the civil religious heritage. But it is not only to the past that we can look to make up for Mr. Nixon's lapse. At, of all places, the White House Worship Service that took place the

very morning after the inauguration there was said what needed
to be said but was not said in Mr. Nixon's inaugural address. The
lack was not made up by Rabbi Edgar F. Magnin who called Mr.
Nixon in his brief sermon, "our great leader" and "a beautiful
human being," nor was it made up by the Reverend Dr. Billy
Graham whose remarks were as empty of content though slightly
less fawning than those of Rabbi Magnin, but by Archbishop
Joseph L. Bernardin of Cincinnati. I quote a few excerpts from
his remarks at that service on January 21, 1973:

> Above all, we are challenged to strive without respite for peace
> in the here and now, justice especially for the poor and oppressed,
> both at home and abroad. . . .
>
> It is in the acceptance of this challenge that we will be able to
> eradicate that enervating individualism based on selfish interest that
> often works against the common good. . . .
>
> The philosophy of this extreme individualism is directly counter
> to the spirit of Biblical religion which emphasizes our relationship to
> others, our responsibility to neighbor, which is the expression of our
> response to God. . . .
>
> For our purposes this morning, I would simply emphasize then the
> need to keep alive in our society the profound sense of compassion
> for the poor, the suffering and the oppressed and to cultivate a firm
> and continuing commitment to the cause of world justice and peace.
>
> After the example of the Lord himself, as portrayed in the Gospel,
> we should be appalled at the sight of degrading poverty, racial
> discrimination and all of the other forms of alienation and oppres-
> sion which are still sometimes present in our affluent society.
>
> We must have, as did the Lord, compassion on our less fortunate
> brothers and sisters and more than that, we must pray for the moral
> courage to make whatever personal sacrifices and to adopt whatever
> public measures may be required to enable them to exercise their
> God given rights.

Mr. Nixon did not *say* that, but at least he *heard* that on the morning after his second inauguration.

One of the things I am trying to suggest in these remarks on
the second inauguration of Richard Nixon is that some of those
who have claimed that the civil religion is finished may be a bit
premature. Sydney Ahlstrom has said that patriotic piety was
repudiated in the 1960's. Charles Henderson has said that in the
political phenomenon of Richard Nixon we can see the death of

a national God. I think it would be safer to say that the national
God, and I would quickly point out how offensive that very phrase
would be to at least one major strand of the civil religion, though
sick, is not dead. Sixty percent of the American voters in 1972
supported Richard Nixon, whose most recurrent message was the
one so clearly stated in his inaugural address. Furthermore his
opponent in that election, George McGovern, enunciated throughout his campaign, even more clearly than Mr. Nixon, a version of
the civil religion, replete with Bible quotations and reference to
the great symbols and events of the civil tradition, though it was
a quite different version, one perhaps with more traditional warrant, than the one enunciated by the president. And finally, if one
thinks the civil religion is dead, he need only wait until 1976. Nor
will, I am sure, the Nixonian version of civil piety go uncontested
in the discussions leading up to the bicentennial. What I am
suggesting is that American civil religion is a present fact and
one we will likely contend with in the future, and not only in its
one-dimensional form but in a whole series of competing and conflicting versions. Nevertheless what Ahlstrom, Henderson, and
others have been saying is serious and cannot be lightly dismissed.

3

We are still too close to the decade of the sixties to evaluate it
adequately. Sydney Ahlstrom boldly asserts that it makes a fundamental turning point in our national history, indeed in the history
of Western culture. He says that it marks the end of the Puritan
era. Certainly much that happened would substantiate such a
judgment. Never before had so many aspects of our history and
our culture been critically examined and found wanting. From
our traditional sexual and marital mores to our treatment of minorities, from our impact on the natural environment to our
military posture in the world, we stood condemned. The very
passage I read from Nixon's inaugural, in its defensive contrast
of shame and pride, gives evidence of the depth of the challenge.
And it was indeed the case that there was a profound failure of
nerve at the top, an uncertainty as to the meaning and value of
our institutions and an inability to move resolutely to meet our
problems. And it was also the case that an important segment of

our student and youth population opted out of established society, adopted strange oriental religions, developed alternative lifestyles that seemed to threaten both our sex ethic and our work ethic. Major ethnic groups, blacks, Spanish-speaking Americans, Indians, for the first time on a large scale publicly questioned the American consensus and demanded different sorts of solutions from what ethnic groups had ever demanded before. What may yet prove to be the most profoundly disturbing force of all, the women's movement, was reborn in the 1960s and has led to the questioning of every espect of our emotional, familial, and occupational life.

Even in early 1973, when we saw a partial recovery of nerve at the top and a partial recession of the "counter-culture" and the political "movement" below, it was far too soon to say that the traumas of the sixties were healed. A profound undermining of authority, of respect for our inherited values and beliefs, has taken place that will not be easily reversed, even though what has been offered instead is often shoddy and distasteful. From such a seismic shaking it will take, we may be sure, much more than the platitudes of Norman Vincent Peale's long-time friend, Richard M. Nixon, to restore us. What place, we may ask, after such a shaking, in the future that lies ahead, does the tradition of the American civil religion have? Does it have any place at all? I believe that is a very serious question, one to which I do not know the answer, but one I think we would be well advised to consider carefully.

In order to amplify that question in all its seriousness, I would like to read to you a series of questions that a friend of mine, a man who was working very intensely in the McGovern campaign, sent me during the summer of the campaign:

Could it be that the old myths have run out? Could it be that there is so little power in the old myths left that they are no longer able either to preserve the old culture or inculcate a revolutionary step within old forms? Isn't the malaise that everyone feels today the result of the fact that old values no longer have meaning and no new ones have taken their place?

Maybe we don't need a second coming of Lincoln's new birth of freedom. Maybe that won't work any more. Maybe the answer is not to recreate the old myths in a more humane context. Maybe that can no longer be done. Maybe we have to go through a period of living an atonal cultural life where it is not clear where home base really is. Maybe the attempt of George McGovern and people like myself to humanize American culture within the present social framework will fail. What then? Do we really want a new Jefferson —who will not own slaves? Can we have him if we wish? Maybe we will be served only by something we have never seen before.

No more than my friend am I sure of the answers to those questions or whether the statements following his many maybe's are true. But I am sure that that position must be taken very seriously. If our past culture and our past myths can no longer speak to us, no longer aid us in our hour of need, then so be it. We must look elsewhere. Clinging to a past that is really dead can lead only to despair. Still, not to ask the past questions that it can still answer or not to ask actively and critically so that the answers themselves are partly new and partly our own creation would be equally foolish.

Under three conditions we can perhaps still learn from the civil religious tradition, or at least under these conditions it is worth the effort to try to learn. They are (1) that we search the whole tradition from its earliest beginnings on and its heretical byways as well as its mainstream; (2) that we subject everything we find to the most searing criticism, something that goes far beyond simply distinguishing the good tradition from the bad tradition, but a criticism that sees the seeds of the bad in the good and vice versa; and (3) that we open up our search entirely beyond the ambit of our own tradition to see what we can learn from radically different traditions that may supplement blind spots in even the noblest strands of our own tradition. Part of the implication of the third condition is that we relativize our own tradition and see it as only one part of the movement toward human liberation in the late twentieth century.

4

There is obviously not space here to do more than suggest how this program might be carried out. In emphasizing that we must push our search for a viable tradition well back into the past, I am motivated by the feeling that it is more than the Puritan era

that is coming to an end (indeed we may be at the beginning of
a new, rather different Puritan era); it may be industrial society
in the form we have known it that is coming to an end, choked by
its own wastefulness and destructiveness. Our pre-industrial past
may be helpful, then, not as a simple blueprint, but as suggestive
of directions we must soon go or choke on our own ever accumulat-
ing wastes. Even the present back-to-the-land movement is, I think,
though not a practical answer, a useful witness.

There is a passage from the very beginning of American history
that I have found worth returning to many times and that is, I
think, more instructive in our present predicament than anything
Richard Nixon said in January 1973, though it is not so far from
what Archbishop Bernardin said. It comes from a sermon preached
in 1630 by John Winthrop, leader of the Massachusetts Bay
colonists, while still on board ship before landing in Boston
Harbor.

> Now the onely way to avoyde shipwracke and to provide for our
> posterity is to followe the Counsel of Micah, to doe Justly, to love
> mercy, to walke humbly with our God. For this end, wee must be
> knitt together in this worke as one man, wee must entertaine each
> other in brotherly Afeccion, wee must be willing to abridge our
> selves of our superfluities, for the supply of others necessities, wee
> must uphold a familiar Commerce together in all meeknes, gentlenes,
> patience and liberality, wee must delight in each other, make others
> Condicions our owne, rejoyce together, mourne together, labour
> and suffer together, allwayes haveing before our eyes our Commis-
> sion and Community in the worke, our Community as members of
> the same body, soe shall wee keepe the unitie of the spirit in the
> bond of peace, the Lord will be our God and delight to dwell among
> us as his owne people and will commaund a blessing upon us in all
> our wayes, soe that wee shall see much more of his wisdome, power,
> goodness and truthe than formerly we have beene acquainted with.
> Wee shall finde that the God of Israell is among us, when tenn of
> us shall be able to resist a thousand of our enemies, when hee shall
> make us a prayse and glory, that men shall say of succeeding
> plantacions: the lord make it like that of New England: for wee must
> Consider that wee shall be as a Citty upon a Hill, the eies of all
> people are uppon us; soe that if wee shall deale falsely with our god
> in this worke wee have undertaken and soe cause him to withdrawe

his present help from us, we shall shame the faces of many of gods
worthy servants, and cause theire prayers to be turned into Curses
upon us till wee be consumed out of the good land wither wee are
goeing: And to shutt upp this discourse with that exhortation of
Moses, that faitheful servant of the Lord in his last farewell to
Israell, Deut. 30. Beloved there is now sett before us life, and good,
deathe and evill in that wee are Commaunded this day to love the
Lord our God, and to love one another, to walke in his wayes and
to keep his Commaundements and his Ordinance, and his lawes,
and the Articles of our Covenant with him that wee may live and be
multiplied, and that the Lord our God may blesse us in the land
whither we goe to possesse it: But if our heartes shall turne away
soe that wee will not obey, but shall be seduced and worship . . .
other Gods, our pleasures, and profitts, and serve them; it is pro-
pounded unto us this day, wee shall surely perishe out of the good
land whither wee passe over this vast Sea to possesse it;

> Therefore lett us choose life,
>   that wee, and our Seede,
>   may live; by obeyeing his
>   voyce, and cleaving to him,
>   for hee is our life, and
>   our prosperity.

It may be surprising in view of our usual generalizations about
Protestant individualism to find there in the very beginning and
core of the Protestant tradition in this country so vivid an expression of a communal ethic: we must be knit together as one
man, we must entertain each other in brotherly affection, we must
be willing to abridge ourselves of our superfluities for the supply
of others' necessities, we must make others' conditions our own,
for we are one community as members of the same body. Only if
we do that do we have a chance to survive in this wilderness. If
instead we follow our pleasures and our profits—concerning ourselves, I might add, only with what we can do for ourselves—we
shall surely perish out of this good land. That message is in a
sense more urgent today than in 1630, for the communal ethic
that Winthrop could take for granted has long since been eroded.
A new sense of community may be a precondition if a viable
human society is to continue on this continent.

There are other places I would look for guidance in constructing that new ethic, though I cannot now do more than name a few of them: the late-eighteenth-century effort to build a viable Republic on the basis of personal self-discipline and contribution to the common good; the mid-nineteenth-century abolitionist movement with its attempt in the 14th amendment to the Constitution to include all of the population within the structure of republican liberty; the early Socialist Party from 1890 to 1919 that tried to bring the destructive forces of industrial capitalism under some kind of collective popular control. Some of these movements failed and none of them succeeded completely, but all of them can instruct us. Some of them have much more to teach us than the more recent ideology of technocratic liberalism whose only answer to our problems is ever proliferating bureaucratic control.

But not one of these aspects of the tradition can be appropriated directly and uncritically. Not one of them is above suspicion. Not one of them is viable today in its original form. Even those noble words of John Winthrop contain a grain of bitterness when he says, "We shall finde that the God of Israell is among us, when tenn of us shall be able to resist a thousand of our enemies." From that seed would grow the terrible sense of our righteousness in the face of our enemies that would allow Americans with a clean conscience to use the most dreadful weapons and tactics of the day—from the massacre of Indians to the lynching of Negroes to the atom-bombing of Japanese to the napalming of Vietnamese children. Nothing in our past can escape the searing fire of radical criticism. We know that Washington, Jefferson, and Lincoln, each in his own way, were racists. This does not mean that we cannot continue to learn from them, respect them and even love them. But we must not deify them, for even our greatest men have been as all men are, profoundly sinful. We need a deeper anthropology and a deeper theology than one that would proclaim that the heart of America is good. It is good and it is evil in a complex and tragic mixture that we must finally face if we are to survive at all. But in that realization, in the destruction of all our simple pieties and the obliteration of our primary naïvetés, as Paul Ricoeur would call them, we may come up against a moment of despair, of the experience of nothingness, to use Michael Novak's words. But there is no other way: that very experience is the only beginning of our healing.

The experience of nothingness suggests my third point about reappropriating our past: not only must we search the whole tradition, not only must we subject it to merciless criticism, but we must also be prepared to recognize that even at its best it has gaps and weaknesses that may need supplementing from other sources entirely outside of it. Little in our own tradition has prepared us to face the chasm of emptiness that has opened in our culture in recent years, yet certain other traditions, for example one that I have long studied, namely Japanese Buddhism, know much about emptiness and nothingness about both the dangers and the creative potentialities of those places. From them we have much to learn that is either absent or faint in our own tradition. Similarly and even closer to hand the American Indians and especially those still functioning with some degree of integrity like the Hopi and the Navaho have much to tell us about the relation between man and the natural environment, things that are either missing in the Western biblical tradition or only vestigial among those of its representatives who came to the new world. These are only two of many possible examples. They point out to us that though we are the bearers of a tradition that has its own integrity, it is not a self-sufficient tradition. The survival of all of us on earth today, a survival that, as Norman O. Brown has pointed out, is itself only a utopian hope, depends on our pooling of all man's cultural resources. If America can have any meaning and value in the future it is only a relative value, only as part of a greater encompassing whole. It is in this sense that I would interpret Charles Long when he says of the American experience that "there is no center" or "there are many centers."

5

And yet for all that I do not think the American civil religion is dead or dying. Every community is based on a sense of the sacred and requires a context of higher meaning. Our nation is a community of fate on which we and to some extent the world, for good or ill, depend. Its enormous power is not likely to be easily divested of the numinous. Nor is its secularization wholly desirable. When the Protestant ethic becomes the work ethic, I have visions of what

Max Weber described when he said that the spirit of capitalism, divested of its last religious inspiration, becomes a cloak of steel, an iron cage. Nor does American foreign policy divested of its idealistic self-righteousness (not that it ever quite is) and tricked out in the garb of game theory and power politics appear any more attractive. Religion and morality and politics are not the same things, and confusing them can lead to terrible distortions. But cutting all links between them can lead to even worse distortions. The concept of civil religion simply points to the fact that some links between them seem to exist in all societies. At its best civil religion would be realized in a situation where politics operates within a set of moral norms, and both politics and morality are open to transcendent judgment.

6

In this final section I feel compelled to add some comments on what came to light in the Watergate hearings about the administration and the person of Richard Nixon, who is so central in this essay. If Mr. Nixon's claims to pristine innocence looked hollow in February 1973, they lay in utter desolation at the end of the year. Whatever particular illegal acts he may or may not have had knowledge of before or after they occurred, it is clear that his entire conduct in office displayed a corrupt use of power unprecedented in American history. Isolating himself like a Bronze Age divine king behind a wall of taboos, he proceeded to a purely personal exercise of power, through the agency of faceless men entirely dependent on his pleasure, that has no resemblance to leadership in a democratic society. It was indeed, as Senator Sam Ervin implied, a form of despotism as classically understood. In his opening remarks at the Watergate hearings Senator Ervin said:

> The founding fathers, having participated in the struggle against arbitrary power, comprehended some eternal truths respecting men and government. They knew that those who are entrusted with power are susceptible to the disease of tyrants, which George Washington rightly described as "love of power and the proneness to abuse it." For that reason, they realized that the power of public officers should be defined by laws which they, as well as the people, are obligated

to obey, a truth enunciated by Daniel Webster when he said that "whatever government is not a government of laws is a despotism, let it be called what it may."

Whatever restraints have operated to check the despotic tendencies of the Nixon administration, respect for law as such does not seem to have been one of them.

We are faced, then, with the rather grim prospect that the second centennial celebration of the founding of the American union will be presided over either by the most politically corrupt president in American history or by the successor to the first successfully impeached president. In either case the bicentennial will inevitably be less a time for national rejoicing and self-congratulation than it will be a time of national self-questioning and repentance. For many Americans, of course, the list of national crimes and short-comings is far older and more serious than even the broadest implications of the Watergate scandal. For them the salience of the recent scandal will only ensure a mood at the bicentennial that was long warranted in any case. Indeed if we look back one hundred years we will see that the centennial was itself celebrated in a gloomy mood in the final year of the most corrupt administration up to that time, that of President Grant. Our troubles, then, are not of recent vintage. The burgeoning of uncontrolled corporate capitalism in the years just after the Civil War, which accounts in large part for the Grant scandals, has gone on apace in the subsequent century and has aggravated our deepening problems in every sphere. Above all we must ask the question whether a Republic founded on Puritan and republican commitment to the common good can survive in a society ever more devoted to power and wealth as ends in themselves.

The disclosures of the Watergate hearings do not cause me to change my analysis. They only lead me to believe that the crisis in the civil religion is deepening even more rapidly than I had expected.

Related Books and Articles

Ahlstrom, Syndey E., "The National Faith, Where Did It Go? How Can We Find It in 1973?" *Yale Alumni Magazine* Vol. 36, No. 4 (January 1973), pp. 8-9.

————, "Requiem for Patriotic Piety," *Worldview,* Vol. 15, No. 8.

Alley, Robert S., *So Help Me God: Religion and the Presidency, Wilson to Nixon.* Richmond: John Knox, 1972.

Arieli, Yehoshua. *Individualism and Nationalism in American Ideology.* Baltimore, Md.: Penguin Books, 1964.

Bellah, Robert N., "Civil Religion in America," *Daedalus,* Vol. 96, No. 1 (Winter 1967), pp. 1-21. Reprinted with commentary and rejoinder in *The Religious Situation, 1968,* ed. Donald R. Cutler. Boston: Beacon Press, 1968, pp. 331-393.

Berger, Peter, *The Noise of Solemn Assemblies.* Garden City, N. Y.: Doubleday & Co., 1961, chap. II, Sections 3 and 4.

Bonnell, John Sutherland, *Presidential Profiles.* Philadelphia: Westminster Press, 1972.

Boorstin, Daniel, *The Genius of American Politics.* Chicago: University of Chicago Press, 1953, chap. V.

Brogan, D. W., *The American Character.* New York: Vintage Books, 1944.

Cherry, Conrad, "American Sacred Ceremonies," *American Mosaic,* eds. Phillip E. Hammond and Benton Johnson. New York: Random House, 1970, pp. 303-316.

————, *God's New Israel: Religious Interpretations of American Destiny,* Englewood Cliffs, N.J.: Prentice-Hall, 1971.

Clebsch, William A., *From Sacred to Profane America: The Role of Religion in American History.* New York: Harper & Row, 1968.

Daedalus, Journal of the American Academy of Arts and Sciences, Vol. 9 b, No. 1 (Winter 1967). Special issue on "Religion in America."

Demerath, Nicholas J. and Phillip E. Hammond, *Religion in Social Context: Tradition and Transition.* New York: Random House,

1969, chap. VI, "Forms and Frustrations of Religious Influence in Contemporary Society."

Dohen, Dorothy, *Nationalism and American Catholicism*. New York: Sheed and Ward, 1967.

Eckardt, Roy, *The Surge of Piety in America*. New York: Association Press, 1958.

Ferm, Robert L., ed., *Issues in American Protestantism*. Garden City, N.Y.: Anchor Books, 1969.

Fox, Matthew, *Religion U.S.A.; An Inquiry into Religion and Culture by Way of Time Magazine*. Dubuque, Iowa: Listening Press, 1971.

Gabriel, Ralph Henry, *The Course of American Democratic Thought*. New York: The Ronald Press, 1956.

Geertz, Clifford, "Religion as a Culture System," with commentary by Talcott Parsons in *The Religious Situation, 1968,* ed. Donald R. Cutler. Boston: Beacon Press, 1968, pp. 639-694.

Gellner, Ernest, *Thought and Change*. Chicago: University of Chicago Press, 1965.

Greeley, Andrew M., "Civil Religion and Ethnic Americans," *Worldview,* No. 16, No. 2 (February 1973), pp. 21-27.

———, *The Denominational Society: A Sociological Approach to Religion in America*. Glenview, Ill.: Scott, Foresman, 1972, chap. 7, "The Civil Religion."

Hammond, Phillip E., "Religion and the 'Informing' of Culture," *Journal for the Scientific Study of Religion,* Vol. 3, Fall 1963.

Handy, Robert T., *A Christian America: Protestant Hopes and Historical Realities*. New York: Oxford University Press, 1971.

Harding, Vincent, "Black Power and the American Christ," in *The Black Power Revolt,* ed. F. B. Barbour. New York: Collier, 1968.

Harland, Gordon, "American Protestantism; Its Genius and Its Problem," *Drew Gateway,* Vol. 34, No. 2 (Winter 1964), pp. 71-82.

———, "The American Protestant Heritage and the Theological Task," *Drew Gateway,* Vol. 32, No. 2 (Winter 1962), pp. 71-93.

Hatfield, Mark, "Civil Religion and Biblical Faith." An address delivered Feb. 1, 1973. Available 463 Old Senate Office Building, Washington, D.C.

Hayes, Carlton J. H. *Nationalism: A Religion*. New York: Macmillan, 1960.

Heimert, Alan and Reinhold Niebuhr, *A Nation So Conceived*. New York: Charles Scribner's Sons, 1963.

Henderson, Charles P., *The Nixon Theology*. New York: Harper & Row, 1972.

Herberg, Will, "Integration of the Jew into America's Three-religion Society," *Journal of Church and State,* Vol. No. 5 (May 1963), pp. 28-40.

————, "The Limits of Pluralism." *National Review,* Vol. 23 (Feb. 23, 1971), pp. 198-199.

————, *Protestant, Catholic, Jew: An Essay in American Religious Sociology.* New ed., rev. Garden City, N. Y.: Anchor Books, 1960.

————, "Religion and Culture in Present Day America," in *Roman Catholicism and the American Way of Life,* ed. Thomas T. McAvoy. Notre Dame, Ind.: University of Notre Dame Press, 1960. Reprinted in *Issues in American Protestantism,* ed. Robert L. Ferm. Garden City, N.Y.: Anchor Books, 1969, pp. 350-368.

————, "The Religion of Americans and American Religion," in *Religious Conflict in America,* ed. Earl Raab. Garden City, N.Y.: Anchor Books, 1964, pp. 101-125.

Howe, Mark DeWolfe, *The Garden in the Wilderness.* Chicago: University of Chicago Press, 1965.

Hudson, Winthrop S., "Fast Days and Civil Religion," in *Theology in Sixteenth and Seventeenth Century England.* University of California, Los Angeles: William Andrews Clark Memorial Library, 1971, pp. 3-24.

————, *Nationalism and Religion in America.* New York: Harper & Row, 1970.

Jessup, John K. and editors of *Life* Magazine, *The National Purpose.* New York: Holt, Rinehart and Winston, 1960.

Lee, Robert, *The Social Sources of Church Unity.* Nashville: Abingdon Press, 1960.

Luckmann, Thomas, *The Invisible Religion.* New York: Macmillan, 1967.

Lynn, Robert W., "Civil Catechetics in Mid-Victorian America: Some Notes about American Civil Religion, Past and Present," *Religious Education,* Vol. 58, No. 1 (January-February 1973), pp. 5-27.

————, "The Eclipse of a Public," in *Theology and Church in Times of Change,* ed. Edward LeRoy Long, Jr., and Robert T. Handy. Philadelphia: Westminster Press, 1970.

Maclear, James F., "The True American Union of Church and State, the Reconstruction of the Theocratic Tradition," *Church History,* Vol. 28, No. 1 (March 1959), pp. 41-62.

McLoughlin, William G. and Robert N. Bellah, eds., *Religion in America.* Boston: Houghton Mifflin, 1968. (Reissue of *Daedalus* special issue on "Religion in America.")

Marty, Martin E., "Ethnicity; the Skeleton of Religion in America," *Church History*, Vol. 41, No. 1 (March 1972), pp. 5-21.

————, *The Modern Schism: Three Paths to the Secular.* New York: Harper & Row, 1969.

————, *The New Shape of American Religion.* New York: Harper & Brothers, 1959.

————, "The Protestant Reinterpretation of American Life," in *Outbursts That Await Us: Three Essays on Religion and Culture in the United States,* by Arthur Hertzberg, *et al.* New York: Macmillan, 1963, pp. 1-60.

————, *Protestantism.* New York: Holt, Rinehart and Winston, 1972.

————, *Religion and Social Conflict.* Based upon Lectures Given at the Institute of Ethics and Society at San Francisco Theological Seminary, ed. with Robert Lee. New York: Oxford University Press, 1964.

————, *Righteous Empire: The Protestant Experience in America.* New York: Dial Press, 1970.

————, "Status of Societal Religion in the United States," *Concordia Theological Monthly,* Vol. 36, No. 10 (November 1965), pp. 687-705.

Mead, Sidney E., "In Quest of America's Religion," *Christian Century,* Vol. 85 (June 17, 1970), pp. 752-756. Reprinted in *Theological Crossings,* ed. Alan Geyer and Dean Peerman. Grand Rapids, Mich.: William B. Eerdmans, 1971, pp. 85-95.

————, *The Lively Experiment: The Shaping of Christianity in America.* New York: Harper & Row, 1963.

————, "The Nation with the Soul of a Church," *Church History,* Vol. 36, No. 3 (September 1967), pp. 262-283.

————, "The Post-Protestant Concept and America's Two Religions," *Religion in Life,* Vol. 33 (Spring 1964), pp. 191-204. Reprinted in Robert L. Ferm, ed., *Issues in American Protestantism.* Garden City, N.Y.: Anchor Books, 1969, pp. 369-388.

————, "Prospects for the Church in America," *The Future of the American Church,* ed. P. J. Hefner. Philadelphia: Fortress Press, 1968.

Michaelsen, Robert, "Common School, Common Religion? A Case Study in Church-State Relations, Cincinnati, 1869-70," *Church History* Vol. 38, (June 1969), pp. 201-215.

————, *Piety in the Public Schools: Trends and Issues in the Relationship Between Religion and the Public School in the U.S.* New York: Macmillan, 1970.

Miller, William, *Piety Along the Potomac: Notes on Politics and Morals in the Fifties*. Boston: Houghton Mifflin, 1964.

———, "Religion and the American Way of Life," in *Religion and the Free Society*. New York: Fund for the Republic, 1958.

Newhaus, Richard J., "The War, the Churches and Civil Religion," *Annals of the American Academy of Political and Social Science*, Vol. 387, No. 1 (January 1970), pp. 129-140.

Niebuhr, H. Richard, "The Idea of Covenant and American Democracy," *Church History*, Vol. 23, No. 2 (June 1954), pp. 126-135.

———, *The Kingdom of God in America*. Chicago: Harper & Row, 1937.

———, "The Protestant Movement and Democracy in the U.S.," in *The Shaping of American Religion*, ed. James W. Smith and A. Leland Jamison. Princeton, N.J.: Princeton University Press, 1961, pp. 20-71.

Nicholas, James Hastings, *Democracy and the Churches*. Philadelphia: Westminster Press, 1951.

Pfeffer, Leo and Anson Phelps Stokes, *Church and State in the United States*. New York: Harper & Row, 1950, especially chap. 19.

Richardson, Herbert W., "Martin Luther King—Unsung Theologian," *Commonweal*, Vol. 90, No. 8 (May 3, 1968). Reprinted in *New Theology, No. 6*, ed. Martin Marty. New York: Macmillan, 1969, pp. 178-184.

———, *Toward an American Theology*. New York: Harper & Row, 1967.

———, *Transcendence*, ed. with Donald R. Cutler. Boston: Beacon Press, 1969.

Reimer, Neal, "The Civil Religion and Prophetic Politics," *Drew Gateway*, Vol. 44 (Fall 1973).

Rose, Stephen C., "Culture Religion: Competitor to Christian Faith," *Social Action*, Vol. 37, No. 6 (February 1971), pp. 6-14.

Sharlemann, Robert, "Political and Denominational Religion: A Structure Crisis," *Dialog*, Vol. 10, No. 3 (Summer 1971), pp. 176-181.

Smith, Elwyn A., ed., *Church-State Relations in Ecumenical Perspective*. Pittsburgh: Duquesne University Press, 1966.

———, ed., *The Religion of the Republic*. Philadelphia: Fortress Press, 1971.

———, *Religious Liberty in the United States: The Development of Church-State Thought Since the Revolutionary Era*. Philadelphia: Fortress Press, 1972.

Smylie, James H., "Presbyterian Clergy and Problems of 'Dominion' in the Revolutionary Generation," *Journal of Presbyterian History* Vol. 48, No. 3 (Fall 1970), pp. 161-175.

Smylie, John E., "National Ethos and the Church," *Theology Today*, Vol. 20, No. 3 (October 1963), pp. 313-321.

Stauffer, Robert E., "More on Civil Religion," *Journal for the Scientific Study of Religion,* Vol. 12, No. 4 (December 1973), pp. 414-425.

Trueblood, Elton, *The Future of the Christian.* New York: Harper & Row, 1971, chap. V, "Civil Religion."

Tuveson, Ernest L., *Redeemer Nation: The Idea of America's Millennial Role.* Chicago: University of Chicago Press, 1968.

Tyack, David, "The Kingdom of God and the Common School: Protestant Ministers and the Educational Awakening in the West," *The Harvard Educational Review,* Vol. XXXVL (1966), pp. 447-469.

Verba, Sidney, "The Kennedy Assassination and the Nature of Political Commitment," in Bradley S. Greenberg and Edwin B. Parker, eds., *The Kennedy Assassination and the American Public.* Stanford: Stanford University Press, 1965.

Warner, William Lloyd, *American Life: Dream and Reality.* Chicago: University of Chicago Press, 1957.

Williams, J. Paul, *What Americans Believe and How They Worship,* rev. ed., New York: Harper & Row, 1962.

Williams, Robin M., Jr., *American Society: A Sociological Interpretation.* New York: Alfred A. Knopf, 1952.

Wilson, John F., *Church and State in American History.* Boston: D. C. Heath, 1965.

Wolf, William J. *The Almost Chosen People: A Study of the Religion of Abraham Lincoln.* Garden City, N.Y.: Doubleday, 1959.